Barcelona
2010

WHAT'S NEW | WHAT'S ON | WHAT'S BEST

www.timeout.com/barcelona

Contents

Barcelona by Area

Essentials

Published by Time Out Guides Ltd
Universal House
251 Tottenham Court Road
London W1T 7AB
Tel: + 44 (0)20 7813 3000
Fax: + 44 (0)20 7813 6001
Email: guides@timeout.com
www.timeout.com

Managing Director Peter Fiennes
Editorial Director Ruth Jarvis
Business Manager Daniel Allen
Editorial Manager Holly Pick
Assistant Management Accountant Ija Krasnikova

Time Out Guides is a wholly owned subsidiary of Time Out Group Ltd.

© **Time Out Group Ltd**
Chairman Tony Elliott
Chief Executive Officer David King
Group General Manager/Director Nichola Coulthard
Time Out Communications Ltd MD David Pepper
Time Out International Ltd MD Cathy Runciman
Time Out Magazine Ltd Publisher/Managing Director Mark Elliott
Production Director Mark Lamond
Group IT Director Simon Chappell
Marketing & Circulation Director Catherine Demajo

Time Out and the Time Out logo are trademarks of Time Out Group Ltd.

This edition first published in Great Britain in 2009 by Ebury Publishing
A Random House Group Company
Company information can be found on www.randomhouse.co.uk
Random House UK Limited Reg. No. 954009
10 9 8 7 6 5 4 3 2 1

Distributed in the US by Publishers Group West
Distributed in Canada by Publishers Group Canada

For further distribution details, see www.timeout.com

ISBN: 978-1-84670-135-1

A CIP catalogue record for this book is available from the British Library.

Printed and bound in Germany by Appl.

The Random House Group Limited supports The Forest Stewardship Council (FSC), the
leading international forest certification organisation. All our titles that are printed on
Greenpeace approved FSC certified paper carry the FSC logo. Our paper procurement
policy can be found at www.rbooks.co.uk/environment.

Time Out carbon-offsets all its flights with Trees for Cities (www.treesforcities.org).

Barcelona Shortlist

The **Time Out Barcelona Shortlist 2010** is one of a series of annual guides that draws on Time Out's background as a magazine publisher to keep you current with everything that's going on in town. As well as Barcelona's key sights and the best of its eating, drinking and leisure options, it picks out the most exciting venues to have opened in the last year and gives a full calendar of events from September 2009 to December 2010. It also includes features on the important news, trends and openings, all compiled by locally based editors and writers. Whether you're visiting for the first time in your life or the first time this year, you'll find the *Time Out Barcelona Shortlist* contains all you need to know, in a format that is both portable and easy-to-use.

The guide divides central Barcelona into seven areas, each containing listings for Sights & Museums, Eating & Drinking, Shopping, Nightlife and Arts & Leisure, and maps pinpointing their locations. At the front of the book are chapters rounding up these scenes city-wide, and giving a shortlist of our overall picks. We also include itineraries for days out, plus essentials such as transport information and hotels.

Our listings give phone numbers as dialled within Barcelona. From abroad, use your country's exit code followed by 34 (the country code for Spain) and the number given.

We have noted price categories by using one to four euro signs (**€-€€€€**), representing budget, moderate, expensive and luxury. Major credit cards are accepted unless otherwise stated. We also indicate when a venue is NEW , and give Event highlights.

All our listings are double-checked, but businesses do sometimes close or change their hours or prices, so it's a good idea to call a venue before visiting. While every effort has been made to ensure accuracy, the publishers cannot accept responsibility for any errors that this guide may contain.

Venues are marked on the maps using symbols numbered according to their order within the chapter and colour-coded as follows:

❶ Sights & Museums
❶ Eating & Drinking
❶ Shopping
❶ Nightlife
❶ Arts & Leisure

Map key	
Major sight or landmark	
Hospital or college	
Railway station	
Park	
River	
Carretera	
Main road	
Main road tunnel	
Pedestrian road	
Airport	✈
Church	✚
Metro station, FGC station	Ⓜ �
Area name	EIXAMPLE

Time Out **Barcelona** Shortlist 2010

EDITORIAL
Editor Sally Davies
Deputy Editor Anna Norman
Proofreader Kieron Corless
Indexer Rob Norman

DESIGN
Art Director Scott Moore
Art Editor Pinelope Kourmouzoglou
Senior Designer Henry Elphick
Graphic Designers Kei Ishimaru,
  Nicola Wilson
Advertising Designer Jodi Sher

Picture Editor Jael Marschner
Deputy Picture Editor Lynn Chambers
Picture Researcher Gemma Walters
Picture Desk Assistant Marzena Zoladz
Picture Librarian Christina Theisen

ADVERTISING
Commercial Director Mark Phillips
International Advertising Manager
  Kasimir Berger
International Sales Executive Charlie Sokol
Advertising Sales (Barcelona) Craig Sanders

MARKETING
Marketing Manager Yvonne Poon
**Sales & Marketing Director, North America
  & Latin America** Lisa Levinson
Senior Publishing Brand Manager
  Luthfa Begum
Art Director Anthony Huggins

PRODUCTION
Production Manager Brendan McKeown
Production Controller Damian Bennett
Production Co-ordinator Kelly Fenlon

CONTRIBUTORS
This guide was researched and written by Sally Davies, Nadia Feddo, Alex Phillips,
Tara Stevens, Mary-Ann Gallagher and Stephen Burgen.

PHOTOGRAPHY
Photography by Greg Gladman, except: pages 7, 28, 29, 43, 44, 45, 48, 82, 102,
159 Elan Fleisher; pages 8, 11, 22, 144, 152, 153 Scott Chasserot; pages 33, 35,
36 Pep Herrero; pages 46, 53 Natalie Pecht; page 88 David Campos; page 140 Olivia
Rutherford. The following images were provided by the featured establishments/artists:
pages 27, 31, 158, 161, 162.

Cover image: Cap de Barcelona by Roy Lichtenstein, Plaza Antonio Lopez, Moll de la Fusta.
© CW Images/Alamy.

MAPS
JS Graphics (john@jsgraphics.co.uk).

About **Time Out**

Founded in 1968, Time Out has expanded from humble London beginnings into the
leading resource for those wanting to know what's happening in the world's greatest
cities. As well as our influential what's-on weeklies in London, New York and Chicago,
we publish nearly 30 other listings magazines in cities as varied as Beijing and
Mumbai. The magazines established Time Out's trademark style: sharp writing,
informed reviewing and bang up-to-date inside knowledge of every scene.

Time Out made the natural leap into travel guides in the 1980s with the City Guide
series, which now extends to over 50 destinations around the world. Written and
researched by expert local writers and generously illustrated with original photography,
the full-size guides cover a larger area than our Shortlist guides and include many
more venue reviews, along with additional background features and a full set of maps.

Throughout this rapid growth, the company has remained proudly independent,
still owned by Tony Elliott over four decades after he started Time Out London as a
single fold-out sheet of A5 paper. This independence extends to the editorial content
of all our publications, this Shortlist included. No establishment has been featured
because it has advertised, and no payment has influenced any of our reviews. And,
for our critics, there's definitely no such thing as a free lunch: all restaurants and
bars are visited and reviewed anonymously, and Time Out always picks up the bill.
For more about the company, see www.timeout.com.

Don't Miss 2010

Sights & Museums

Barcelona has not had an easy time of it in these economically troubled times, with tourism dropping by about 20 per cent between 2008 and 2009. As the state tightens its belt, the most interesting new openings have been private endeavours or those run by foundations, such as the fabulous art collections of the Fundación Alorda Derksen (p125) and the Fundació Suñol (p125).

Pressure to pull in tourists has, however, prompted existing museums and galleries to revamp their collections, and the Museu Picasso (p76) and the MNAC (p113) have both invested in several new pieces to bolster their holdings. The Centre d'Art Santa Mònica (p57) and the MACBA (p88) both have new directors appointed to act as brooms, Fundación Francisco

Goya has moved to larger premises, while other centres have added strings to their bows, such as the Casa Amatller's new guided tours (see box p124).

Many projects, though, have been put on hold until the current climate improves. Norman Foster's spectacular Gaudí-inspired overhaul of the Nou Camp stadium is one such, along with Frank Gehry's makeover of the La Sagrera station and creation of a new transport museum, and Richard Rogers' reworking of the Las Arenas bullring into a leisure and office complex.

Plans for a grand Museu del Disseny (Design Museum) in the Plaça de les Glòries have also been stalled, though there has been some movement. The idea is that it will incorporate the clothing, ceramics and decorative arts museums, along

Disseny Hub Barcelona p154

SHORTLIST

Best newcomers
- Fundación Alorda Derksen (p125)

Best revamps
- Centre d'Art Santa Mònica (p57)
- Disseny Hub Barcelona (p154)
- MACBA (p88)

Neat transport
- Catamaran Orsom (p107)
- Telefèric de Montjuïc (p116)
- Tramvia Blau (p156)

Best churches
- Cathedral (p56)
- Sagrada Família (p129)
- Sant Pau del Camp (p90)
- Santa Maria del Mar (p77)

Quirky collections
- Museu de Carrosses Fúnebres (p127)
- Museu del Calçat (p57)
- Museu del Perfum (p127)
- Museu Frederic Marès (p58)

Picnic spots
- Parc de la Ciutadella (p77)
- Park Güell (p141)

Kids' stuff
- L'Aquàrium (p106)
- CosmoCaixa (p154)
- Zoo de Barcelona (p78)

Glorious Gaudí
- Casa Batlló (p121)
- Palau Güell (p90)
- Sagrada Família (p129)

Best for free
- CaixaForum (p111)
- Centre d'Art Santa Mònica (p57)
- Fundació Joan Brossa (p125)
- Palau Güell (p90)
- Park Güell (p141)

with several smaller collections. For the meantime, the Museu Tèxtil has moved from its longstanding home in a Born mansion to the Palau Reial de Pedralbes, which it shares with the Museu de Ceràmica and the Museu de les Arts Decoratives. These are now known as the Disseny Hub Barcelona (p154).

Barrio by barrio

The medieval Barri Gòtic, with the cathedral at its heart, is the starting point for most visitors. A stroll through its narrow alleyways and secluded squares is the best possible introduction to the city, combined, of course, with a wander down La Rambla, frenetic and commercial, but with a certain charm.

The last decade or so has been very kind to the districts of the Born and Sant Pere, and where moneyed Catalans once feared to tread, they now covet property. The two neighbourhoods are divided by C/Princesa, which runs from metro Jaume I to the verdant Parc de la

Airline flights are one of the biggest producers of the global warming gas CO_2. But with **The CarbonNeutral Company** you can make your travel a little greener.

Go to **www.carbonneutral.com** to calculate your flight emissions then 'neutralise' them through international projects which save exactly the same amount of carbon dioxide.

Contact us at **shop@carbonneutral.com** or call into the office on **0870 199 99 88** for more details.

Ciutadella. The Born's main artery, the wide, pedestrianised Passeig del Born, is a former jousting ground and one of Barcelona's prettiest thoroughfares, bookended by the magnificent wrought-iron 19th-century market building and the glorious 14th-century Santa Maria del Mar church.

Once considered a no-go area for tourists, the Raval is undergoing a dramatic transformation, which began in 1995 with the addition of Richard Meier's monumental white MACBA, housing the city's principal collection of modern art, and in 2008 saw the erection of the five-star, futuristic Barceló hotel, smack in the centre of this previously rundown area. Some of its gems have been around for much longer – Gaudí's medievalist Palau Güell was an early, brave attempt towards gentrification.

The city's seafront was famously ignored until the 1992 Olympics, when the makeshift restaurants and illegal dwellings were controversially swept aside and thousands of tons of sand laid down; the city now has seven kilometres of golden sands running from the bustling Port Vell to the upscale Port Olímpic and beyond. The former fishermen's district of Barceloneta still retains its local feel but is home to some of the city's best seafood restaurants.

It's often left off visitors' itineraries, but the hill of Montjuïc merits at least a day's wander. The Fundació Joan Miró is as impressive for its Corbusier-influenced building as its collection, while Montjuïc's lesser-known museums are a varied bunch, dedicated to themes as diverse as archaeology and sport.

The Eixample (literally 'the expansion'), with its grid layout, was created in 1854 and became a Modernista showcase. Its buildings include the Sagrada Família, La Pedrera and the Hospital de Sant Pau. Bisecting the area is the elegant Passeig de Gràcia; the area to its right is the fashionable Dreta, while to the left is the more down-at-heel Esquerra.

Fundación Francisco Godia p126

Beyond the Eixample lies the low-rise, studenty *barrio* of Gràcia, which, like workaday Sants and well-heeled Sarrià, was once an independent town swallowed up as Barcelona spread; despite this, you'll find each area retains a distinct and separate identity. Above Gràcia is Gaudí's Park Güell. Other notable areas outside the centre include the former industrial neighbourhood of Poblenou, touted by many as Barcelona's answer to the Meatpacking District, though this transformation is very much a work in progress.

Getting around

Barcelona is a breeze to navigate. Many major sights are within walking distance of each other, and the natural enclosure formed by the sea and the mountains mean it's hard to get too lost. Remember that uphill is *muntanya* (mountain) and downhill is *mar* (sea) – locals often give directions with these terms. As well as using your feet or the cheap, user-friendly metro and bus systems (for a map of the metro, see the back flap; the subterranean tourist information office in Plaça Catalunya provides a very good bus map), you can also choose to get around in a variety of increasingly bizarre contraptions (see box p60).

The city council runs walking tours on various themes (from Picasso to Modernisme, gourmet to Gothic) at weekends and occasional other days. These tours start in the Plaça Catalunya tourist office, and take 90 minutes to two hours, excluding the museum trip. For more information, see www.barcelonaturisme.com.

There are two tourist buses seen all over town: the orange Barcelona Tours (93 317 64 54, www.barcelonatours.es) and the white Bus Turístic (www.barcelona turisme.com). The former is less frequent but less popular, so you won't have to queue, while the latter gives a book of discounts for various attractions. Both visit many of the same sights and cost much the same.

Discounted passes

The Articket (www.articketbcn. org, €20) gives free entry to seven major museums and galleries (one visit per venue over six months): Fundació Miró, MACBA, the MNAC, La Pedrera, Fundació Tàpies, the CCCB and the Museu Picasso. The Barcelona Card (www.barcelonacard.com) allows unlimited transport on metro and buses, and gives discounts on sights, cable cars and on the airport bus. It costs €24 for a two-day pass, €29 for three days, €33 for four and €36 for five. The Tiquet Ciència allows entry to Cosmocaixa, the Zoo, Museu Marítim, the Jardí Botànic, the Museu de Ciències Naturals and a couple of others outside Barcelona, for a bargain €19. All these tickets are available from participating venues and tourist offices.

A word of warning

While the situation has improved of late, Barcelona's reputation for muggings is not completely without justification. You are very unlikely to be physically assaulted, but bag-snatching and pickpocketing are rife, especially in the Old City, on the beach and on public transport. Leave whatever you can in your hotel, keep your wallet in your front pocket, wear backpacks on the front and be wary of anyone trying to clean something off your shoulder, sell you a posy or get you to point something out on a map.

Stush & Teng p133

WHAT'S BEST
Eating & Drinking

Thus far, Barcelona's dining scene has proved itself remarkably resilient to recession, and despite the drop in tourism, a good unreserved table is as impossible to bag on a Friday night as it ever was. Bars and cafés also seem to be weathering the crisis, with few closures and no perceptible slowdown in business.

This is partly explained by local habits. Catalans tend not to entertain at home, so the bar is as crucial a meeting place as ever, while restaurants are kept afloat by the continuing brisk trade in lunchtime *menús del dia* for the workers – the sandwich habit has never really caught on in Spain.

At the luxury end of the spectrum, many of Barcelona's top chefs have responded to the situation by creating diffusion lines – some are now offering catering for people to eat at home, and others have opened lower-key, more affordable eateries. As ever, superchef Ferran Adrià was at the vanguard, with his fast-food restaurant Fast Good (p131), followed shortly afterwards by Michelin-starred chef Carles Abellán opening a tapas restaurant, Tapaç24 (p133). More recently, top chefs Carlos Gaig and Fermi Puig have opened what they term 'bistros' – Fonda Gaig (p131) and Petit Comité (p133) – though don't go expecting much change from €60 a head.

Elsewhere, the expats have it, with Australian-owned El Atril (p78) becoming a hit in the Born, Jamaican Stush & Teng (p133) offering something very different from the Barcelona norm, Au Port de la Lune (p90) adding a little French savoir faire to a scruffy square behind the Boqueria, and

Make the most of London life

the excellent Routa (see box p71) flying the flag for New Nordic.

Drink up

If you want draught beer, ask for a *caña*, which is a small measure; tourists invariably request *cerveza*, which is a bottled beer. Recently there has been a welcome comeback for Moritz beer, brewed in Barcelona and preferred by many to the ubiquitous Estrella. Shandy (*clara*) is also popular, here made with bitter lemon and very refreshing in summer. *Sangria* is rarely offered outside tourist traps.

Catalan wines are becoming better known internationally as they improve, and it's worth looking out for the local DOs Priorat, Montsant, Toro and Costers del Segre, as well as the commonplace Penedès. Most wine drunk here is red (*negre/tinto*), apart from the many cavas, which run from *semi-sec* ('half-dry', but actually pretty sweet) to *brut nature* (very dry). Freixenet is the best known, but there are better cavas around, including Parxet and Albet i Noya.

Coffee in Barcelona is mostly strong and mostly good. The three basic types are *solo* (also known simply as *café*), a small strong black coffee; *cortado*, the same but with a little milk, and *café con leche*, the same with more milk. An *americano* is black coffee diluted with more water and *carajillo* is a short, black coffee with a liberal dash of brandy. Decaffeinated coffee (*descafeinado*) is popular and widely available, but specify *de máquina* (from the machine) unless you want instant (*de sobre*).

Tea is pretty poor and generally best avoided. If you can't live without it, ask for cold milk on the side ('*leche fría aparte*') or run the risk of getting a glass of hot milk and a teabag.

SHORTLIST

Best new Catalan
- Fonda Gaig (p131)
- Patxoca (p81)
- Petit Comité (p133)

Best new global
- El Atril (p78)
- Routa (p71)
- Stush & Teng (p133)
- La Xina (p96)

Best new cafés
- Bar del Convent (p78)
- Drac Café (p79)
- Fragments Café (p151)

Best new tapas bars
- Fragments Café (p151)
- Re-Pla (p81)
- Tapaç24 (p133)

Best for kids
- Bar Kasparo (p91)
- El Jardí (p93)
- La Nena (p146)

Best vegetarian
- La Báscula (p78)
- Buenas Migas (p92)
- Juicy Jones (p93)

Best for tea and cake
- Baraka (p92)
- Caj Chai (p62)
- La Granja (p63)
- La Nena (p146)

Best for seafood
- Cal Pep (p79)
- Can Majó (p102)
- Kaiku (p104)
- La Paradeta (p81)

Best for winos
- Ginger (p83)
- La Vinateria del Call (p66)
- La Vinya del Senyor (p81)

www.treesforcities.org

Trees for Cities
Charity registration number 1032154

Travelling creates so many lasting memories.

Make your trip mean something for years to come - not just for you but for the environment and for people living in deprived urban areas.

Anyone can offset their flights, but when you plant trees with Trees for Cities, you'll help create a green space for an urban community that really needs it.

To find out more visit www.treesforcities.org

Leave Your Mark

Create a green future for cities.

Re-Pla p81

Tapas tips

Tapas are not especially popular in Barcelona, though there are some excellent options, Inopia (p132), Quimet i Quimet (p117) and Tapaç24 (p133) among them. The custom of giving a free tapa, or just a saucer of crisps and nuts, with a drink is almost unheard of in Catalonia.

Slightly different from the archetypal Spanish tapas bars are *pintxo* bars – their Basque origin means that the word is always given in Euskera – such as Euskal Etxea (p79). A *pintxo* (be careful not to confuse it with the Spanish term *pincho*, which simply refers to a

very small tapa) consists of some ingenious culinary combination on a small slice of bread. Platters of them are usually brought out at particular times, often around 1pm and again at 8pm. *Pintxos* come impaled on toothpicks, which you keep on your plate so that the barman can tally them up at the end. Unfortunately, the British are the holders of the worst reputation for abusing this eminently civilised system by 'forgetting' to hand over all their toothpicks.

Without a decent grasp of the language, tapas bars can be quite intimidating unless you know exactly what you want. Don't be afraid to seek guidance, but some of the more standard offerings will include *tortilla* (potato omelette), *patatas bravas* (fried potatoes in a spicy red sauce and garlic mayonnaise), *ensaladilla* (Russian salad), *pinchos morunos* (small pork skewers), *champiñones al ajillo* (mushrooms fried in garlic), *gambas al ajillo* (prawns and garlic), *mejillones a la marinera* (mussels in a tomato and onion sauce), *chocos* (squid fried in batter), *almejas al vapor* (steamed clams with garlic and parsley), *pulpo* (octopus) and *pimientos del padrón* (little green peppers, one or two of which will kick like an angry mule, in a vegetable Russian roulette).

Order, order

The concept of 'rounds' is unknown here; instead, drinks are tallied up and paid for when you leave. There are some exceptions, mostly in tourist-oriented or very busy places, where you may be asked to pay as you order, particularly if you sit out on the terrace. To attract a waiter's attention, a loud but polite '*oiga*' or, in Catalan, '*escolti*' is acceptable. On the vexed question of throwing detritus on the floor (cigarette ends, olive pits and so on), it's safest to keep an eye on what the locals are doing.

Kitchens usually open around 1.30 or 2pm and go on until roughly 3.30 or 4pm; dinner is served from about 9 until 11.30pm or midnight. Some restaurants open earlier in the evening, but arriving before 9.30 or 10pm generally means you'll be dining alone or in the company of other foreigners. Reserving a table is generally a good idea: not only on Friday and Saturday nights, but also on Sunday evenings and Monday lunchtimes, when few restaurants are open. Many also close for holidays, including about a week over Easter, and the month of August. We have listed closures of more than a week wherever we can, but restaurants are fickle.

Costs & tipping

For US and UK visitors particularly, eating out in Barcelona is not as cheap as it used to be, but low mark-ups on wines keep the cost relatively reasonable. The majority of restaurants serve an economical, fixed-price *menú del día* at lunchtime; this usually consists of a starter, main course, dessert, bread and something to drink.

Laws governing the issue of prices are often flouted, but, legally, menus must declare if the seven per cent IVA (VAT) is included in prices or not (it rarely is), and also if there is a cover charge (generally expressed as a charge for bread). Tipping is not seen as obligatory, and is generally modest, but always appreciated.

Stush & Teng p133

Capricho de Muñeca p83

Shopping

Strolling down the golden retail belts of Portal de l'Angel, Rambla de Catalunya or Passeig de Gràcia you would never know there was a recession. Down the sidestreets, however, owners of small shops have had to adapt to survive: the new breed of themed concept stores such as Lobby (p84) and Still Light (p96) have triumphed through diversity, offering not only clothes but also music, beauty products and homewares. Small designers have sought safety in numbers, forming collectives and making their clothes in workshops attached to the store front. Vintage stores are also growing steadily in popularity, particularly in the Raval and Gràcia, with many stocking repurposed and recycled garments on the side.

The Ajuntament has responded to the retail crisis by creating Barcelona Comerç, a council-backed credit card with all manner of consumer perks, and has even attempted to throw money at the problem – splashing out a million euros on extra Christmas lights around the municipal markets to boost spending.

Depêche mode

To widespread consternation, Bread & Butter, the titan of Barcelona fashion fairs, upped sticks and returned to its roots in Berlin in 2009, but an ever-expanding cast of one-day markets, pop-up shops and other niche shopping events keep Barcelona's fickle fashion scene on the move.

Wanted.
Jumpers, coats and people with their knickers in a twist.

From the people who feel moved to bring us their old books and CDs, to the people fed up to the back teeth with our politicians' track record on climate change, Oxfam supporters have one thing in common. They're passionate. If you've got a little fire in your belly, we'd love to hear from you. Visit us at **oxfam.org.uk**

Be Humankind (X) Oxfam

Pulgas Mix (www.pulgasmix.net) combines indie designer clothes stalls with music and urban art three times a year at the Convent Sant Agustí in the Born; the international Fashion Freak Festival (www.fashionfreak.es) is more of a roving nightclub event with clothes stalls and DJs late into the night; while the biannual Changing Room (www.changing room.org) takes place at the Chic & Basic Hotel, where 25 designers take over rooms for one day with their designs, while Sinnamon Records takes care of the soundtrack. More established designers such as El Delgado Buil and Josep Abril are on offer at Maremàgnum's Pop Up Fashion(www.maremagnum.es/ fashionpopup), which runs for the month of May.

Wining ways

Everybody and his dog seems to be taking evening classes in wine tasting these days, and entering a wine shop has become a statement about your lifestyle choice rather than a quick foray to grab a bottle of plonk. Wine shops are no longer fusty old *bodegas* where customers have to poke about and rely on guesswork: shops such as Vila Viniteca (p85), Torres (C/Nou del a Rambla 25, Raval, 93 317 32 34, www.vinosencasa.com) and Vinus & Brindis (C/Torrent de l'Olla 147, Gràcia, 93 218 30 37, www.vindus brindis.com) have expanded and reinvented themselves to offer taster spaces, designer tapas to complement the wines, wine courses, vineyard tours and all manner of gourmet food products such as artisan olive oils and pâtés. Inverting the paradigm, many gourmet food shops now offer wines to complement their products – try a combination of fine Iberian ham and wine at Jamonísimo (p136).

SHORTLIST

Best new concept shops
- Lobby (p84)
- Still Light (p96)

Best for books
- Altaïr (p134)
- Casa del Llibre (p134)
- FNAC (p135)
- Hibernian Books (p148)

Best for street chic
- Capricho de Muñeca (p83)
- Free (p96)
- Holala Ibiza! (p96)

Best malls
- Barcelona Glòries (p159)
- Diagonal Mar (p159)
- Maremàgnum (p105)

Best food forward
- Camper (p134)
- Mango (p137)
- Muxart (p137)

Best for arts and crafts
- Arlequí Mascares (p67)
- El Ingenio (p69)
- Xilografies (p70)

Best emblematic design
- Camper (p134)
- Custo Barcelona (p83)
- Vinçon (p137)

Best local chains
- Camper (p134)
- Mango (p137)

Best for kids
- Du Pareil au Même (p135)
- Imaginarium (p136)
- El Ingenio (p69)

Most historical
- Caelum (p68)
- Cereria Subirà (p69)
- Formatgeria La Seu (p69)
- Herboristeria del Rei (p69)

Still Light p96

Small is beautiful

It is Barcelona's wealth of tiny independent shops that really make it unique as a shopping destination, although it can be hard to see how the shops devoted to a single obscure speciality such as felt dolls or retro vinyl can survive. Look out for the dressmakers and one-off fashion boutiques in the Born; the indie art galleries of the upper Raval; the traditional artisans, antique shops and speciality food stores of the Barri Gòtic and the quirky jewellery workshops or vintage clothes shops of Gràcia. These shops are also among the most photogenic in the city, often holding treasures such as the ancient butter-making machinery in Formatgeria La Seu (p69), the old toasting ovens at Casa Gispert (pC/Sombrerers 23, Born, 93 319 75 35) or the medieval Jewish baths at Caelum (p68).

Market forces

In the Ajuntament's book, a revamped local market is the first step on the road to urban regeneration. This was true for the Mercat Santa Caterina in Sant Pere and the Mercat de la Barceloneta, both spectacular pieces of architecture in their own right and the catalysts for reinventing previously downtrodden neighbourhoods. In an attempt to fuse modern and traditional approaches to shopping, the new markets tend to hold far fewer actual stalls than before, with more space turned over to supermarkets and restaurants. The largest current project is the complete overhaul of the Mercat Sant Antoni, set to include three new subterranean floors and provide a new home for the traditional Els Encants flea market, while retaining its spectacular iron Modernista shell. While building work takes place, the market stalls and Els Encants have been moved to provisional buildings on the Ronda de Sant Antoni between C/Casanova and C/Urgell.

Finding an outlet

A new trend in outlet shopping is for temporary guest spots, such as the Casita de Wendy outlet label periodically on sale at Duduá (C/Rossic 6, Born, 93 315 04 01), a shop-cum-gallery-cum-creative workshop.

One of Barcelona's hotspots for bargain clothes shopping is C/Girona. In particular, the two blocks between C/Ausiàs Marc and Gran Via de les Corts Catalanes are crammed with remainder stores and factory outlets of varying quality. By far the most popular is the Mango Outlet (C/Girona 37, 93 412 29 35), with plenty of girls willing to brave the brutal lighting and rails heaving with last season's unsold stock.

Shop tactics

Most small independent stores still open 10am-2pm and 5-8pm Monday to Saturday, but high-street shops tend to stay open through the siesta period. Markets mostly open only until 2 or 3pm, though some stay open into the evening from Thursday to Saturday.

Sales (*rebaixes* or *rebajas*) generally run from 7 January to late February, and again during July and August.

Tourist offices stock free Shopping Guide booklets, with a map and advice on everything from how to get your VAT refund to using the Barcelona Shopping Line bus.

Sala Monasterio p106

WHAT'S BEST
Nightlife

There's an energy and creativity in Barcelona's nightlife that's hard to find anywhere else, demonstrated by the anything-goes mix of people in bars, the willingness to experiment with sound and art, and the continued devotion to innovation in interior bar design. But a night out in Barcelona is greater than the sum of these parts; it's a spiritual matter. It's a vibe, created and fostered by a population who party well, knowing when to go for it and when to call it quits, when to clap and when to soft-shoe… but most of all understanding that going out – like eating – is a necessary (and pleasurable) part of life that should be done right.

While battles between club owners and the town hall continue to inspire an apocalyptic image in local media, the exaggerated rumours of the death of the city's music scene are gradually fading. In a long-awaited move, officials have simplified convoluted licencing laws and offered financial support of €600,000 to those owners willing to soundproof their spaces.

Millions of words have already been spent lamenting the iconic clubs and smokehouse bars that have fallen victim to the municipal government's recent, and potent, anti-noise campaign, with the future of some of its best-loved bars and clubs (the legendary La Paloma among them, p97) hanging in the balance in 2009. The good news is that the venues springing up to fill the void, such as the eclectic Lotus Theatre club (p138) and live venues such as La [2] (p118) and Sala BeCool (p157), have given a much-needed shot in the arm to the scene.

DON'T MISS: 2010

Live acts

There is further evidence that all is not as bad as it seems: local acts continue to pop up like toast, their success and profligacy attesting to Barcelona's tenacious relevancy on the wider Spanish music scene. Live electro group Love of Lesbian, trip-hop pioneers Najwajean, hipster-folk favourites Fisheart, and Cineplexx & the Odeons and chirpy electro-popsters The Pinker Tones are some names to look out for. There are also more active metal-core bands than you can shake a death rattle at, if that's your thing, and a slew of internationally minded musicians drawing from a blend of rock, flamenco, rai, hip hop and various South American, Asian and African styles – the best known among them are Ojos de Brujo, Raval's 08001 and CaboSanRoque, who played to an enamoured audience at last year's Sónar festival.

The main venue for international names (as well as hotly tipped unknowns and local musicians) is

Discover the city from your back pocket

Essential for your weekend break, 25 top cities available.

POCKET SIZED
from £6.99 /
$11.95

Lotus Theatre p138

the multi-faceted industrial space
Razzmatazz (p159), which has
recently hosted everything from
Kaiser Chiefs and Kings of Leon
to where-are-they-now bands like
The Stranglers or Sisters of Mercy.
Moving into fallback position,
the mall-like Bikini (p151) still
nets some top-notch international
names and plenty of local stars.
For weirder and less well-known
acts, the old dancehalls Sala Apolo
(p119) and Luz de Gas (p156) host
several concerts a week. Global
superstars perform in Montjuïc's
sports stadiums or at the sprawling
Fòrum, where even 44,000 people
at Primavera Sound can't seem to
fill the space.

Times & tickets

Going out happens late here, with
people rarely meeting for a drink
much before 11pm – if they do,
it's a pre-dinner thing. Bars tend
to close around 2am, or 3am at
weekends, and it's only after this
that the clubs get going, so many
offer reduced entrance fees or free
drinks to those willing to be seen

inside before 1am. And if you're
still raring to go at 6am, just ask
around – more often than not
there'll be an after-party party
catering to the truly brave.

For concert information, see
the weekly listings magazine
Time Out Barcelona or the
Friday papers, which usually
include listings supplements.
Look in bars and music shops
for free magazines such as *Go*,
AB, *Mondo Sonoro* (all mostly
independent pop/rock/electronica)
and *Batonga!* (which covers world
music). *Punto H* and *Suite* are
good for keeping up to date on
the club scene.

Try web listings sites www.
infoconcerts.cat, www.atiza.com,
www.salirenbarcelona.com,
www.barcelonarocks.com and
www.clubbing spain.com. For
festivals, try www.festivales.com
and www.whatsonwhen.com.
You can also get information
and tickets from Tel-entrada
and Servi-Caixa, and FNAC.
Specialist record shops, such as
those on C/Tallers in the Raval,
are good for info and club flyers.

Arts & Leisure

A steady stream of new performing arts venues such as the Fabra i Coats centre for theatre and dance, and the recently inaugurated Auditori in La Pedrera, show that despite hard economic times, there is always enthusiasm and funding for the arts in Barcelona. Major projects in the pipeline are the Illa Philips, an enormous new dance space due to open in 2010; the 12-million euro Filmoteca projected to open in the Raval in 2012; and yet another extension to the L'Auditori (p139), which can't seem to build new performance spaces fast enough.

The most warmly received new arts festival to hit the scene in 2008 was Montjuïc de Nit, a night of over 50 free cultural activities ranging from cinema to circus; inspired by similar nights in other European cities, Barcelona characteristically took a good idea and improved on it, concentrating all events on the magic mountain of Montjuïc and cementing its image as a new cultural hotspot.

Film

Dubbing is a huge industry in Barcelona and although it is generally very well done, economic considerations mean that most imports are dubbed into Castilian Spanish rather than Catalan. A sense of linguistic regional pride combined with an increasing mastery of English has greatly encouraged the local trend for subtitles over dubbing, even in large commercial cineplexes such as the Yelmo Icària. This is all good news for the foreign filmgoer and new additions to the cinemas that show films in *versió original* (VO) include the Casablanca-Gràcia,

Palau de la Música Catalana p76

ever-expanding Auditori (p139), providing concert and rehearsal space for the Banda Municipal de Barcelona and other Auditori residents such as the Quartet Casals, the classical ensemble BCN 216, the Capella Reial de Catalunya and the Orquestra Àrab.

Performing Arts

Showcasing Barcelona's knack for appropriating unlikely spaces for innovative purposes is the disused Fabra i Coats textile factory (C/Sant Adrià 18-24) in the outlying neighbourhood of Sant Andreu, which has been sleekly reinvented as a space for performing arts. The dance and theatre programmes are particularly strong with a much-needed emphasis on children's

Casablanca-Kaplan and Boliche (p157). Subtitled indie flicks are also shown at occasional outdoor cinema cycles, such as the Sala Montjuïc (www.salamontjuic.com) or Gandules in the patio of the CCCB (p88), both in July and August.

Classical music

In recent years there has been a huge increase in the range of classical music on offer, thanks to the opening of new facilities, such as the recently inaugurated Auditori in Gaudí's landmark La Pedrera (p128), the Liceu opera house's subterranean Conservatori, and the modern extension to the Modernista Palau de la Música Catalana (p76). All of these spaces offer an alternative to the classical canon with dynamic and sometimes surprisingly daring programmes of chamber opera, recitals and contemporary compositions.

An injection of state funding for local projects, known as the Plan Zapatero, is also paying for a new four-floor extension to the

SHORTLIST

Best for indie flicks
- Cinemes Méliès (p139)
- La FilmoTeca (p139)
- Renoir-Floridablanca (p139)

Best dance venues
- Fabra i Coats (p29)
- Mercat de les Flors (p119)
- Teatre Nacional (p139)

Best for kids
- L'Aquàrium (p106)
- CosmoCaixa (p154)
- Nou Camp (p151)

Best cultural freebies
- Festes de la Mercè (p34)
- Montjuïc de Nit (p40)

Best classical music venues
- L'Auditori (p139)
- Auditori de La Pedrera (p128)
- Gran Teatre del Liceu (p72)
- Palau de la Música Catalana (p76)

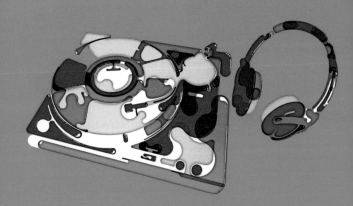

NYC

Ask New York City about New York City all night

nycgo.com

L'Auditori p139

productions. The next project to redress the city's current lack of major dance venues is the 600sq m Illa Philips, based in Zona Franca, which is currently being transformed into the Centre de Creació de la Dansa and is due to open in 2010. Other major performing art venues include the Teatre Nacional (p139), for large-scale pieces by big names such as Pina Bausch or Nacho Duato, and the Mercat de les Flors (p119), with its concentration on the kookier end of the scale with plenty of offbeat and experimental performances.

Kids

In Barcelona, children are never too young to get their first taste of opera or classical music and L'Auditori, the Liceu and the Palau de la Música all offer very popular family sessions that might include anything from percussion for under-twos to a specially adapted version of Stravinsky's 'Firebird'. Other fun educational treats include learning about anything from geckos to gravity at CosmoCaixa (p154), a trip to the

Zoo (p78) or L'Aquàrium (p106), or even making chocolate figures at the Museu de la Xocolata (p74). To let off steam, there's always fun to be had at the beach, the Parc de la Ciutadella, or a day at the Tibidabo Funfair (p152).

Sports

The biggest sporting event of 2010 is, without a doubt, the European Athletics Championships (see box p41) in July, but the city's excellent Olympic facilities attract a steady stream of events throughout the year.

The main focus of local sporting life, however, is football, and the Nou Camp stadium, already the biggest in Europe, may be about to get even bigger. It has been earmarked for a controversial €250m facelift by Norman Foster, which will increase its capacity from 98,000 to 106,000 and coat it with an outer shell of multi-coloured screens, to reflect the style of Antoni Gaudí. Another major draw is the Formula One Spanish Grand Prix; the big new name in 2010 is local (and frighteningly young) driver Dani Clos.

WHEREVER CRIMES AGAINST HUMANITY ARE PERPETRATED.

Across borders and above politics.
Against the most heinous abuses
and the most dangerous oppressors.
From conduct in wartime
to economic, social, and cultural rights.
Everywhere we go,
we build an unimpeachable case
for change and advocate action
at the highest levels.

HUMAN RIGHTS WATCH TYRANNY HAS A WITNESS

WWW.HRW.ORG

HUMA
RIGHT
WATC

Calendar

The festival story in 2009 was one of many more foldings than openings, so check these events before you set off. Information and exact dates can be found nearer the time from the *Time Out Barcelona* magazine (www.timeout.cat), along with flyers and seasonal guides available from tourist offices (p185). For gay and lesbian events, look out for free magazines such as *Nois* and *Shanguide*.

Dates highlighted in **bold** are public holidays.

September 2009

Festival L'Hora del Jazz
Various venues
www.amjm.org
Three-week festival of local jazz acts, with free daytime concerts.

11 Diada Nacional de Catalunya
All over Barcelona
Flags and marches affirm cultural identity on Catalan National Day.

19-20 **Hipnotik**
CCCB (p88)
www.cccb.org or
www.hipnotikfestival.com
A two-day festival of all things hip hop.

Late Sept **Festival Asia**
Various venues
www.casaasia.es/festival
Shows, music, workshops and stalls from 17 Asian countries, over a week.

Week of 24 Sept
Barcelona Arts de Carrer
Various venues
www.bcn.cat/cultura/artsdecarrer.org
Three-day street performance festival.

Week of 24 Sept **Mostra de Vins i Caves de Catalunya**
Moll de la Fusta, Port Vell
Tasting fair of local wines and cavas.

Week of 24 Sept **Barcelona Acció Musical (BAM)**
Various venues
www.bam.es

Around 40 concerts, mostly from local acts, and many of which are free.

Week of 24 Sept
Festes de la Mercè
All over Barcelona
www.bcn.cat/merce
Barcelona's biggest, brightest festival with human castles, giants, concerts, an airshow and fireworks on the beach.

24 La Mercè

End Sept **Festa Major de la Barceloneta**
All over Barceloneta
www.cascantic.net
Festival fever fills the fishing quarter, over a long weekend.

30-4 Oct **Docúpolis**
CCCB (p88)
www.docupolis.org
International documentary festival.

October 2009

Ongoing Docúpolis (see Sept)

LEM Festival
Various venues, Gràcia
www.gracia-territori.com
Month-long festival of multimedia art and experimental electronica.

Festival de Músiques del Món
L'Auditori (p139)
www.auditori.org
Three-week world music festival featuring 20 concerts and related exhibitions.

12 Dia de la Hispanitat

17-18 **Caminada Internacional de Barcelona**
www.euro-senders.com/internacional
The International Walk is conducted along different routes of varying lengths.

Mid Oct **Festival de Tardor Ribermúsica**
Various venues, Born
www.ribermusica.org
Over 100 free music performances, held in squares, churches, bars and shops.

29-1 Nov **Art Futura**
Mercat de les Flors (p119)
www.artfutura.org
Digital and cyber art festival.

29-8 Nov **In-Edit Beefeater Festival**
Various venues, Eixample
www.in-edit.beefeater.es
Film festival of musical documentaries.

31-1 Nov **La Castanyada**
All over Barcelona
All Saints' Day and the evening before are celebrated with piles of roast chestnuts and floral tributes at cemeteries.

November 2009

Ongoing La Castanyada (see Oct); Art Futura (see Oct); In-Edit Beefeater Festival (see Oct)

Nov **Festival Internacional de Jazz de Barcelona**
Various venues
www.theproject.es
Jazz from bebop to big band.

Nov **Wintercase Barcelona**
Sala Razzmatazz 1, C/Almogàvers 122, Poblenou
www.wintercase.com
Big-name indie bands.

1 Tots Sants (All Saints' Day)

2 Nov-31 Dec **BAC!**
CCCB (p88) & other venues
www.cccb.org
www.bacfestival.com
Contemporary art festival.

13-21 **L'Alternativa**
CCCB (p88)
www.alternativa.cccb.org
Indie film festival.

December 2009

Ongoing BAC! (see Nov)

Els Grans del Gospel
Various venues
www.theproject.es
A three-week festival of gospel music.

Night of the coolhunter

It may have started in St Petersburg with the 24-hour 'White Nights' celebrations that take place around the summer solstice during its period of famously long days, or it might have kicked off in Paris when dynamic Mayor Bernard Delanoë organised the first all-night Nuit Blanche in 2002. It seems a pity not to give Delanoë the credit; his enthusiasm was such that even after he survived an assassination attempt during the event, he insisted that the festivities should continue regardless.

Whatever its origins, the celebrations have spread across Europe, mostly with a similar name (in many languages, a 'white night' is a sleepless night) and generally offering a mix of cultural offerings and parties, with museums staying open late and live music in the most unlikely of venues.

Barcelona was a little late to the party but has now put on its own version, called **Montjuïc de Nit** (p40) until such time as it might become citywide. While Rome, Paris, Brussels and others hold their dusk-to-dawn entertainments in early October, the date was felt to be uncomfortably close to the city's Mercè celebrations. Instead, a quiet weekend in July was picked for a vibrant selection of music, theatre, dance, cinema and art on the hill, with museums staying open until around 3am.

Among myriad other entertainments, the Magic Fountain (p111) pulled out all the stops on its sound and light spectacular; the castle hosted a night of rumba; the ethnology and archaeology museums jointly laid on a night of African dance, music, food and culture, and the Poble Espanyol put on a Chinese puppet show. The 'Night of the Bat' was a Bacardi-sponsored marathon of shows, from the DJs of the moment to the ineffable La Fura dels Baus dance/theatre troupe. Barcelona being Barcelona, there was also a fabulously cool chill-out option for the party-weary, with ambient music and video projections in the moonlit Grec amphitheatre.
■ www.bcn.cat/cultura/montjuicnit

Montjuïc de Nit p40

1-24 Fair of Sant Eloi
www.bcn.cat
C/Argenteria, Born
A Christmas street fair with artisans selling their wares. Live music is performed from 6-8pm.

2-23 Fira de Santa Llúcia
Pla de la Seu & Avda de la Catedral, Barri Gòtic
www.bcn.cat/nadal
Fira de Santa Llúcia is a Christmas market with trees, decorations and nativity-scene figures.

6 Día de la Constitución

8 La Immaculada

18-20 Drap Art
CCCB (p88)
www.drapart.org
A creative recycling fest, with concerts, workshops and a Christmas market.

Late Dec BAF (Belles Arts Festival)
Sala Apolo (p119)
One day avant-garde, non-commercial art and performance festival.

25 Nadal (Christmas Day)

26 Sant Esteve (Boxing Day)

28 Día dels Inocents
Local version of April Fool's Day, with paper figures attached to the backs of unsuspecting victims.

31 Cap d'Any (New Year's Eve)
Swill cava and eat a grape for every chime of the clock at midnight. Wear red underwear for good luck.

January 2010

1 Any Nou (New Year's Day)

5 Cavalcada dels Reis
All over Barcelona
www.bcn.cat/nadal
The three kings (Melchior, Gaspar and Balthasar) head a grand parade around town from 5-9pm.

6 Reis Mags (Three Kings)

17 Festa dels Tres Tombs
Around Mercat Sant Antoni & Raval
www.xarxantoni.net/festamajor
Neighbourhood festival celebrating St Anthony's day.

Last weekend Sa Pobla a Gràcia
Gràcia, around Plaça Diamant
www.bcn.cat/gracia
Two days of festivities drawn from Mallorcan folk culture.

February 2010

Feb Festival Internacional de Percussió
L'Auditori (p139)
www.auditori.org
International percussion festival.

Week of 12 Feb Santa Eulàlia
All over Barcelona
www.bcn.cat/santaeulalia
Blowout winter festival in honour of Santa Eulàlia, co-patron saint of the city and a particular favourite of children. Expect many kids' activities.

13-17 Carnival
All over Barcelona
www.bcn.cat/carnaval
King Carnestoltes leads the fancy dress parades and street parties before being burned on Ash Wednesday.

16-26 Barcelona Visual Sound
Various venues
www.bcnvisualsound.org
Ten-day showcase for untried film talent covering shorts, documentaries, animation and web design.

Late Feb Minifestival de Música Independent de Barcelona
La [2] (p118) & Convent de Sant Agustí, Born
www.minifestival.net
Two-day festival of eclectic indie and folk sounds.

March 2010

Nous Sons – Músiques Contemporànies
L'Auditori (p139) & CCCB (p88)
www.auditori.org
International contemporary music at the three-week New Sounds festival.

3 Festes de Sant Medir de Gràcia
Gràcia
www.santmedir.org
People riding decorated horse-drawn carts shower the crowds with blessed boiled sweets.

7 Marató Barcelona
Starts & finishes at Plaça de Espanya
www.maratobarcelona.com
City marathon.

Week of 17 March El Feile
Various venues
www.elfeile.com
Irish festival of music, dance and stand-up comedy for Saint Patrick's.

29-5 Apr Setmana Santa (Holy Week)
Palm fronds are blessed at the cathedral on Palm Sunday at the start of Holy Week, and children receive elaborate chocolate creations.

April 2010

Ongoing Setmana Santa (see Mar)

Apr-June Festival Guitarra
Various venues
www.theproject.es
Guitar festival spanning everything from flamenco to jazz.

2 Divendres Sant (Good Friday)

Festival del Grec p40

**6 Dilluns de Pasqua
(Easter Monday)**

23 **Sant Jordi**
La Rambla & all over Barcelona
Feast day of Sant Jordi (St George), the
patron saint of Catalonia. Couples
exchange gifts of red roses and books.

End Apr-early May **BAFF
Barcelona Asian Film Festival**
Various venues
www.baff-bcn.org
Digital cinema, non-commercial films
and anime from Asia.

Late Apr **Dia de la Terra**
Passeig Lluís Companys, Born
www.diadelaterra.org
Two-day eco-festival.

Late Apr-early May
Feria de Abril de Catalunya
Fòrum area
www.fecac.com
Satellite of Seville's famous fair with
decorated marquees, flamenco and
manzanilla sherry, over a week.

Late Apr-May **Festival
de Música Antiga**
L'Auditori (p139)
www.auditori.org
Cycle of ancient music.

May 2010

Ongoing Festival Guitarra
(see Apr), BAFF Barcelona Asian
Film Festival (see Apr), Feria
de Abril de Catalunya (see Apr),
Festival de Música Antiga
(see Apr)

1 Dia del Treball (May Day)
Various venues
Mass demonstrations across town,
led by trade unionists.

11 **Sant Ponç**
C/Hospital, Raval
www.bcn.cat
Street market of herbs, honey and can-
died fruit to celebrate the day of Saint
Ponç, patron saint of herbalists.

Mid May **Festival Internacional
de Poesia**
All over Barcelona
www.bcn.cat/barcelonapoesia
Week-long city-wide poetry festival,
with readings in English.

15 **Nit dels Museus**
All over Barcelona
www.museus2010.cat
Late-night and free entrance to the
city's museums.

Mid May **Festa Major
de Nou Barris**
Nou Barris
www.bcn.cat
Neighbourhood festival famous for
outstanding flamenco.

Mid May **Loop Festival**
Various venues
www.loop-barcelona.com
Experimental video art festival.

18 **Dia Internacional dels Museus**
All over Barcelona
www.museus2010.cat
Free entrance to the city's museums
during the daytime.

Late May **La Cursa del Corte Inglés**
All over Barcelona
www.cursaelcorteingles.com
Over 50,000 participants attempt the
seven-mile race.

Late May **Festival de Flamenco
de Ciutat Vella**
CCCB (p88)
www.flamencociutatvella.com
Four-day flamenco festival, with concerts, films and children's activities.

Late May **La Tamborinada**
Parc de la Ciutadella, Born
www.fundaciolaroda.net
A one-day festival of concerts, workshops and circus performances.

Late May **Primavera Sound**
Fòrum area
www.primaverasound.com
Big-name three-day music festival and
the Soundtrack Film Festival.

31 Segona Pascua (Whitsun)

June 2010

Ongoing Festival Guitarra (see Apr)

June-Aug **Música als Parcs**
Various venues
www.bcn.cat/parcsijardins
Free alfresco music in Barcelona's parks:
jazz on Wednesday and Friday nights,
classical on Thursday and Sunday.

Early June **Festa dels Cors
de la Barceloneta**
Barceloneta
www.bcn.cat
Choirs sing and parade on Saturday
morning and Monday afternoon.

3-5 **L'Ou com Balla**
Cathedral cloisters & other venues
www.bcn.cat/icub
Corpus Christi processions and the
L'Ou Com Balla – hollowed-out eggs
dancing on decorated fountains.

Mid June **Sónar**
Various venues
www.sonar.es
Four-day festival of electronic music,
urban art and media technologies.

Mid June **Festa de la Música**
All over Barcelona
www.bcn.cat/festadelamusica
Free international music festival with
amateur musicians from 100 countries.

Late June **Gran Trobada
d'Havaneres**
Passeig Joan de Borbó,
Barceloneta
www.bcn.cat/icub
Sea shanties with fireworks and cremat
(flaming spiced rum) over a few days.

23-**24** **Sant Joan**
All over Barcelona
Summer solstice means cava, all-night
bonfires and fireworks.

Late June-Aug **Festival del Grec**
Various venues
www.bcn.cat/grec

Two-month spree of dance, music and
theatre all over the city.

July 2010

Ongoing Música als Parcs (see
June), Festival del Grec (see June)

July **B-estival**
Poble Espanyol (p115)
www.b-estival.com
Three weeks of blues, soul, R&B and
more in a 'festival of rhythm'.

Early July **Dies de Dansa**
Various venues
www.marato.com
Several days of dance performances in
public spaces dotted around the city.

Early July **Montjuïc de Nit**
Montjuïc
www.bcn.cat/cultura/montjuicnit
See box p35.

Mid July **Festa Major del Raval**
Raval
www.bcn.cat/icub
Over three days, events include giants,
a fleamarket, children's workshops and
free concerts on the Rambla del Raval.

Mid July **Downtown Reggae
Festival**
Camp de Futbol La Satalia,
Passeig de la Exposició, Poble Sec
www.downtownreggae.net
A free Jamaican music festival puts on
dancehall reggae from 5pm-2am.

Mid July **Summercase**
Parc del Fòrum
www.summercase.com
Cancelled in 2009, the future of this exc-
cellent big-name music festival is sadly
uncertain.

August 2010

Ongoing Música als Parcs (see
June), Festival del Grec (see June)

Aug **Mas i Mas Festival**
Various venues
www.masimas.com

Wildly varied festival, with acts from Latin to chamber music.

Every Wed **Summer Nights at CaixaForum**
CaixaForum (p111)
www.fundacio.lacaixa.es
All exhibitions are open until midnight with music, films and other activities.

Every Tue-Thur **Gandules**
CCCB (p88)
www.cccb.org
A series of outdoor film screenings held on the deckchair-strewn patio of the CCCB.

15 L'Assumpció (Assumption Day)

Week of 16 Aug **Festa de Sant Roc**
Barri Gòtic
www.bcn.cat
The Barri Gòtic's party with parades, fireworks, traditional street games and fire-running.

Late Aug **Festa Major de Gràcia**
Gràcia
www.festamajordegracia.org
A best-dressed street competition, along with giants and human castles.

Late Aug **Festa Major de Sants**
Sants
www.festamajordesants.org
Traditional neighbourhood festival consisting of street parties, concerts and fire-running.

September 2010

Ongoing Mas i Mas Festival (see July)

Sept **Festival L'Hora del Jazz**
See above Sept 2009.

11 Diada Nacional de Catalunya
See above Sept 2009.

Mid Sept **Hipnotik**
See above Sept 2009.

Sports days

The 2010 European Athletics Championships.

Ever since the success of the 1992 Olympics, Barcelona has been keen to market itself as the go-to destination for sporting events, particularly in the field of athletics. The city now hosts 350 sporting events every year but the current most eagerly awaited and relentlessly marketed is the 20th edition of the European Athletics Championships. Scheduled to take place between 26 July and 1 August 2010, this is the only major athletics competition that has never been staged in Spain and the award of the event to Barcelona allows the Spanish Athletics Federation to finally complete its collection.

Snappily branded 'B10', the Barcelona leg of these four-yearly continental Olympics already has the requisite tub-thumping anthem in production, local sports ambassadors to promote the event abroad and, of course, its very own mascot. In a departure from the animal mascots previously used for this event, Barni is a puffy, white figure who currently bears a startling resemblance to the Pillsbury Doughboy but who will grow fitter and more muscled during the run-up to the games in an earnest municipal bid to encourage local children to enjoy sports.

Most of the games are to be held in the 1992 Olympics stadium high on the hill of Montjuïc, with the exception of the walking and marathon events which will run on the flat ground of the city streets below.
■ www.bcn2010.org

Late Sept **Festival Asia**
See above Sept 2009.

Week of Sept 24 **Barcelona Arts de Carrer**
See above Sept 2009.

Week of Sept 24 **Mostra de Vins i Caves de Catalunya**
See above Sept 2009.

Week of Sept 24 **Barcelona Acció Musical (BAM)**
See above Sept 2009.

Week of Sept 24 **Festes de la Mercè**
See above Sept 2009.

24 La Mercè

End Sept **Festa Major de la Barceloneta**
See above Sept 2009.

October 2010

LEM Festival
See above Oct 2009.

Festival de Músiques del Món
See above Oct 2009.

Early Oct **Docúpolis**
See above Sept 2009.

12 Dia de la Hispanitat

Mid Oct **Caminada Internacional de Barcelona**
See above Oct 2009.

Mid Oct **Festival de Tardor Ribermúsica**
See above Oct 2009.

Late Oct **Art Futura**
See above Oct 2009.

Late Oct-early Nov **In-Edit Beefeater Festival**
See above Oct 2009.

31-1 Nov **La Castanyada**
See above Oct 2009.

November 2010

Ongoing La Castanyada (see Oct); In-Edit Beefeater Festival (see Oct)

Festival Internacional de Jazz de Barcelona
See above Nov 2009.

Wintercase Barcelona
See above Nov 2009.

1 Tots Sants (All Saints' Day)

Nov-Dec **BAC!**
See above Nov 2009.

Mid Nov **L'Alternativa**
See above Nov 2009.

December 2010

Ongoing Festival de Jazz de Barcelona (see Nov), BAC! 2009 (see Nov)

Els Grans del Gospel
See above Dec 2009.

1-24 **Fair of Sant Eloi**
See above Dec 2009.

2-23 **Fira de Santa Llúcia**
See above Dec 2009.

6 Día de la Constitución

8 La Immaculada

Mid Dec **Drap Art**
See above Dec 2009.

Late Dec **BAF (Belles Arts Festival)**
See above Dec 2009.

25 Nadal (Christmas Day)

26 Sant Esteve (Boxing Day)

28 **Día dels Inocents**
See above Dec 2009.

31 **Cap d'Any (New Year's Eve)**
See above Dec 2009.

Itineraries

Tales of the City

From cathedral confession boxes to brothels, from medieval alleyways to modern industrial parks, Barcelona in all its glory and its grimness has been immortalised in numerous novels and books. An exhaustive literary tour of the city would take weeks, but this full-day itinerary covers a few of the highlights, travelling uptown from the Born to the neighbourhood of Gràcia.

The tour starts in the Born district at the basilica of **Santa Maria del Mar** (p77), focus of Ildefonso Falcones' recent bestseller, *Cathedral of the Sea*. Set in medieval times, the thriller follows the fortunes of Arnau Estanyol and is dominated by the construction of Santa Maria del Mar. Young Arnau joins the stonemasons' guild and helps to build the church, while his adopted brother Joan studies to become a priest and eventually joins the

Inquisition. When Arnau falls in love with a forbidden Jewish woman (cunningly also named Mar), he is hauled before none other than his own brother, facing execution just as his beloved Cathedral of the Sea is finally completed.

Turn down C/Canvis Vells and on to Pla de Palau to catch the 59, 64 or 157 bus to the bottom of **La Rambla**. Standing with your back to the sea, the **Barri Xinès** (Barrio Chino) lies to the left. This seedy downtown district retains a little of its edge from the 1930s, when Jean Genet prowled its streets as a rent boy among the 'whores, thieves, pimps and beggars' that populate his memoir, *The Thief's Journal*. From La Rambla, walk along to the end of the narrow C/Arc del Teatre to what is now the **Plaça Jean Genet**, where Genet shared a bed in a *pensión* with 'six other

Santa Maria del Mar

vagrants', including his lover Salvador and a one-armed pimp named Stilitano.

While you're in the area, you could pick a worse guide than Pepe Carvalho, the gourmet sleuth of Manuel Vázquez Montalbán's famous series of detective novels. Carvalho's wanderings through the Chino neighbourhood take him past familiar local bars, shops and characters, such as his prostitute girlfriend, Charo, and his informant, Bromide the shoeshine man – replaced in the later books by El Mohammed, marking the new wave of North African immigrants in the area.

Walk up from Plaça Jean Genet along Avda Drassanes to the **Rambla del Raval** to see the square named in Montalbán's honour, inaugurated in February 2009. The square is located a few steps from the apartment where he was born and grew up, although we can hardly imagine that the staunchly socialist Montalbán would appreciate today's side view of the luxurious new Barceló hotel.

Even Barcelona's Mayor, Jordi Hereu, acknowledged that the writer would be less than delighted, particularly given his dislike of what are known as Barcelona's 'hard squares'. A more appropriate way to commemorate the great writer would be to nip next door for a slap-up fish lunch in Carvalho's favourite restaurant, **Casa Leopoldo** (C/Sant Rafael 24, 93 441 30 14).

At the top of the Rambla de Raval, turn right on to C/Hospital and when you hit La Rambla again, turn left. Here, in his *Homage to Catalonia*, George Orwell famously documented his part in the Civil War and his time spent fighting for the Trotskyist POUM party, entrenched on the Raval side of La Rambla. In May 1937, Orwell spent three days on the roof of the **Teatre Poliorama** (no.115) with its high observatory and twin domes, defending the POUM headquarters from the Guardia Civil barricaded inside the Café Moka, an ersatz version of which still stands opposite at no.126. 'I think few experiences could be more sickening, more disillusioning or, finally, more nerve-racking than those evil days of street warfare,' wrote Orwell of his time in Barcelona.

Turn off La Rambla on to C/Canuda, turn right at Portal del Angel and continue to the **Gothic Cathedral**. A confession box surrounded by tourists is the unlikely setting for one of the funniest sex scenes in Quim Monzó's *The Enormity of the Tragedy*. Probably Catalonia's most prominent contemporary writer, Monzó has written the Catalan answer to *Portnoy's Complaint*, telling the story of Ramón Maria, a middle-aged trumpet player who wakes up one day with a permanent erection.

Exit the cathedral through the cloisters and head down C/Sant Sever, turning right into **Plaça Sant Felip Neri**. This quiet, melancholy square is the setting for a key scene in Carlos Ruiz Zafón's blockbuster thriller *The Shadow of the Wind*. Here, young Daniel Sempere meets and falls for Núria Monfort, daughter of the keeper of the Cemetery of Forgotten Books and 'the typical woman that I think we all fall in love with', as she is sitting and reading by the walls of the Baroque church to escape the damp oppressiveness of her nearby apartment. If you need a caffeine fix at this point, backtrack to C/Canuda for a quick coffee at the delightful first-floor café of the Ateneu library, another pivotal *Shadow of the Wind* spot, where Daniel meets Gustavo Barceló.

Continue back past the cathedral and turn right on to Via Laietana to catch the metro from Plaça de Sant

Plaça Sant Felip Neri

Jaume. Take line 4 to Passeig de Gràcia, change on to line 2 and get off at **Sagrada Família**. Gaudí's iconic temple (p129) is the setting for the latest *Da Vinci Code* clone: *The Gaudi Key* by local boys Esteban Martín and Andreu Carranza. The preposterous premise is that Gaudí was one of the mysterious Knights of Moriah, who guard a fabulous pre-Christian relic. Generations after Gaudí was fatally pushed under a tram by members of an evil sect, doctoral candidate María Givell and her boyfriend Miguel (a mathematician and dashing swordsman, naturally) dodge baddie bullets and hunt for clues to Gaudí's symbolic message to the Catholic world hidden within the architectural fabric of his Sagrada Família.

Back on the metro again, take line 2 to Diagonal and change over to line 3; get off at Fontana and walk along C/Astúries until you arrive at **Plaça del Diamant**, on the right. This square is the setting for several pivotal scenes in Mercè Rodoreda's *The Time of the Doves* (in Catalan, *La Plaça del Diamant*), one of the most acclaimed Catalan novels of all time. Here, Natalia and Quimet meet and fall in love just before the Civil War breaks out; the commemorative bronze statue of **La Colometa** ('Little Dove', Quimet's nickname for Natalia) depicts her fleeing Quimet's pet doves, which have become symbols of her suffering. The Bar Monumental where they eat and drink vermouth together in the novel is long gone, but the quiet **Bar Diamant** on the corner (C/Astúries 67, 93 237 25 98) is as good a place as any to curl up with a copy of the book that put the neighbourhood of Gràcia, and indeed all of Barcelona, firmly on the literary map.

Route with a View

Once the bedrock of a feared bastion of suppression by a brutal faraway government, then a vast area of pleasure gardens for the idle rich and, more recently, the stage for the fabulously successful 1992 Olympics, the hill of Montjuïc has played many roles over the centuries. Nowadays, its formidable castle is being converted into the Centre for Peace, and access has been improved so that all citizens can make the most of its well-tended parks and treasury of museums and sculptures.

The possible routes are numerous, but following this one you can stroll around many of its attractions in an hour or two. If you plan to step into any of the museums, however, we'd allow a full day. Bear in mind too that eating options are limited up here, and carry water in summer.

Start at the lower entrance to the Poble Sec metro station and head up C/Badas to the gardens of the **Teatre Grec**, then take the gateway to the right of the amphitheatre. From here, head up to the **Fundació Joan Miró** (p111) via the **Escales del Generalife**, a series of trickling fountains flanked by stone steps, olive trees and benches, named after the water gardens of Granada's Alhambra palace. Instead of taking the steps, however, turn right into the **Jardins Laribal**, designed – like the Escales – by French landscape architect Jean-Claude Nicolas Forestier at the start of the last century. Ahead lie the **Colla de l'Arròs** rose gardens, at their best in late spring. From here, a long pergola leads up to the **Font del Gat** (*Fountain of the Cat*), a clearing on the slope with the rather modest fountain itself and a small restaurant – the perfect lunch stop if you've decided to spend an hour or two at the nearby Miró.

With your back to the restaurant follow the path east towards the Miró and you'll arrive at a clearing, in the middle of which is Josep Viladomat's bronze **Noia de la Trena** (*Girl with a Plait*). Straight ahead is the stone **Repòs**, also by

Viladomat, a scaled-up version of a Manolo Hugué figure, which Hugué was too ill to finish.

Turn right on to the Avda Miramar where, opposite the Miró museum, you'll find a flight of steps which lead up and around to the **Tres Pins nursery**, where grow the city's plants. From here the Avda Miramar runs seaward, past the **Plaça Dante Alighieri**. In front of Dante, and in contrast to his stern salute, stands Josep Llimona's curvaceous and coquettish **Bellesa** (*Beauty*).

At the end of this road is the Miramar area, fronted by formal gardens, the station for the cablecar, and slightly south and below it, the **Costa i Llobera** cactus gardens. Backtracking, a road leads behind the hotel up the hill towards the castle, passing the **Joan Brossa gardens** en route. These were created on the site of the old fairground, and some of the statues from the time (like Charlie Chaplin) are still in place. Just outside the gardens is the **Sardana** sculpture, a representation of the Catalan national dance. Cross the road here to walk up via the fountains and ceramic mosaics of the **Mirador de l'Alcalde**. From here, the **Camí del Mar**, with great views out to sea, runs alongside the **castle** and, after five minutes or so, eventually to the **Mirador del Migdia**, one of the few places in Barcelona from which you can watch the sun set. There is a picnic area or, if you're lucky, **La Caseta de Migdia**, a wonderful outdoor café, might be open.

From here a path runs around the landward side of the castle – follow this until you reach the **cablecar** station and take the steps down on the left. Follow as straight a path as you can, cutting across various flights of steps, and turn right on the road at the bottom, which then curves round to the left. Here you'll arrive at an entrance to the **Jardins Mossèn Cinto**. The gardens are dedicated to the poet Jacint Verdaguer and specialise in bulbous plants and various types of waterlilies, with a series of terraced ponds running down the hillside to a small lake.

Exiting from the lower side of these gardens, turn left to catch the funicular down the hill to Avda Paral·lel and the metro.

Fundació Joan Miró p47

Lay of the Sand

Barcelona never had much of a beach culture until the 1992 Olympics opened the city's eyes to the commercial potential of its location. What little sand there was before then was grey and clogged with private swimming baths and *xiringuitos* (beach restaurants) that served seafood on trestle tables set up on the sand; the rest was given over to heavy industry and waste dumps, cut off from the rest of the city by a strip of rail track, warehouses and factories. For the grand Olympic makeover, the beaches were swiftly cleared and filled with tons of golden sand, imported palm trees and landscaped promenades, and nowadays the city's seven kilometres of sand pulls in millions of visitors every year.

For a day at the beach that involves more than just soaking up the rays, take bus no.14 or 41 from Plaça Catalunya to the **Platja Mar Bella** ('*platja*' means beach in Catalan). This is one of the more lively beaches, with basketball nets, volleyball courts, table-tennis tables and a half-pipe for BMXers and skaters. A focal point is the **Base Nàutica de la Mar Bella** (Avda Litoral, 93 221 04 32, www.basenautica.org) at the southerly end of this beach, where you can hire a kayak for an hour or so of messing about in boats. Experienced surfers can also hire boards, subject to a proficiency test. For pleasures of a more cerebral sort, an alternative is the **Cementiri de Poblenou**, a short walk back from the beach. The cemetery contains some impressive examples of funerary art, many of which were built at the height of the romantic-Gothic craze at the end of the 19th century. A leaflet or larger guide (€15) sold at the entrance suggests a route around 30 of the more interesting monuments.

Back on the shoreline, the next beach along is the **Platja de Bogatell**, which really comes into its own after dark, when its *xiringuitos* light torches among the loungers and their soundsystems pump out the latest beats. This

Estel Ferit

beach leads to the broader stretch
of sand at **Nova Icària** and,
beyond, the flashy marina of the
Port Olímpic. The port and the
Vila Olímpica neighbourhood
behind it were created to house the
athletes during the 1992 Games,
and these days draw a curious mix
of well-heeled Catalan residents of
the area and drunk, scantily clad
tourists attracted to the tawdry
bars around the port.

Behind the port rise the landmark
twin towers of the Mapfre insurance
building and the luxurious Hotel
Arts (p171), while just in front of
the Arts you'll see Frank Gehry's
vast, glittering **Fish** sculpture. By
now it should be lunchtime, so drop
down to the beach just below *Fish*,
and after a hundred metres or so
you'll find **Agua** (p102), a relaxed
restaurant with globally influenced
dishes and tables on a terrace
giving on to the beach. If Agua is
full, backtrack to Italian sister
restaurant **Bestial** (p102) or, for
more old-fashioned fish dishes and
paella, head to one of any number
of restaurants in Barceloneta.

After lunch comes the most
relaxing part of the day. Just
along from Agua on the sheltered
walkway running alongside the
beach, you'll find the **Centre de la
Platja** (Passeig Marítim s/n, 93 224
75 71; see box p103), a new beach
centre with a small library that
lends books, magazines and papers
(some in English) along with beach
toys from June to September. Take
a passport to borrow some reading
material and repair to the beach for
some late afternoon sun.

This area has been the
beneficiary of a staggering amount
of sculpture, mostly as part of the
drive to prettify it for the Olympics;
the most obvious (and therefore the
beach meeting point of choice) is
Rebecca Horn's tower of rusty
cubes, **Estel Ferit** (*Wounded
Star*), which pays homage to the
much-missed *xiringuitos* that lined
the sands in pre-Olympic days.
Stroll past this to the end of the
Platja Barceloneta to Juan Muñoz's
disturbing sculpture of five caged
figures known as **Una habitació
on sempre plou** (*A Room Where*

It Always Rains) at the top of **Passeig Joan de Borbó**. This maritime promenade separates the Port Vell from the tight-knit seaside community of **Barceloneta**, which is slowly metamorphosing from a working-class neighbourhood dependent on fishing and heavy industry into a node of leisured bucket-and-spade tourism, with ever greater numbers of bars, restaurants and holiday flats.

The district was created in the 18th century to rehouse workers left homeless when the area now occupied by the Ciutadella park was razed to make way for the hated citadel. Narrow rows of cheap housing were set around a central square (now home to the recently redesigned Mercat de la Barceloneta) and the two-storey houses became home to fishermen, sailors and dockers. With the arrival of factories and shipbuilding yards in the 19th century, the area soon became so overcrowded with workers that the houses were split in half and later quartered. The infamous 'quarts de casa' typically measured no more than 30 square metres (320 square feet), had no running water until the 1960s and often held families of ten or so. Most were later built up to six or more storeys, but even today, many of the flats remain cramped and in bad condition despite their brightly painted façades.

Back on Passeig Joan de Borbó, walk down the broad portside esplanade looking down for Mario Merz's **Crescendo Appare** (*Growing in Appearance*) halfway down. These neon numbers set below glass represent the Fibonacci sequence, and were part of the 1992 sculptural bonanza, as was, further along, Lothar Baumgarten's **Rosa dels Vents** (*Wind Rose*), which features the names of Catalan sea winds embedded in the pavement.

For a better view of it, take the lift to the rooftop café of the **Museu d'Història de Catalunya** (p99; admission to the café is free) in the Palau de Mar, the only remaining warehouse from the area's industrial past, which has been stylishly converted into offices, restaurants and the museum. From here you also get a great panorama that takes in the Port Vell leisure marina (heralded with Roy Lichtenstein's pop art *Barcelona Head*), the hill of Montjuïc and across the city. Just over the grassy slopes in front is the **Ictineo II**, a replica of the world's first combustion-powered submarine, created by Narcis Monturiol and launched from Barcelona port in 1862. The Virgin in the foreground as you look to Montjuïc tops the Mercè church in the Barri Gòtic, and the towering column to its left is the **Monument a Colom** (p99). Pull up a seat for a restorative *caña* (draught beer) while admiring the view, and there should just be time to head back into town to shower off the sand before dinner.

ITINERARIES

1000 ways to
spend your
weekends

**TIME OUT GUIDES
WRITTEN BY
LOCAL EXPERTS**
visit timeout.com/shop

Barcelona by Area

La Rambla

Barri Gòtic
& La Rambla

Roughly at the centre of
the Gothic Quarter is the
cathedral, surrounded by a knot
of medieval streets and small,
shady squares. A triumvirate of
more imposing squares nearby
comprises the Plaça Sant Jaume,
which now hosts the municipal
government (**Ajuntament**) and
the Catalan regional government
(Generalitat) buildings, the well-
preserved Plaça del Rei, which
houses the **Museu d'Història de
la Ciutat**, the Escher-esque 16th-
century watchtower (Mirador del
Rei Martí) and the Capella de Santa
Àgata and, finally, the arcaded
Plaça Reial, known for its bars,
cheap backpacker hostels and
rather scuzzy atmosphere at night.
The *plaça* has the Tres Gràcies
fountain in the centre, and lamp-
posts designed by the young Gaudí.

The Barri Gòtic is flanked to
the east by La Rambla, the famed,
mile-long boulevard that leads from
Plaça Catalunya to the sea. In the
absence of any great buildings
or museums, it's the people who
provide the spectacle: from flower-
sellers to living statues, opera-goers
to clubbers, market shoppers to
tango dancers, all human life is
here. On its west side is the Palau
de la Virreina exhibition and
cultural information centre, and
the superb **Boqueria** market. A
little further down is the pavement
mosaic created in 1976 by Joan
Miró and recently restored to its
original glory. On the left is the
extraordinary Bruno Quadros
building (1883); a former umbrella
shop, it is decorated with roundels
of open parasols and a Chinese
dragon carrying a Peking lantern.

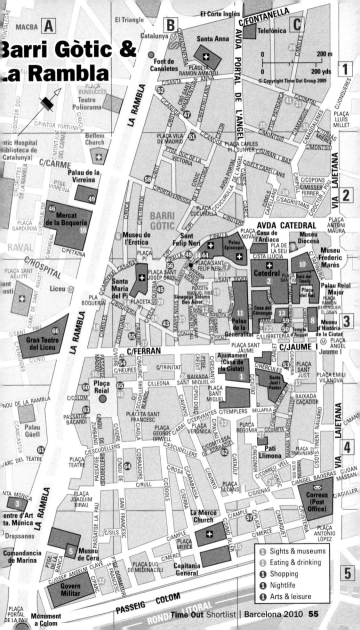

Museu de l'Eròtica

Sights & museums

Ajuntament (City Hall)

*Plaça Sant Jaume (93 402 70 00/
special visits 93 402 73 64/www.
bcn.cat). Metro Jaume I or Liceu.*
Open *Office 8.30am-2.30pm Mon-
Fri. Visits 10.30am-1.30pm Sun.*
Admission *free.* **Map** p55 C3 ❶

The Ajuntament's centrepiece is the
famous Saló de Cent, where the Consell
de Cent ruled the city between 1372 and
1714. The Saló de Cròniques is filled
with Josep Maria Sert's immense black-
and-gold mural (1928), depicting the
early 14th-century Catalan campaign in
Byzantium and Greece. Full of art and
sculptures by the great Catalan masters
from Clarà to Subirachs, the interior of
the city hall is open for guided tours (in
different languages) on Sundays.

Catedral

*Pla de la Seu (93 342 82 60/
www.catedralbcn.org). Metro Jaume I.*
Open *Combined ticket 1-5pm Mon-Sat;
2-4.45pm Sun. Church 8am-12.45pm,
5.15-7pm Mon-Fri; 8am-12.45pm, 5.15-
6pm Sat; 8am-12.45pm, 5.15-6pm Sun.*
*Cloister 9am-12.30pm, 5-7pm daily.
Museum 10am-12.30pm, 5.15-7pm daily.*
Admission *Combined ticket €5. Church
& cloister free. Museum €2. Lift to roof
€2.50. Choir €2.20.* No credit cards.
Map p55 C3 ❷

Construction on Barcelona's Gothic
cathedral began in 1298, but, although
the architects remained faithful to
the vertical Nordic lines of the 15th-
century plans, the façade and central
spire were not finished until 1913.
Inside, it is a cavernous and slightly
forbidding place, but many paintings,
sculptures and an intricately carved
central choir from the 1390s shine
through the gloom. The cathedral
is dedicated to Saint Eulàlia, whose
remains lie in the dramatically lit
crypt, in an alabaster tomb carved
with torture scenes from her martyr-
dom. The cloister is famous for its
13 geese and half-erased floor engrav-
ings. The cathedral museum, which is
housed in the 17th-century chapter-
house, includes paintings and sculptures by local Gothic masters. A
combined ticket (*visita especial*) has a
timetable that's intended to keep

tourists and worshippers from bothering one another. From 1-4.30pm, the entry fee is obligatory; however, ticket-holders have the run of the cloister, church, choir and lift, and can enter some chapels and take photos (normally prohibited).

Centre d'Art Santa Mònica

La Rambla 7 (93 316 28 10/ www.artssantamonica.cat). Metro Drassanes. **Open** 11am-8pm Tue-Sat; 11am-3pm Sun. **Admission** free. **Map** p55 A4 ❸

In a controversial move, the Generalitat has appointed new director Vicenç Altaió to pump up the lacklustre visitor numbers for this contemporary art space. Altaió vowed to create 'a multidisciplinary centre for art, science, thought and communication', although detractors fear that the governmental hijacking of the management will mean diluted programming. After remodelling, the museum reopened in March 2009. There are plans to move the CASM to a new contemporary art centre in 2010 once a venue is decided.

Dalí Barcelona
Real Cercle Artístic

C/Arcs 5 (93 318 17 74/www. dalibarcelona.com). Metro Jaume I or Liceu. **Open** 10am-10pm daily. **Admission** €8; €6 reductions; free under-7s. **Map** p55 C2 ❹

This private collection of Dalí sculptures looks right at home amid the red velvet curtains and high Gothic arches of the Palau Pignatelli. In his later years, Dalí signed his name to almost anything, but these 44 pieces were moulded by his own hands in wax by the pool at his house in Port Lligat and show he was just as accomplished at sculpting as painting. Broadly divided into themes such as eroticism, Don Quixote and mythology, they include such gems as a small bronze that's simultaneously a swan, a dragon and an elephant, and an erotic vision of Dulcinea, Quixote's reluctant lady.

Museu de Cera

Ptge de la Banca 7 (93 317 26 49/ www.museocerabcn.com). Metro Drassanes. **Open** *Mid July-mid Sept* 10am-10pm daily. *Mid Sept-mid July* 10am-1.30pm, 4-7.30pm Mon-Fri; 11am-2pm, 4.30-8.30pm Sat, Sun. **Admission** €10; €6 reductions; free under-5s. **Map** p55 A5 ❺

A fun but somewhat shabby wax museum, featuring all the usual characters: Frankenstein, Luke Skywalker and Princess Diana (here holding hands with Mother Teresa while Charles and Camilla look smug). Children who've been to Madame Tussauds are unlikely to be impressed.

Museu de l'Eròtica

La Rambla 96 bis (93 318 98 65/ www.erotica-museum.com). Metro Liceu. **Open** *June-Sept* 10am-10pm daily. *Oct-May* 10am-6.50pm daily. **Admission** €7.50; €6.50 reductions. **Map** p55 B2 ❻

The Erotic Museum is a surprisingly limp affair. Expect plenty of filler in the form of Kama Sutra illustrations and airbrushed paintings of naked maidens, with the odd fascinating item such as studded chastity belts or a Victorian walking stick topped with an ivory vagina. Genuine rarities include Japanese drawings, a painful-looking 'pleasure chair' and compelling photos of brothels in the city's Barrio Chino in the decadent 1930s.

Museu del Calçat
(Shoe Museum)

Plaça Sant Felip Neri 5 (93 301 45 33). Metro Jaume I. **Open** 11am-2pm Tue-Sun. **Admission** €2.50; free under-7s. No credit cards. **Map** p55 B2 ❼

Housed in what was once part of the medieval shoemakers' guild, this quirky little museum details the cobbler's craft from practical Roman sandals to tottering 1970s platform boots. The earlier examples are reproductions, although those from the 17th century to the present day are originals, including clogs, swagged musketeers' boots and even celebrity footwear such as the tiny shoes of diminutive cellist, Pau Casals.

Museu d'Història de la Ciutat

Plaça del Rei 1 (93 315 11 11/www. museuhistoria.bcn.cat). Metro Jaume I. **Open** *Apr-Sept* 10am-8pm Tue-Sat; 10am-3pm Sun. *Oct-Mar* 10am-2pm, 4-7pm Tue-Sat; 10am-3pm Sun. Guided tours by appointment. **Admission** *Permanent exhibitions* €6; €4 reductions; free under-16s. *Temporary exhibitions* €3.50; €2 reductions. Both free 4-8pm 1st Sat of mth. No credit cards. **Map** p55 C3 ❽

Stretching from the Plaça del Rei to the cathedral are four sq km (1.5sq miles) of subterranean Roman ruins, including streets, villas and storage vats for oil and wine. The labyrinth is reached via the Casa Padellàs, a merchant's palace dating from 1498. Admission also allows access to the Capella de Santa Àgata – with its 15th-century altarpiece by Jaume Huguet – and the Saló del Tinell. This majestic room began life in 1370 as the seat of the Catalan parliament and was converted in the 18th century into a Baroque church, which was dismantled in 1934. The Rei Martí watchtower is still closed to the public while it awaits reinforcement. Tickets for the museum are also valid for the convent at Pedralbes.

Museu Diocesà

Avda de la Catedral 4 (93 315 22 13). Metro Jaume I. **Open** 10am-2pm, 5-8pm Tue-Sat; 11am-2pm Sun. **Admission** €6; €3 reductions; free under-7s. No credit cards. **Map** p55 C2 ❾

A hotchpotch of religious art, including 14th-century alabaster virgins, altarpieces by Bernat Martorell and wonderful Romanesque murals. The building itself is also something of a mishmash; it includes the Gothic Pia Almoina, an almshouse and soup kitchen founded in 1009 and stuck on to a Renaissance canon's residence complete with Tuscan columns, which

in turn was built inside an octagonal Roman defence tower. The museum has space for two temporary exhibitions, usually dedicated to local artists, photographers and architects.

Museu Frederic Marès

Plaça Sant Iu 5-6 (93 310 58 00/ www.museumares.bcn.cat). Metro Jaume I. **Open** 10am-7pm Tue-Sat; 10am-3pm Sun. **Admission** €3; €1.50 reductions; free under-16s. Free 3-7pm Wed, 1st Sun of mth. No credit cards. Guided tours noon Sun. **Map** p55 C3 ❿

Kleptomaniac and magpie, Frederic Marès (1893-1991) 'collected' everything he laid his hands on, from hairbrushes to opera glasses and gargoyles. His collection is divided into three main sections. The basement, ground floor and first floor are devoted to sculpture dating from the pre-Roman era to the 20th century, including a vast array of polychromatic religious carvings, tombs, capitals and entire church portals, all exquisitely carved. On the second floor sits the Sentimental Museum, with objects from everyday life; look out for the Ladies' Room, filled with fans, sewing scissors and perfume flasks, and the Entertainment Room, with mechanical toys, puppets and a room dedicated to smoking paraphernalia. Also on the second floor, comprising the third main collection, is a room devoted to photography, as well as Marès' study and library, filled with sculptures.

Palau de la Generalitat

Plaça Sant Jaume (93 402 46 17/ www.gencat.cat/generalitat). Metro Jaume I or Liceu. **Guided tours** every 30-40mins approx 10.30am-1pm, 2nd & 4th Sun of mth; 9.30am-1pm Fri-Sun by appt. **Admission** free. **Map** p55 C3 ⓫

The home of Catalan government has a Gothic side entrance on C/Bisbe with a beautiful relief of St George, patron saint of Catalonia, made by Pere Johan in 1418. Inside the building, the finest

Museu d'Història de la Ciutat

BARCELONA BY AREA

features are the first-floor Pati de Tarongers (Orange Tree Patio), and a magnificent 15th-century chapel. The Generalitat is open to the public on Sant Jordi (23 April), La Diada (11 September) and La Mercè (24 September). The guided tours are generally in Spanish or Catalan, so it's best to call ahead for an English-speaking guide.

Sinagoga Shlomo Ben Adret

C/Marlet 5 (93 317 07 90/www. calldebarcelona.org). Metro Jaume I or Liceu. **Open** 11am-2.30pm, 4-6.30pm Mon-Fri; 11am-2.30pm Sat, Sun. **Admission** €2. No credit cards. **Map** p55 B3 ⑫

The main synagogue of the Call until the pogrom in 1391, this tiny basement space lay abandoned for many years until its rediscovery in recent times. Once again a working synagogue, one of the two rooms is a place of worship with several interesting artefacts, the other holds the 14th-century dyeing vats used by the family that lived here until their status as crypto-Jews was

discovered. The façade of the building, slightly skewing the street, fulfils religious requirements by which the synagogue has to face Jerusalem; the two windows at knee height allow light to enter from that direction.

Temple Romà d'Augusti

C/Paradis 10 (93 315 11 11). Metro Jaume I. **Open** 10am-8pm Tue-Sat; 10am-3pm Sun. **Admission** free. **Map** p55 C3 ⑬

Four stunning fluted Corinthian columns dating from the first century BC soar out of their podium in the most unlikely of places: a back patio of the Mountaineering Centre of Catalonia. Part of the rear corner of the temple devoted to the Roman emperor Augustus (who after his death was elevated to the pantheon), the columns were discovered and isolated from the structure of a medieval building in 1835.

Eating & drinking

Ácoma

C/Boqueria 21 (93 301 75 97/ www.acomacafe.com). Metro Liceu.

Them's the brakes

A number of quirky new tours have hit town.

Go Car

Segways

Strap on your reflector shades and join a convoy of Segway 'personal transporters'. These robust two-wheelers glide you around the maritime area on a two-hour tour (€60).
Pros: plans are afoot to take in the fresh air on Montjuïc.
Cons: does not look cool.
Top speed: 20km/hr (12.5mph).
■ www.spainglides.com

Rickshaws

Offbeat tours on Funky Cycles with comfy bench-seats (€30/hr).
Pros: eco-friendly.
Cons: bulky and slow.
Top speed: decreases rapidly as time passes.
■ www.funkycycle.es

Pedicab

Bright and bulky three-wheeler cabs, the driver aided by an electric motor (€18/hr).
Pros: relaxing. Generally people look at the driver, and not at you.

Cons: you are a moving ad for an omnipresent clothes brand.
Top speed: 11km/hr.
■ www.trixitour.com

Kickbike

The same company offers Kickbike tours, on a scooter/bike hybrid. Tailored tours start at €20.
Pros: use of pedestrian zones.
Cons: tiring.
Top speed: with a tailwind, it's a dream. In the summer humidity, it's a killer.

In-line skates

Skating school Rodats do a sweeping two-hour tour of the top Modernista sights.
Pros: fantastic fun.
Cons: you need to have a good grip on skating.
Top speed: fast as you like.
■ www.rodats.com

Mopeds

Cooltra offer two- (€25) or four-hour (€45) moped tours. You can even rent a Harley.
Pros: get all over the city, fast.
Cons: traffic can get hairy.
Top speed: 50km/hr (officially).
■ www.cooltra.com

Go Car

Looking like an errant yellow dodgem, the GPS-guided, petrol-run Go Car (€45/hr) is fun, but scary even for practised drivers. Steered like a moped, with an irreverent inbuilt 'talking' guide.
Pros: irritating to taxi drivers.
Cons: irritating to taxi drivers.
Top speed: 50km/hr (allegedly).
■ www.gocartours.es

Open 9.30am-12.30am daily.
Café. Map p55 B3
A regular enough looking bar from the street, Ácoma is almost unique in the Old City for its sheltered patio at the back. Here there are tables in the shade of an orange tree and the rear of the Santa Maria del Pi church, and a small pond from which bemused fish and turtles can observe singer-songwriters and small groups perform for a young and merry foreign crowd. Salads, burgers, burritos and the like are served from midday to 11.30pm.

Bar Celta

C/Mercè 16 (93 315 00 06). Metro Drassanes. **Open** noon-midnight Tue-Sun. **€**. **Tapas**. Map p55 C5
Celta's unapologetically 1960s interior is fiercely lit, noisy and not recommended for anyone feeling a bit rough. It is, however, one of the more authentic experiences to be had in the Gòtic. A Galician tapas bar, it specialises in food from the region, such as *lacón con grelos* (boiled gammon with turnip tops) and good seafood, accompanied by crisp Albariño wine served in traditional white ceramic bowls. A characterful place.

Bar Pinotxo

La Boqueria 466-467, La Rambla 89 (93 317 17 31). Metro Liceu. **Open** 6am-5pm Mon-Sat. Closed 3wks Aug. No credit cards. **Bar**. Map p55 A2
Just inside the entrance of the Boqueria, on the right-hand side, is this essential market bar, run by Juanito, one of the city's best-loved figures. In the early morning the place is popular with ravenous night owls on their way home and, at lunchtime, foodies in the know. Various tapas are available, along with excellent daily specials such as tuna casserole or scrambled eggs with clams.

Cafè de l'Acadèmia

C/Lledó 1 (93 319 82 53). Metro Jaume I. **Open** 9am-noon, 1.30-4.30pm, 8.45pm-11.30pm Mon-Fri. Closed 3wks Aug. **€€**. **Catalan**. Map p55 C3
An assured approach to the classics of Catalan cuisine, combined with the sunny terrace tables on the pretty Plaça Sant Just, make this one of the best-value restaurants around. The set lunch changes daily, but eat à la carte for quail stuffed with duck's liver and *botifarra* with wild mushroom sauce, or duck confit with poached onion and orange sauce.

El Portalón p65

La Vinateria del Call p66

Café de l'Opera

La Rambla 74 (93 317 75 85).
Metro Liceu. **Open** 8am-2.30am Mon-
Thur, Sun; 8am-3am Fri, Sat. **Café**.
Map p55 A3 ⑱
Cast-iron pillars, etched mirrors and
bucolic murals create an air of fading
grandeur at Café de l'Opera, which now
seems incongruous among the fast-
food joints and tawdry souvenir shops.
Coffee, pastries and a handful of tapas
are served by attentive bow-tied waiters to a largely tourist clientele, but
given the atmosphere (and the opposi-
tion), there's no better place for a coffee on La Rambla.

Caj Chai

*C/Sant Domènec del Call 12 (mobile 610
334 712). Metro Jaume I.* **Open** 3-10pm
Mon; 10.30am-10pm Tue-Sun. No credit
cards. **Tea house**. **Map** p55 B3 ⑲
A cosy tearoom, where first-flush
Darjeeling is approached with the rev-
erence afforded to a Château d'Yquem.
A range of leaves comes with tasting
notes describing not only the origins,
but giving suggestions for maximum
enjoyment. It has recently begun serving *bocadillos* and breakfasts.

Can Culleretes

*C/Quintana 5 (93 317 30 22). Metro
Liceu.* **Open** 1.30-4pm, 9-11pm Tue-Sat;
1.30-4pm Sun. Closed 3wks July, 1wk
Aug. €. **Catalan**. **Map** p55 B3 ⑳
The rambling dining rooms at the
'house of teaspoons' have been packing
'em in since 1786. The secret to this
restaurant's longevity is a straightforward one: honest, hearty cooking and
decent wine served at the lowest possible prices. Under huge oil paintings
and a thousand signed black-and-white
photos, diners munch sticky boar stew,
tender pork with prunes and dates,
goose with apples, partridge escabeche
and superbly fresh seafood.

Cervecería Taller de Tapas

C/Comtal 28 (93 481 62 33/www.
tallerdetapas.com). Metro Catalunya.
Open 9am-midnight Mon-Thur; 9am-
1am Fri, Sat; noon-midnight Sun. €€.
Tapas. **Map** p55 C1 ㉑
Although strictly speaking a tapas bar,
with a wide range and a useful menu
in English, the Cervecería has tried to
fill a gap in the market by providing a
reasonable selection of beers from
around the world. The list provides a

refreshing alternative to the ubiquitous Estrella, with Argentine Quilmes, Brazilian Brahma (this one, admittedly, via Luton), Bass Pale Ale, Leffe and Hoegaarden, among others.

Gelaaati!

C/Llibreteria 7 (93 310 50 45). *Metro Jaume I.* **Open** 11am-midnight daily. Closed Jan. No credit cards. **Ice-cream. Map** p55 C3 ㉒

One of the more recent gelateries, Gelaaati! has built up a loyal following quickly, and with good reason. All its flavours are made on the premises every day, using natural ingredients – no colourings, no preservatives. Especially good are the hazelnut, pistachio and raspberry ice-creams; unusual flavours include soya bean, celery, and avocado.

Ginger

C/Palma de Sant Just 1 (93 310 53 09). *Metro Jaume I.* **Open** 7pm-2.30am Tue-Thur; 7pm-3am Fri, Sat. Closed 3wks Aug. **Bar. Map** p55 C4 ㉓

Ginger manages to be all things to all punters: art deco cocktail bar with comfortable buttercup yellow banquettes; purveyor of fine tapas and wines; and, above all, a superbly relaxed place to chat and listen to music. Admittedly the foreigner quotient has risen in recent years, but it would be short-sighted to dismiss this little gem for that.

El Gran Café

C/Avinyó 9 (93 318 79 86). Metro Liceu. **Open** 1-4.30pm, 7.30pm-midnight daily. €€. **Mediterranean. Map** p55 B3 ㉔

The fluted columns, bronze nymphs, suspended globe lamps and wood panelling help El Gran replicate a classic Parisian vibe. The cornerstones of brasserie cuisine – onion soup, duck magret, tarte tatin and even crêpes suzette – are all present and correct. The imaginative Catalan dishes spliced into the menu also work, but the distinctly non-Gallic attitude towards the hastily assembled set lunch is less convincing.

La Granja

C/Banys Nous 4 (93 302 69 75). Metro Liceu. **Open** June-Sept 9.30am-1.30pm, 5-9pm Mon-Sat. Oct-May 9.30am-1.30pm, 5-9pm Mon-Sat; 5-9pm Sun. Closed Aug. No credit cards. **Café. Map** p55 B3 ㉕

La Granja is an old-fashioned café filled with yellowing photos and antiques, which has its very own section of Roman wall. You can stand your spoon in the tarry-thick hot chocolate, which won't be to all tastes; but the *xocolata amb café*, a mocha espresso, or the *xocolata picant*, chocolate with chilli, pack a mid-afternoon energy punch.

Machiroku

C/Moles 21 (93 412 60 82). Metro Catalunya. **Open** 1.30-3.30pm, 8.30-11.30pm Mon-Fri; 8.30-11.30pm Sat. Closed Aug. €€. No credit cards. **Japanese. Map** p55 C1 ㉖

A cosy, modest space decorated with Japanese wall hangings and prints. Service is charming and friendly and the various set menus at lunchtime offer good value, featuring rice and miso soup and then a choice of sushi, teriyaki, *yakinuku* (chargrilled beef) or a bento box with vegetable and prawn tempura. A short wine list has some excellent options.

Matsuri

Plaça Regomir 1 (93 268 15 35). Metro Jaume I. **Open** 1.30-3.30pm, 8.30-11.30pm Mon-Fri; 8.30pm-midnight Sat. €€. **Asian. Map** p55 C4 ㉗

A welcoming space painted in tasteful shades of ochre and terracotta, with the obligatory trickling fountain, wooden carvings and wall-hung candles, but saved from eastern cliché by some thoroughly occidental jazz in the background. Reasonably priced tom yam soup and pad thai feature, while the less predictable choices include *pho bo*, a Vietnamese broth with meat and spices, and *sake niku*, a delicious beef dish with wok-fried broccoli and a lightly perfumed soy sauce.

Mesón Jesús

C/Cecs de la Boqueria 4 (93 317 46 98).
Metro Jaume I or Liceu. **Open** 1-4pm,
8-11pm Mon-Fri. Closed Aug. **€**.
Spanish. Map p55 B3 ㉓
Old-school Castilian, with gingham
tablecloths, oak barrels and cartwheels
aplenty. The menu is limited and never
changes, but the dishes are reliably
good and inexpensive to boot – try the
sautéed green beans with ham to start,
then the superb grilled prawns or a
tasty *zarzuela* (fish stew). The wait-
resses are incessantly cheerful with a
largely non-Spanish-speaking clientele, and especially obliging when it
comes to dealing with children.

Milk

C/Gignas 21 (93 268 09 22/
www.milkbarcelona.com). *Metro
Jaume I.* **Open** *Aug* 7pm-3am Mon-
Fri; 11am-3am Sat, Sun. *Sept-July*
6pm-3am Mon-Fri; 11am-3am Sat,
Sun. **€€**. **Fusion/cocktails**.
Map p55 C4 ㉙
Still unchallenged in the Old City in
its provision of a decent brunch,
Milk's fry-ups, pancakes and smoothies are sadly only available at weekends (until 4pm). Its candlelit, low-key
baroque look, charming service and
cheap prices make it a good bet at any
time, however, with solid homemade
bistro grub from Caesar salad to
fish and chips.

Neri Restaurante

C/Sant Sever 5 (93 304 06 55/
www.hotelneri.com). *Metro Jaume I.*
Open 1.30-4pm, 8.30-11pm daily.
€€€€. **Catalan**. Map p55 B3 ㉚
These days, any Barcelona restaurant
worth its fleur de sel has an alumnus
of acclaimed chef Ferran Adrià head-
ing up its kitchens, and the Neri is no
exception. Jordi Ruiz has eschewed
the wilder excesses of molecular gas-
tronomy, however, and cooks with a
quiet assurance in tune with the som-
bre gothic arches, crushed velvet and
earthy tones of his dining room.

Onofre

C/Magdalenes 19 (93 317 69 37/
www.onofre.net). *Metro Urquinaona.*
Open 10am-5pm, 8pm-12.30am Mon-
Fri; 1pm-5pm, 8pm-1.30am Sat. Closed
Aug. **€€**. **Tapas**. Map p55 C1 ㉛
It's tiny and not especially well known,
but Onofre has a merited following
among local gourmands for its impec-
cably sourced wines, cured meats,
pâtés, hams and artisanal cheeses
from around the country. Increasingly,
it provides more elaborate dishes
too, such as a scallop gratin with
caramelised onion, or a pear tatin with
melted goat's cheese and Mallorcan
sobrassada sausage.

El Paraguayo

C/Parc 1 (93 302 14 41). *Metro
Drassanes.* **Open** 1-4pm, 8pm-midnight
Tue-Sun. **Main courses** €17.
Set lunch €12 Tue-Fri. **€€€**.
Paraguayan. Map p345 A5 ㉜
The only way to go at El Paraguayo is
to order a fat juicy steak, a bottle of good
cheap house Rioja and a bowl of piping
hot yucca chips. The rest is largely
menu filler. As to which steak, a helpful
chart walks you through the various
cuts, but a *bife de chorizo* should satisfy
the ravenous. The place itself is cosy
and wood-panelled, brightened with
Botero-esque oil paintings of buxom
madams and their dapper admirers.

Peimong

C/Templers 6-10 (93 318 28 73). *Metro
Jaume I.* **Open** 1-4pm, 8-11.30pm Tue-
Sat; 1-4pm Sun. Closed 2wks Aug. **€**.
Peruvian. Map p55 B4 ㉝
Not, perhaps, the fanciest-looking restaurant around (think Peruvian gimcracks,
strip lighting and tapestries of Macchu
Pichu) or indeed the fanciest-looking
food, but it sure tastes like the real thing.
Start with a pisco sour and a dish of
yucca chips or maybe some spicy corn
tamales, and then move on to ceviche
or the satisfying *lomo saltado* – pork
fried with onions, tomatoes and coriander. There are two types of Peruvian

La Boqueria p67

beer and even – for the very nostalgic or the hypoglycaemic – Inca Kola.

El Portalón

C/Banys Nous 20 (93 302 11 87). Metro Liceu. **Open** 9am-midnight Mon-Sat. Closed Aug. **€**. **Tapas**. **Map** p55 B3 ㉞

A rare pocket of authenticity in the increasingly touristy Barri Gòtic, this traditional tapas bar is located in what were once medieval stables, and it doesn't seem to worry too much about inheriting the ancient dust. The tapas list is long, but the torrades are also good: toasted bread topped with red peppers and anchovy, cheese, ham or whatever takes your fancy. House wine comes in terracotta jugs.

Els Quatre Gats

C/Montsió 3 bis (93 302 41 40/ www.4gats.com). Metro Catalunya. **Open** 10am-1am daily. **€€€**. **Café/Catalan**. **Map** p55 C1 ㉟

The essence of fin-de-siècle Barcelona, the 'Four Cats' was designed by Modernista heavyweight Puig i Cadafalch and patronised by the cultural glitterati of the era, most notably Picasso, who hung out here with Modernista painters Santiago Rusiñol and Ramon Casas. These days it's mostly frequented by tourists, but is nonetheless an essential stop for a coffee or a reasonable set lunch.

Les Quinze Nits

Plaça Reial 6 (93 317 30 75). Metro Liceu. **Open** 1-3.45pm, 8.30-11.30pm daily. **€**. **Spanish**. **Map** p55 A3 ㊱

The staggering success of the Quinze Nits enterprise (there are countless branches here in Barcelona and now in Madrid too, along with a handful of hotels) is down to one simple concept: style on a budget. All the restaurants have a certain Manhattan chic, yet you'll struggle to pay much more than €20 a head. The food plays second fiddle and is a hit-and-miss affair, but order simple dishes and at these prices you can't go far wrong.

Schilling

C/Ferran 23 (93 317 67 87). Metro Liceu. **Open** *Sept-July* 10am-2am Mon-Thur; 10am-3am Fri, Sat; noon-2.30am Sun. *Aug* 6.30pm-3am daily. **Café**. **Map** p55 B3 ㊲

BARCELONA BY AREA

Schilling's large windows that face on to the main thoroughfare connecting La Rambla with the Plaça Sant Jaume were once the spot to see and be seen, and although it's lost some of its cachet, it's still undeniably elegant – the high ceilings, bookshelves and traditional air contrasting with the fiercely modern young waiting staff. Weave through to the back for more intimate seating.

Shunka

C/Sagristans 5 (93 412 49 91). Metro Jaume I. **Open** 1.30-3.30pm, 8.30-11.15pm Tue-Fri; 2-3.30pm, 8.30-11.15pm Sat, Sun. Closed Aug & 1wk Xmas. **€€€. Japanese. Map** p55 C2 ③⑧
The speciality here, one of few good Japanese restaurants in the Old City, is prime-grade *toro*, fatty and deliciously creamy tuna belly. It's wildly expensive as a main, but you can sample it as nigiri-zushi. The house salad with raw fish also makes for a zingy starter, then you'll find all the usual staples of the sushi menu, along with heartier options like udon *kakiage*, a broth of langoustine tempura, vegetables and noodles.

Taller de Tapas

Plaça Sant Josep Oriol 9 (93 301 80 20/ www.tallerdetapas.com). Metro Liceu. **Open** 9am-midnight Mon-Fri; 10am-1am Sat; noon-midnight Sun. **€€.** **Tapas. Map** p55 B3 ③⑨
At its best, Taller de Tapas is an easy, multilingual environment, with plentiful outdoor seating, in which to try tapas from razor clams to local wild mushrooms. At busy periods, however, the service can be hurried and unhelpful, with dishes prepared in haste and orders confused, so it pays to avoid the lunchtime and evening rush hours.

Taxidermista

Plaça Reial 8 (93 412 45 36). Metro Liceu. **Open** 1.30-4pm, 7.30pm-12.30am Tue-Sun. Closed 3wks Jan. **€€.** **Mediterranean. Map** p55 B4 ④⓪
When this was a taxidermist's, Dalí ordered 200,000 ants, a tiger, a lion and a rhinoceros – the latter was wheeled into the Plaça Reial so that he could be photographed atop the beast. Those who leave here stuffed nowadays are mostly tourists, but standards remain reasonably high. À la carte offerings include foie gras with quince jelly; langoustine ravioli with seafood sauce; and some slightly misjudged fusion elements (wok-fried spaghetti with vegetables).

Tokyo

C/Comtal 20 (93 317 61 80). Metro Catalunya. **Open** 1.30-4pm, 8-11.30pm Mon-Sat. Closed Aug. **€€€. Japanese. Map** p55 C1 ④①
A small and simple space, where suspended beams, plastic plants and slatted wooden partitions are used to clever effect and the walls are lined with photos and drawings from grateful clients. The speciality is edomae (hand-rolled nigiri-zushi), but the meat and vegetable sukiyaki, which is cooked at your table, is also good, while the *menú* of sushi and tempura is great value. The red bean and green tea mochi rolls to finish are something of an acquired taste.

La Vinateria del Call

C/Sant Domènec del Call 9 (93 302 60 92). Metro Jaume I or Liceu. **Open** 8.30pm-1am Mon-Sat; 8.30pm-midnight Sun. **€€€. Tapas. Map** p55 B3 ④②
An atmospheric little bar, which places a high priority on the sourcing of its wine, hams and cheeses, and which has excellent homemade dishes, like a delicious fig ice-cream. Despite the antique fittings and dusty bottles, the staff – like the music they play – are young and lively, and some speak English.

Shopping

Almacenes del Pilar

C/Boqueria 43 (93 317 79 84/www. almacenesdelpilar.com). Metro Liceu. **Open** 10am-2pm, 4-8pm Mon-Sat. Closed 2wks Aug. **Map** p55 B3 ④③
An array of traditional Spanish fabrics and accessories is on display in this

L'Arca de l'Àvia

colourful, shambolic interior, dating all the way back to 1886. You'll find the richly hued brocades used for Valencian *fallera* outfits and other rudiments of folkloric dress from various parts of the country. Lace mantillas, and the high combs over which they are worn, are stocked, along with fringed, hand-embroidered pure silk shawls and colourful wooden fans.

L'Arca de l'Àvia

C/Banys Nous 20 (93 302 15 98/ www.larcadelavia.com). Metro Liceu. **Open** 5-8pm Mon; 10.30am-2pm, 5-8pm Tue-Fri; 11am-2pm Sat. Closed 2wks Aug. **Map** p55 B3 ㊹
Specialising in antique textiles, the 'Grandmother's Ark' smells of cloves and freshly ironed linen and is bursting with both antique and reproduction curtains, bed linen, table cloths, clothes and a snowstorm of handmade lace. It's particularly popular with brides seeking original veils, and is also the perfect place for a lace mantilla (headdress) or lavishly embroidered *mantones* (fringed silk shawls).

Arlequí Mascares

Plaça Sant Josep Oriol 8 (93 317 24 29/ www.arlequimask.com). Metro Liceu. **Open** 10.30am-8.30pm Mon-Sat; 10.30am-4.30pm Sun. **Map** p55 B3 ㊺
The walls here are dripping with masks, crafted from papier mâché and leather. Whether gilt-laden or in feathered commedia dell'arte style, simple Greek tragicomedy styles or traditional Japanese or Catalan varieties, they make striking fancy dress or decorative staples. Other trinkets and toys include finger puppets, mirrors and ornamental boxes.

La Boqueria

La Rambla 89, Raval (93 318 25 84/ www.boqueria.info). Metro Liceu. **Open** 8am-8.30pm Mon-Sat. **Map** p55 A3 ㊻
Thronged with tourists searching for a little bit of Barcelona's gastro magic, and usually ending up with a pre-sliced quarter of overpriced pineapple, Europe's biggest food market is still an essential stop. Admire the orderly stacks of ridged Montserrat tomatoes,

Caelum

the wet sacks of snails and the oozing razor clams on the fish stalls. If you can't or don't want to cook it all yourself, you can eat instead at several market tapas bars.

Visit in the morning for the best produce, including the smallholders' fruit and veg stalls in the little square attached to the C/Carme side of the market, where prices tend to be cheaper. But if you come only to ogle, remember that this is where locals come to shop. Don't touch what you don't want to buy, ask before taking photos and watch out for vicious old ladies with ankle-destroying wheeled shopping bags.

Le Boudoir

C/Canuda 21 (93 302 52 81/www. leboudoir.net). Metro Catalunya.
Open *Sept-July* 10am-8.30pm Mon-Fri; 10.30am-9pm Sat. *Aug* 11am-9pm Mon-Sat. **Map** p55 B1 ⓸⓻
Make like Dita Von Teese with feather boas, stockings, masks, gloves and, of course, racks of sexy bras, knickers, basques and suspender belts. To show you how to use it all, the shop runs monthly striptease classes.

Caelum

C/Palla 8 (93 302 69 93). Metro Liceu.
Open 5-8.30pm Mon; 10.30am-8.30pm Tue-Thur; 10.30am-11pm Fri, Sat; 11.30am-9pm Sun. Closed 1wk Aug.
Map p55 B2 ⓸⓼
Spain's monks and nuns have a naughty sideline in traditional sweets including *'pets de monja'* (little chocolate biscuits known as 'nuns' farts') candied saints' bones, and drinkable goodies such as eucalyptus and orange liqueur, all beautifully packaged. If you'd like to sample before committing to a whole box of Santa Teresa's sugared egg yolks, there's a café downstairs on the site of the medieval Jewish thermal baths.

Casa Beethoven

La Rambla 97 (93 301 48 26/www. casabeethoven.com). Metro Liceu.
Open 9am-2pm, 4-8pm Mon-Fri; 9am-1.30pm, 5-8pm Sat. Closed 3wks Aug.
Map p55 A2 ⓸⓽

The sheet music and songbooks on sale in this old shop cover the gamut from Wagner to the White Stripes, with a focus on opera. Books cover music history and theory, while CDs are particularly strong on both modern and classical Spanish music.

Cereria Subirà

Baixada de Llibreteria 7 (93 315 26 06). Metro Jaume I. **Open** 9am-1.30pm, 4-7.30pm Mon-Fri; 9am-1.30pm Sat. **Map** p55 C3 ⑳

With a staircase fit for a full swish from Scarlett O'Hara, this exquisite candle shop dates back to the pre-electric days of 1716 when candles were an everyday necessity at home and in church. These days, the votive candles sit next to novelties such as After Eight-scented candles and candles in the shape of the Sagrada Família.

Decathlon

C/Canuda 20 (93 342 61 61/www. decathlon.es). Metro Catalunya. **Open** 9.30am-9.30pm Mon-Sat. **Map** p55 B2 ㉑

Whether you need boxing gloves or a bivouac, a beach volleyball or a bicycle lock, this multi-storey French chain will probably be able to see you right. Additional services include bike repair and hire, and team-kit stamping.

Flora Albaicín

C/Canuda 3 (93 302 10 35). Metro Catalunya. **Open** 10.30am-1pm, 5-8pm Mon-Sat. **Map** p55 B1 ㉒

This tiny boutique is bursting at the seams with brightly coloured flamenco frocks, polka-dotted shoes, head combs, bangles, shawls and everything else you need to dance the sevillanas in style.

Formatgeria La Seu

C/Dagueria 16 (93 412 65 48/www. formatgerialaseu.com). Metro Jaume I. **Open** 10am-2pm, 5-8pm Tue-Thur; 10am-3.30pm, 5-8pm Fri, Sat. Closed Aug. No credit cards. **Map** p55 C3 ㉓

This is the only shop in the country to specialise in Spanish-only farmhouse

Herboristeria del Rei

cheeses. Scottish owner Katherine McLaughlin hand-picks her wares, such as a Manchego that knocks the socks off anything you'll find in the market, or the truly strange Catalan Tupí. She also stocks six varieties of cheese ice-cream and some excellent-value olive oils.

Herboristeria del Rei

C/Vidre 1 (93 318 05 12). Metro Liceu. **Open** 4-8pm Tue-Fri; 10am-8pm Sat. Closed 1-2wks Aug. **Map** p55 B3 ㉔

Designed by a theatre set designer in the 1860s, this atmospheric shop hides myriad herbs, infusions, ointments and unguents for health and beauty. More up-to-date stock includes vegetarian foods, organic olive oils and organic mueslis; it's also a good place to buy saffron.

El Ingenio

C/Rauric 6 (93 317 71 38/www.el-ingenio.com). Metro Liceu. **Open** 10am-1.30pm, 4.15-8pm Mon-Fri; 11am-2pm, 5-8.30pm Sat. **Map** p55 B3 ㉕

At once enchanting and disturbing, El Ingenio's handcrafted toys, tricks and costumes are reminders of a pre-digital world where people made their own entertainment. Its cabinets are full of practical jokes and curious toys; its fascinating workshop produces the oversized heads and garish costumes used in Barcelona's traditional festivities.

Joguines Monforte

Plaça Sant Josep Oriol 3 (93 318 22 85/ www.joguinesmonforte.com). Metro Liceu. **Open** 9.30am-1.30pm, 4-8pm Mon-Fri; 10am-2pm, 4.30-8.30pm Sat. **Map** p55 B3 ❺❻

This venerable toy shop has been selling traditional toys, board games and everything you need for a game of billiards since 1840. Try the Spanish version of snakes and ladders (*el juego de la oca*, or the 'goose game') and ludo (*parchís*) along with chess, jigsaws, painted tin toys and outdoor games such as croquet and skittles.

Papabubble

C/Ample 28 (93 268 86 25/www. papabubble.com). Metro Barceloneta or Drassanes. **Open** 10am-2pm, 4-8.30pm Tue-Fri; 10am-8.30pm Sat; 11am-7.30pm Sun. Closed 2wks Aug. **Map** p55 C5 ❺❼

Push through the crowds to watch the Australian owners stretch, roll and chop their kaleidoscopic rock candy into lollies, sticks, humbugs and novelty sculptures. The goodies come in any flavour from strawberry to lavender or passion fruit.

Women's Secret

C/Portaferrissa 7-9 (93 318 92 42/ www.womensecret.com). Metro Liceu. **Open** 10am-9pm Mon-Sat. **Map** p55 B2 ❺❽

There are some sexy pieces at Women's Secret, but the stock is mostly versatile strap bras, brightly printed cotton PJs and a funky line of under-/outerwear in cartoonish stylings: skimpy shorts, miniskirts and vest tops.

Xilografies

C/Freneria 1 (93 315 07 58). Metro Jaume I. **Open** 10am-2pm Mon-Sat. Closed Aug. No credit cards. **Map** p55 C3 ❺❾

Using painstakingly detailed 18th-century carved boxwood blocks that have been passed down in her family for generations, Maria creates ex libris stickers for books, notepaper, address books and prints. She also sells pens, birthday cards, prints of 18th-century maps and reproduction pocket sundials.

Nightlife

Barcelona Pipa Club

Plaça Reial 3, pral (93 302 47 32/ www.bpipaclub.com). Metro Liceu. **Open** 11pm-3am daily. **Admission** free. No credit cards. **Map** p55 A3 ❻⓪

A converted flat on Plaça Reial, decorated with oak, velvet, Sherlock Holmes-style memorabilia and a bar that's often impossible to get anywhere near, despite the high prices. For all its genteel decor, it has a semi-underground quality and is rammed with young Americans and their Catalan friends. Ring the bell downstairs to get in.

Fellini

La Rambla 27 (93 272 49 80/www. clubfellini.com). Metro Liceu. **Open** July-mid Sept 12.30am-5am Mon-Thur; 12.30am-6am Fri, Sat. Mid Sept-June 12.30am-5am Mon, Thur; 12.30-6am Sat. **Admission** free before 1.30am Mon-Sat; €9 (with flyer), €9 Mon-Wed; €12 (with flyer), €15 Thur-Sat. No credit cards. **Map** p55 A4 ❻❶

For a club on La Rambla, Fellini draws a remarkably mixed and local crowd to its two floors of tech-house and the Red Room, where you might find rock, '80s or hip hop. The space is great (huge, well divided and remarkably devoid of typical nightclub tack), the bar staff efficient and the guest DJs some of the world's best. Shame about the meat-market vibe and the quick-to-anger, truck-shaped bouncers.

Northern exposure

Scandinavian culture comes in from the cold.

Still Light

New Nordic is sweeping Barcelona. It started with Scandinavian concept stores, which have cropped up over the city, where cool northern minimalism meshes nicely with slick Barcelona styling.

Up in Gràcia, **Snö Mito Nórdico** (C/Sèneca 33, Gràcia, 93 218 08 59, www.snobarcelona.com) offers a smörgåsbord of clothing, hair and skincare products, jewellery and household design objects from internationally recognised Nordic labels. Most have not yet been introduced to Spain, and include Rodebjer, House of Dagmar, Ole Hendrikson and Rika, as well the store's signature label, Snö. A collective of designers create and sell their clothes in **Still Light** (p96), which also exhibits artwork, plays the latest Nordic sounds and stocks magazines, books and design

items, as does more youth-oriented sister shop **Bingo** (C/Roger de Llúria 45, Eixample, 93 467 62 86, www.bingoshop barcelona.com). Over in the Born, **Å-Copenhagen** (C/Ribera 8, Born, mobile 625 152 655, www.acopenhagen.com) offers mostly Danish fashion labels including Baum und Pferdgarten, Filippa K, Bruuns Bazaar and Mads Nørgaard.

Barcelona's exposure to Nordic cuisine has come a long way from the Swedish meatballs at IKEA. Young Finnish chefs Matti Romppanen and Tero Siltanen recently opened **Routa** (C/Enric Granados 10, Eixample, 93 451 19 97, www.restaurant-routa.com), Barcelona's first high-level Scandinavian restaurant, which employs traditional techniques of smoking, salting and pickling in delicacies such as smoked herring ravioli and ice-cream, or sweetbreads with horseradish gel and beetroot risotto. For organic, old-style Scandinavian baked goods such as oat cakes, spelt bread and rye bread, head to **Barcelona Reykjavik** (C/Doctor Dou 12, Raval, 93 302 09 21, www. barcelonareykjavik.com). A less wholesome experience is on offer at the kitschy **Edda Nordisk Bar** (C/Blasco de Garay 15, Poble Sec, 93 443 24 44, www. eddanordiskbar.com) where Barcelona's Scandinavian community bond over shots of Aquavit, Swedish Kopparberg cider and Finnish Lapin Kulta at themed Eurovision nights.

BARCELONA BY AREA

Harlem Jazz Club

C/Comtessa de Sobradiel 8 (93 310 07 55). Metro Jaume I. **Open** *July-Sept* 8pm-4am Tue-Thur; 8pm-5am Fri, Sat. *Oct-June* 8pm-4am Tue-Thur, Sun; 8pm-5am Fri, Sat. *Gigs* 10.30pm, midnight Tue-Thur, Sun; 11.30pm, 1am Fri, Sat. Closed 2wks Aug. **Admission** free Tue-Thur; (incl 1 drink) €7.50 Fri-Sun. No credit cards. **Map** p55 B4 ⑫

Despite the DJ booth, live music is what the Harlem Jazz Club does best, so it's no surprise that it's a regular hangout for not-so-cashed-up musicians, buffs and students alike. A lot of local musical history's gone down at Harlem, and some of the city's greatest talents have emerged from here. Jazz, klezmer, funk and flamenco get a run in a venue that holds no musical prejudices.

Jamboree/Los Tarantos

Plaça Reial 17 (93 319 17 89/www. masimas.com). Metro Liceu. **Open** 8pm-11am daily. *Shows* Jamboree 9pm, 11pm daily. Tarantos 8.30pm, 9.30pm, 10.30pm daily. **Open** 1-5am Mon-Thur, Sun; 1-6am Fri, Sat. **Admission** *Shows* €6-€12. *Club* €10. Map p55 A4 ⑬

The cave-like Jamboree hosts jazz, Latin or blues gigs by mainly Spanish groups – on Mondays, in particular, the outrageously popular What the Fuck (WTF) jazz jam session is crammed with a young crowd. Upstairs, slicker sister venue Los Tarantos stages flamenco performances, then joins forces with Jamboree to become one fun, cheesy club later on.

La Macarena

C/Nou de Sant Francesc 5 (no phone/ www.macarenaclub.com). Metro Drassanes. **Open** 11.30pm-4.30am Mon-Thur, Sun; 11.30pm-5.30am Fri, Sat. **Admission** free before 1.30am; €5 afterwards (but can vary). No credit cards. **Map** p55 B4 ⑭

La Macarena is smaller than your apartment but has big-club pretensions in the best sense: the music is excellent – minimal electro selected by resident DJs and the occasional big-name guest (who usually appear the day before or after a bigger gig elsewhere) – and complemented by a kicking sound system. Watch your bag and your drink.

Sidecar Factory Club

Plaça Reial 7 (93 302 15 86/www. sidecarfactoryclub.com). Metro Liceu. **Open** 6pm-4.30am Mon-Thur; 6pm-5am Fri, Sat. **Admission** (incl 1 drink) €5 before 2am; €7 after 2am Mon-Thur; €7 Fri, Sat. *Gigs* €5-€15. No credit cards. **Map** p55 B3 ⑮

Sidecar still has all the ballsy attitude of the spit 'n' sawdust rock club that it once was and programming that includes breakbeat, indie, electro and live shows continues to pack in the local indie kids and Interrailers.

Arts & leisure

Gran Teatre del Liceu

La Rambla 51-59 (93 485 99 13/tickets 902 53 33 53/www.liceubarcelona.com). Metro Liceu. **Open** *Information* 11am-2pm, 3-8pm Mon-Fri. *Tickets* vary. **Map** p55 A3 ⑯

Since it opened in 1847, two fires, a bombing and financial crisis have failed to quash the spirit and splendour of the Liceu. A restrained façade opens into an elegant 2,292-seat auditorium of red plush, gold leaf and ornate carvings. The latest mod cons include seat-back subtitles in various languages that complement the Catalan subtitles above the stage. Under the stewardship of artistic director Joan Matabosch and musical director Sebastian Weigle, the Liceu has consolidated its programming policy, mixing co-productions with leading international opera houses with its own in-house productions. Classical, full-length opera is the staple. Opened at the end of 2008, its adjoining six-floor Conservatori (C/Nou de la Rambla 82-88, 93 304 11 13, www.conservatori-liceu.es) lends its 400-seater basement auditorium to classical and contemporary concerts, small-scale operas and even jazz.

Born & Sant Pere

Label-happy cool-hunters throng the Born's pedestrian streets, where museums, restored 13th-century mansions and churches alternate with cafés, galleries and boutiques. Regeneration has come more slowly for the neighbouring area of Sant Pere, north of C/Princesa, which maintains a slightly grungier feel despite the municipal money-pumping. Still, there have been recent large-scale improvements, such as the long Plaça Pou de la Figuera and the spectacularly reinvented Santa Caterina market. The area is demarcated to the east by the glorious Parc de la Ciutadella and to the west by Via Laietana. In 2010, work is due to start on turning over some of the latter's car lanes to pedestrians.

'Born' originally meant 'joust' or 'list', and in the Middle Ages, and for many centuries thereafter, the neighbourhood's main artery, the Passeig del Born, was the focal point of the city's festivals, processions, tournaments, carnivals and the burning of heretics by the Inquisition. At one end of the road is the old Born market, a magnificent 1870s wrought-iron structure, which is to be turned into a cultural centre and museum, although progress is painfully slow. Leading off the Passeig del Born is C/Montcada, lined with a succession of 15th-century merchants' mansions.

BARCELONA BY AREA

Sights & museums

Museu Barbier-Mueller d'Art Precolombí

C/Montcada 14 (93 310 45 16/ www.barbier-mueller.ch). Metro Jaume I. **Open** 11am-7pm Tue-Fri; 10am-7pm Sat; 10am-3pm Sun. **Admission** €3.50; €1.70 reductions; free under-16s & 1st Sun of mth. **Map** p75 B4 ❶

Palau de la Música Catalana p76

Located in the 15th-century Palau Nadal, this world-class collection of pre-Columbian art was ceded to Barcelona in 1996 by the Barbier-Mueller Museum in Geneva. The holdings focus solely on the Americas, representing most of the styles from the ancient cultures of Meso-America, Andean America and the Amazon region. The frequently changing selection of masks, textiles, jewellery and sculpture includes pieces dating from as far back as the second millennium BC running through to the early 16th-century (demonstrating just how loosely the term 'pre-Columbian' can be used).

Museu de Ciències Naturals

Natural History Museum
Passeig Picasso (93 319 69 12/ www.bcn.cat/museuciencies). Metro Arc de Triomf. **Open** 10am-6.30pm Tue-Sat; 10am-2.30pm, 3-8pm Sun. **Admission** All exhibitions & Jardí Botànic €5.30; €3.70 reductions. Free under-16s & 1st Sun of mth. No credit cards. **Map** p75 C3 **②**
The Natural History Museum is split between Domènech i Montaner's turreted Castell dels Tres Dragons and the nearby Museu Martorell, housing the

zoology and geology museums respectively. The first floor of the zoology museum is a spooky hall of stuffed animals, preserved insects and molluscs. Several animals from the collection have enjoyed a moment of fame being lent out for TV and theatre shows and the horned mouflon skull was the direct inspiration for the Oscar-winning faun make-up in the film *Pan's Labyrinth*. Don't expect any multimedia displays – this is an old-school affair of glass cases and formaldehyde jars.

Over in the geology museum, the entrance contains meteorites, gems, crystals, radioactive minerals and rocks from the Earth's lithosphere. Some 300,000 fossils reside in the Palaeontology Hall, alongside 12 full-scale 1917 replicas of large extinct animals. A combined ticket also grants entrance to the Jardí Botànic on Montjuïc (p112).

Museu de la Xocolata

Chocolate Museum
C/Comerç 36 (93 268 78 78/ www.museudelaxocolata.cat). Metro Arc de Triomf or Jaume I. **Open** 10am-7pm Mon, Wed-Sat; 10am-3pm Sun. **Admission** €4.30; €3.75 reductions; free under-7s. **Map** p75 C3 **③**

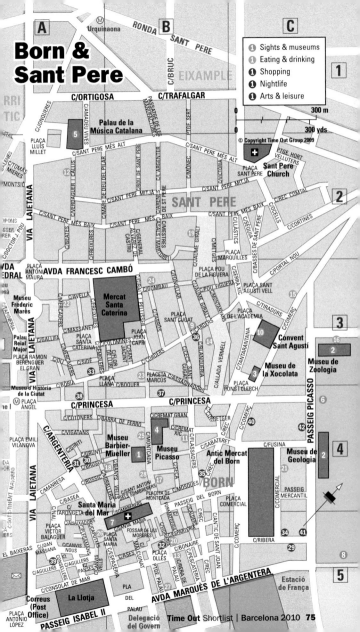

Born &
Sant Pere

A **B** **C**

Urquinaona
RONDA SANT PERE

C/BRUC

EIXAMPLE

1 Sights & museums
1 Eating & drinking
1 Shopping
1 Nightlife
1 Arts & leisure

C/ORTIGOSA   C/TRAFALGAR

1

Palau de la
Música Catalana

5

0   300 m
0   300 yds
© Copyright Time Out Group 2009

PTGE HORT
VELLUTERS

PLAÇA
LLUÍS
MILLET

C/SANT PERE MÉS ALT

PLAÇA
SANT PERE

Sant Pere
Church

C/COMTAL

2

12

C/SANT PERE MÉS ALT

C/SANT PERE MITJÀ

SANT PERE

C/SANT PERE MÉS BAIX

C/CORTINES

PLAÇA
MARQUILLES

19

PLAÇA POU
DE LA FIGUERA

C/BASSES DE SANT PERE

C/PORTAL NOU

AVDA FRANCESC CAMBÓ

PLAÇA
SANT
AGUSTÍ VELL

24

15

Mercat
Santa
Caterina

C/TIRADORS

Museu
Frederic
Marès

PLAÇA
SANT CUGAT

9

PLAÇA
DE L'ACADÈMIA

10

Convent
Sant Agustí

Palau
Reial
Major

36

14

16

2

Museu de
Zoologia

PLAÇA RAMON
BERENGUER
EL GRAN

33

23

PLAÇA
LLANA

3

Museu de
la Xocolata

3

Museu d'Història
de la Ciutat

38

PLAÇETA
MARCUS

PLAÇA
PONS I CLERCH

PASSEIG PICASSO

PLAÇA
ÀNGEL

37

6

C/PRINCESA   C/PRINCESA

C/CREMAT GRAN

40

PLAÇA EMIL
VILANOVA

C/COTONERS   C/BARRA DE FERRO

Museu
Barbier-
Mueller

4

C/CREMAT
XIC

11

42

4

C/ARGENTERIA

1

Museu
Picasso

Antic Mercat
del Born

Museu de
Geologia

2

31 **30**

18

25

28

17

C/FUSINA

C/COMERCIAL

21

PASSEIG
MERCANTIL

Santa Maria
del Mar

7

PLAÇA
SANTA
MARIA

PASSEIG DEL BORN

BORN

PLAÇA
COMERCIAL

PLAÇA
VÍCTOR
BALAGUER

Fossar de les
Moreres

32

34 **41**

C/RIBERA

29

8

PLAÇA
OLLES

13

27

AVDA MARQUÉS DE L'ARGENTERA

Estació
de França

5

Correus
(Post
Office)

La Llotja

PLA
DEL
PALAU

Delegació
del Govern

PLAÇA
ANTONIO
LÓPEZ

PASSEIG ISABEL II

Parc de la Ciutadella

The best-smelling museum in town draws chocoholics of all ages to its collection of chocolate sculptures made by Barcelona's master *pastissers* for the Easter competition. These range from multicoloured models of Gaudí's Casa Batlló to characters from *Chicken Run*, while audio-visual shows and touchscreen computers help lead children through what would otherwise be the dry history of the cocoa bean.

Museu Picasso

C/Montcada 15-23 (93 256 30 00/ www.museupicasso.bcn.cat). Metro Jaume I. **Open** (last ticket 30mins before closing) 10am-8pm Tue-Sun. **Admission** *Annual pass* €10. *All exhibitions* €9; €5.80 reductions. *Temporary exhibition only* €5.80; €4.80 reductions; free under-16s & 1st Sun of mth.* **Map** p75 B4 ❹
The Picasso Museum takes up a row of medieval mansions, with the main entrance now at the Palau Meca. By no means an overview of the artist's work, it's a record of the vital formative years that the young Picasso spent nearby at

La Llotja art school, and later hanging out with the fin-de-siècle avant-garde.

The presentation of Picasso's development from 1890 to 1904, from deft pre-adolescent portraits to sketchy landscapes to the intense innovations of his Blue Period, is seamless and unbeatable; the collection then leaps to a gallery of mature Cubist paintings from 1917. The pièce de résistance, however, is the complete series of 57 canvases based on Velázquez's famous *Las Meninas*, stretching through three rooms. The display ends with a wonderful collection of ceramics. Temporary exhibitions are held under the magnificent coffered ceiling of the Palau Finestres. A new annual pass is excellent value and allows the visitor to skip the interminable queues. **Event highlights** Picasso's erotic prints (5 Nov 2009-14 Feb 2010).

Palau de la Música Catalana

C/Sant Francesc de Paula 2 (93 295 72 00/www.palaumusica.org). Metro Urquinaona. **Open** *Box office* 10am-9pm Mon-Sat. *Guided tours* Sept-July

10am-3.30pm daily. Aug 10am-6pm.
Admission €10; €9 reductions.
Map p75 A2 **⑤**
Commissioned by the nationalistic Orfeó Català choral society, this jaw-dropping concert hall was intended as a paean to the Catalan renaixença and a showcase for the most outstanding Modernista workmanship available. Domènech i Montaner's façade is a frenzy of colour and detail, including a large allegorical mosaic representing the members of the Orfeó Català, and floral tiled columns topped with the busts of Bach, Beethoven and Palestrina on the main façade and Wagner on the side. Indoors, decoration erupts every-where. The ceiling is an inverted bell of stained glass depicting the sun bursting out of a blue sky; 18 half-mosaic, half-relief Muses appear from the back of the stage; winged horses fly over the upper balcony, and Wagnerian Valkyries ride over a bust of Beethoven.

Guided tours are available in English every hour and start with a short film of the Palau's history.

Parc de la Ciutadella
Passeig Picasso (93 413 2400). Metro Arc de Triomf or Barceloneta. **Open** 9am-sunset daily. **Admission** free.
Map p75 C4 **⑥**
Named after the hated Bourbon citadel – the largest in Europe – that occupied this site from 1716 to 1869, this elegant park contains a host of attractions, including the city zoo (p78), the Natural History Museum, a boating lake and more than 30 pieces of imaginative statuary. The giant mammoth statue at the far side of the boating lake is a huge hit with kids, as is the trio of prancing deer by the zoo dedicated to Walt Disney. In the north-east corner is the Cascade, an ornamental fountain topped with Aurora's chariot, on which a young Gaudí worked as assistant to Josep Fontseré, the architect of the park. Not to be missed are Fontseré's slatted wooden Umbracle (literally, 'shade house'), which provides a pocket

Zoo p78

of tropical forest within the city, and the elegant Hivernacle ('winter garden') designed by Josep Amargós in 1884. Outside, on the Passeig Picasso, is Antoni Tàpies's *A Picasso*, which is a giant Cubist monument to the artist.

Santa Maria del Mar
Plaça de Santa Maria (93 310 23 90). Metro Jaume I. **Open** 9am-1.30pm, 4.30-8pm Mon-Sat; 10am-1.30pm, 4.30-8pm Sun. **Admission** free. **Map** p75 B5 **⑦**
One of the most perfect surviving examples of the Catalan Gothic style, this graceful basilica stands out for its characteristic horizontal lines, plain surfaces, square buttresses and flat-topped octagonal towers. Its superb unity of style is down to the fact that it was built relatively quickly, with construction taking just 55 years (1329 to 1384). In the broad, single-nave interior, two rows of perfectly proportioned columns soar up to fan vaults, creating an atmosphere of space around the light-flooded altar. There's also superb stained glass, especially the great 15th-century rose window above the main

door. The original window fell down during an earthquake, killing 25 people. The incongruous modern window at the other end was a 1997 addition, belatedly celebrating the Olympics.

It's perhaps thanks to the group of anti-clerical anarchists who set the church ablaze for 11 days in 1936 that its superb features can be appreciated – without the wooden Baroque furniture that clutters so many Spanish churches, the simplicity of its lines can emerge. **Event highlights** Handel's *Messiah* (Christmas 2009 & 2010); Mozart's *Requiem* (Easter 2010).

Zoo

Parc de la Ciutadella (93 225 67 80/ www.zoobarcelona.com). Metro Barceloneta or Ciutadella-Vila Olímpica. **Open** *Mar, Oct* 10am-6pm daily. *Apr-Sept* 10am-7pm daily. *Nov-Feb* 10am-5pm daily. **Admission** €15.40; €9.30 3-12s; free under-3s. **Map** p75 C5 **8**

The dolphin shows are the big draw, but the decently sized zoo has plenty of other animals, all of whom look happy enough in reasonably spacious enclosures. Favourites include giant hippos, the prehistoric-looking rhino, sea lions, elephants, giraffes, lions and tigers. Child-friendly features include a farmyard zoo, pony rides, picnic areas and two excellent playgrounds.

Eating & drinking

El Atril

NEW *C/Carders 23 (93 310 12 20/ www.atrilbarcelona.com). Metro Jaume I.* **Open** 1.30-4.30pm, 7.30-12.30pm Tue-Sun. €€. **Global**. **Map** p75 B3 **9**

El Atril's handful of tables require a reservation on most nights of the week thanks to some reliably good cooking traversing a broad range of cuisines. On the tapas menu fried green plantains with coriander and lime mayonnaise sit alongside *botifarra* with caramelised onions, while a catholic selection of main courses includes a bowl of Belgian-style mussels and chips.

Bar del Convent

NEW *Plaça de l'Acàdemia (no phone). Metro Arc de Triomf or Jaume I.* **Open** 9am-10pm Mon-Thur; 10am-midnight Fri, Sat. No credit cards. **Café**. **Map** p75 C3 **10**

The 14th-century Convent de Sant Agustí has had a new lease of life in recent years – first with James Turrell's fabulous 'light sculpture' surrounding the C/Comerç entrance, then with the opening of a dynamic civic centre. And now this secluded little café has opened in the cloister. There are croissants, pastries and light dishes available all day, and live music, DJs, storytelling and other performances on Friday and Saturday nights.

La Báscula

C/Flassaders 30 (93 319 98 66). Metro Jaume I. **Open** 7pm-midnight Wed-Fri; 1pm-midnight Sat. €. No credit cards. **Vegetarian**. **Map** p75 B4 **11**

After a sustained campaign, the threat of demolition has been lifted from this former chocolate factory turned café. Just as well, since it's a real find, with good vegetarian food and a large dining room situated out back. An impressive list of drinks runs from chai to Glühwein, taking in cocktails, milkshakes, smoothies and iced tea, and the pasta and cakes are as good as you'll find anywhere.

El Bitxo

C/Verdaguer i Callis 9 (93 268 17 08). Metro Urquinaona. **Open** 7pm-midnight Mon; 1pm-midnight Tue-Thur; 1pm-1am Fri, Sat. No credit cards. €€. **Tapas**. **Map** p75 A2 **12**

A small, lively tapas bar specialising in excellent cheese and charcuterie from the small Catalan village of Oix, along with more outré fare such as salmon sashimi with a coffee reduction. The wine list is steadily increasing and now has around 30 suggestions, all of them good. Being so close to the Palau de la Música, the bar can get packed in the early evening before concerts.

Comerç 24

centre for a young and thrusting scene that attracts DJs from the higher echelons of cool. In the daytime, it's just a nice place for parents to have a cheeky beer on the terrace while the children amuse themselves in the playground just in front.

Comerç 24

C/Comerç 24 (93 319 21 02/www.
comerc24.com). Metro Arc de Triomf.
Open 1.30-3.30pm, 8.30pm-11pm
Tue-Sat. €€€€. **Modern tapas**.
Map p75 C3 ⑮

Carles Abellan trained under Ferran Adrià but now ploughs his own very successful furrow in this sexy restaurant. A selection of tiny playful dishes changes seasonally, but normally includes the ever popular 'Kinder egg' (lined with truffle) and the tuna sashimi and seaweed on a wafer-thin pizza crust. Adrià's latest discoveries continue to affect Abellan's menu, so recently he's been embracing Eastern cuisine.

Cal Pep

Plaça de les Olles 8 (93 310 79 61/
www.calpep.com). Metro Barceloneta.
Open 8-11.45pm Mon; 1.30-4pm,
8-11.45pm Tue-Fri; 1.30-4pm Sat.
Closed Aug & Easter week. €€€.
Seafood. Map p75 B5 ⑬

As much tapas bar as restaurant, Cal Pep is always packed: get here early for the coveted front seats. The affable Pep will take the order, steering the neophytes towards the *trifásico* – a mélange of fried whitebait, squid rings and shrimp. Other faves are the exquisite little *tallarines* (wedge clams), and *botifarra* sausage with beans.

Casa Paco

C/Allada-Vermell 10 (no phone/
www.casapaco.org). Metro Arc de
Triomf or Jaume I. **Open** Apr-Sept
9am-2am Mon-Thur, Sun; 9am-3am
Fri, Sat; Oct-Mar 6pm-2am Tue-Thur,
Sun; 6pm-3am Fri, Sat. No credit cards.
Bar. Map p75 B3 ⑭

Not much more than a hole-in-the-wall with a handful of zinc tables outside, Casa Paco is the improbable nerve

Drac Café

NEW Parc de la Ciutadella, Passeig
Lluis Companys entrance (93 310 76
06/www.draccafe.com). Metro Arc de
Triomf. **Open** 9am-9pm Tue-Sun. €.
No credit cards. **Café**. Map p75 C3 ⑯

With this alfresco terrace café, the Parc de la Ciutadella finally has a healthy alternative to the *kioskos* serving overpriced beer and bags of rainbow popcorn. Not much more than a *kiosko* itself, the friendly 'Dragon Café' serves breakfast all day, along with salads, nachos, guacamole and houmous, served tapas-style.

Euskal Etxea

Placeta Montcada 1-3 (93 310 21 85).
Metro Barceloneta or Jaume I. **Open**
Bar 7pm-midnight Mon; noon-5pm,
7pm-midnight Tue-Sat. Restaurant
8.30-11.30pm Mon; 1.30-4pm, 8.30-
11.30pm Tue-Sat. Closed 1wk Dec-Jan.
€. **Tapas**. Map p75 B4 ⑰

A Basque cultural centre and the best of the city's many *pintxo* bars. Help

BARCELONA BY AREA

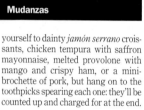

Mudanzas

yourself to dainty *jamón serrano* croissants, chicken tempura with saffron
mayonnaise, melted provolone with
mango and crispy ham, or a mini-
brochette of pork, but hang on to the
toothpicks spearing each one: they'll be
counted up and charged for at the end.

Itztli

*C/Mirallers 7 (93 319 68 75/
www.itztli.es). Metro Barceloneta or
Jaume I.* **Open** noon-11pm Tue-Sun.
€. Mexican. Map p75 B4 ⑱
Fortify yourself in the interminable
queue for entry to the Picasso Museum
with a takeaway chicken burrito from
this nearby Mexican snack bar. Keenly
priced around the €3.50 mark, burritos
also come with beef, chilli con carne or
veg, as do tacos. There's also a good
range of Mexican beers, tinned goods
and fiery chilli sauces for sale.

Mosquito

*C/Jaume Giralt 53 (93 315 17 44).
Metro Arc de Triomf or Jaume I.*
Open 8pm-midnight Mon; 1-4pm,
8pm-midnight Tue-Thur, Sun;

1-4pm, 8pm-1am Fri, Sat. **€.**
Asian. Map p75 B2 ⑲
Rehoused in a bigger, post-industrial
space with an expanded menu to
match, Mosquito continues to turn out
affordable, shareable, Asian 'tapas',
and has added some excellent beers,
some brewed especially for the restaurant; the *trigo* (wheat) is superb. Of the
new dishes, the *xiaolong bao* (steamed
pork dumplings) and crispy duck are
more than toothsome, and the crunchy
potato chaat still heads up the list.

Mudanzas

*C/Vidrieria 15 (93 319 11 37). Metro
Barceloneta or Jaume I.* **Open** *Sept-July*
10am-2.30am Mon-Thur, Sun; 10am-
3am Fri, Sat. *Aug* 5.30pm-2.30am Mon-
Thur, Sun; 5.30pm-3am Fri, Sat. **Bar.**
Map p75 B5 ⑳
Eternally popular with all ages and
nationalities, Mudanzas has a beguil-
ing, old-fashioned look, with marble-
topped tables, a black-and-white
chequered floor and a rack of newspapers and magazines, many of them in
English. It can get very smoky in the

winter months, though relief can be found at the tables on the mezzanine.

La Paradeta

C/Comercial 7 (93 268 19 39/www.laparadeta.com). Metro Arc de Triomf or Jaume I. **Open** 8-11.30pm Tue-Fri; 1-4pm, 8pm-midnight Sat; 1-4pm Sun. **€**. **Seafood**. Map p75 C4 ㉑
Superb seafood, served refectory-style. Choose from glistening mounds of clams, mussels, squid, spider crabs and other fresh treats, decide how you'd like it cooked (grilled, steamed or *a la marinera*), pick a sauce (Marie Rose, spicy local romesco, all i oli or onion), buy a drink and wait for your number to be called. A great and cheap experience for anyone not too grand to clear their own plate.

Patxoca

NEW C/Mercaders 28 (93 319 20 29). Metro Jaume I or Urquinaona. **Open** 8am-2am Mon-Sat. **€€**. **Catalan**. Map p75 A3 ㉒
Describing itself as *'agroecològic'*, Patxoca endeavours to source produce locally (with the curious omission of most of its wines) and buys organic wherever feasible. The cornerstones of Catalan soul food are all present, from *cap i pota* (stew of calves' head and meat) to salt cod, while homesick Brits can take comfort in a local take on shepherd's pie (*pastis de vedella*) or cauliflower cheese.

Re-Pla

NEW C/Montcada 2 (93 268 30 03). Metro Jaume I. **Open** noon-11pm Tue-Sat. **€€€**. **Tapas**. Map p75 B3 ㉓
The fetching new look at this longtime favourite is halfway between a French bistro and tapas joint, with a long marble bar. There are three small dishes and a pudding for €10; otherwise, it's tapas or *raciones* (such as divine pig's trotters with foie, and outstanding *pa amb tomàquet*). Drinks include Mahou on tap, plus some good wines by the glass.

Rococó

C/Gombau 5-7 (93 269 16 58). Metro Jaume I. **Open** Sept-July 9am-midnight Mon-Thur; 9am-1am Fri, Sat. Aug 10am-midnight Mon-Thur; 10am-1am Fri; 6pm-1am Sat. Closed 2wks Aug. **€**. **Café**. Map p75 B3 ㉔
On the ground floor of a nondescript block, Rococó manages to live up to its name thanks to red velvet seating, flock wallpaper and gilt-edged paintings. A wildly varied menu takes in a range of delicious *bocadillos* on homemade ciabatta, gnocchi with wild mushroom sauce, Vietnamese rice-paper rolls and apple crumble. It's one of the few oases left for smokers.

Tèxtil Cafè

C/Montcada 12 (93 268 25 98/www.textilcafe.com). Metro Jaume I. **Open** Nov-Feb 10am-8pm Tue, Wed; 10am-midnight Thur-Sun. Mar-Oct 10am-midnight Tue-Thur, Sun; 10am-1am Fri, Sat. **€**. **Café**. Map p75 B4 ㉕
The Textile Museum has moved up to the Disseny Hub Barcelona in Pedralbes, but the café remains in the 14th-century courtyard of what has become the Barcelona Design Centre. It's a good place for breakfast or lunch, and, for a €5 supplement, has a DJ on Wednesday nights and live jazz on Sundays.

La Vinya del Senyor

Plaça Santa Maria 5 (93 310 33 79). Metro Barceloneta or Jaume I. **Open** noon-1am Mon-Thur; noon-2am Fri, Sat; noon-midnight Sun. **€€**. **Tapas/wine**. Map p75 A5 ㉖
Though many pull up a chair simply to appreciate the splendours of Santa Maria del Mar's Gothic façade, it's a crime to take up the tables of the 'Wine of the Lord' without sampling a few of the excellent vintages on its list, along with some top-quality cheeses, hams and other tapas.

Wushu

Avda Marquès de l'Argentera 1 (93 310 73 13/www.wushu-restaurant.com).

Market days

Santa Caterina

One of the great and unintended tourist attractions of Barcelona is the **Boqueria food market** (p67) on La Rambla. More than 35 years since Les Halles and Covent Garden markets were shunted out to the Paris and London suburbs, the Boqueria remains in the city centre, serving its populace and restaurants for miles around. But the Boqueria is only one of many traditional markets in the city and, in celebration of this fact, the council has devised a series of DIY tours, collectively known as the **Ruta dels Mercats**. Tourist offices have leaflets detailing the routes, or they can be printed out from www.mercatsbcn.com.

The most appealing and accessible is the Ruta dels Mercats Emblemàtics, which takes in six of the most famous, starting with the Boqueria. From there it takes you across to **Santa Caterina**, the city's oldest, rebuilt by the architect Enric Miralles (who was born next door), and reopened in 2005. The city is running a

rolling programme of refurbishing the historic markets; **Barceloneta**, next on the tour, was rebuilt from scratch, although with less architectural finesse than Santa Caterina. The building is entirely powered by solar panels, but somewhere in the process the place lost its neighbourhood ambience. This is not the case, however, with the **Mercat de Sant Antoní**, which lies just outside the line of the old city walls, on the edge of the Raval. Sant Antoní has a truly proletarian feel, selling not just food but cheap clothes, towels and bedlinen. The market is undergoing restoration and the traders have been moved temporarily to a vast marquee in the street outside. The smallest market on the route is **Concepció** in the Eixample, a charming steel-framed structure, with a 24-hour flower market on the upper side. The last stop on the tour is **Els Encants**, the furniture and flea market in Plaça de les Glòries, a lovely sprawl of gems and junk.

Metro Jaume I. **Open** 1pm-midnight Tue-Sat; 1-4pm Sun. **€€**. **Asian**. Map p75 B5 ㉗

Still in the Born, but now in bigger premises, Wushu has managed to maintain its quality while serving three times as many people. Brad Ainsworth learned his trade under Sydney superchef Neil Perry; his healthy Asian cooking ranges from good to delectable, as evinced by the superb laksa, pad Thai, kangaroo yakisoba and Vietnamese rice-paper rolls. Save space for excellent puddings, however.

El Xampanyet

C/Montcada 22 (93 319 70 03). Metro Jaume I. **Open** noon-4pm, 7-11.30pm Tue-Sat; noon-4pm Sun. Closed Aug. **€**. **Tapas**. Map p75 B4 ㉘

The eponymous bubbly is actually a pretty low-grade cava, if truth be told, but a drinkable enough accompaniment to the house tapa; a saucer of Cantabrian anchovies. Lined with coloured tiles, barrels and antique curios, the bar chiefly functions as a little slice of Barcelona history, and has been owned by the same family since the 1930s.

Shopping

Adolfo Domínguez

C/Ribera 16 (93 319 21 59/ www.adolfodominguez.com). Metro Barceloneta. **Open** 11am-9pm Mon-Sat. Map p75 C5 ㉙

The women's department has finally caught up with the men's tailoring that for many years was Domínguez's forte. Expect to find sharp, flattering jackets, with surprisingly adventurous separates in luxurious materials, along with well-made shoes and bags.

Capricho de Muñeca

C/Brosoli 1 (93 319 58 91/www. caprichodemuneca.com). Metro Jaume I. **Open** 5-9.30pm Tue-Fri, 1-9.30pm Sat. Map p75 A4 ㉚

Soft leather handbags in cherry reds, chocolate browns and violet made by hand just upstairs by designer Lisa Lempp. Sizes range from the cute and petit to the luxuriously large. Belts and wallets complement the handbags.

Como Agua de Mayo

C/Argenteria 43 (93 310 64 41/www. comoaguademayo.es). Metro Jaume I. **Open** 10am-8.30pm. Map p75 A4 ㉛

A temple for coquettish Carrie Bradshaw style on a mid-range budget. Think lots of mixing and matching of patterns with plenty of candy-bright shoes. Labels include Amaya Arzuaga, Antik Batik and Miriam Ocáriz; footwear comes courtesy of Otto et Moi, Pedro Garcia and Chie Mihara. You might need to buzz to get in.

Custo Barcelona

Plaça de les Olles 7 (93 268 78 93/ www.custo-barcelona.com). Metro Jaume I. **Open** 10am-10pm Mon-Sat. Map p75 B5 ㉜

The Custo look is synonymous with Barcelona style, and the loud print T-shirts have spawned a thousand imitations. Custodio Dalmau's signature prints can now be found on everything from coats to jeans to swimwear for both men and women, but a T-shirt is still the most highly prized (and highly priced) souvenir for visiting fashionistas. There's also a Custo Vintage (Plaça del Pi 2, Barri Gòtic, 93 304 27 53), with clothes from past seasons.

Hatquarters

Plaça de la Llana 6 (93 310 18 02/ www.hatquarters.com). Metro Jaume I. **Open** 11am-8.30pm Mon-Sat. Map p75 A3 ㉝

You won't find anything as vulgar as a tourist sombrero at Chad Weidmar's tiny temple to the *titfer*. From raffia and tweed cadet caps, leather bucket hats to felt fedoras – by Goorin Bros, Cassel Goorin and Sant Cassel, among others – the simple application of any piece of headwear in this shop will get you past the toughest nightclub bouncer in town.

Electric dreams

Barcelona has seen a surge of activity in the experimental music scene of late, with an emphasis on new technology and putting on a show. Events are well attended by a gaunt but enthusiastic crowd, and even the **MACBA** (p88) has jumped on board with an exhibition on pioneer John Cage in early 2010.

The relatively new **Digressions** festival (www.digressions.es) takes advantage of audiovisual equipment at L'Auditori to programme a few big concerts in April, at least one of which involves contemporary orchestra-in-residence BCN216. Others are tinnitus-inducing rock and/or electronica, or experiment with hi-tech devices, such as local party-piece the reacTable. Played by moving blocks on a table, electrical connections are charted like troop movements on a giant screen. The sound, while not exactly melodic, is evocative, and endorsed by Björk, who bought one.

October's **LEM** festival (www.gracia-territori.com) offers a larger selection of small format shows, which may include spoken word and classical song with a contemporary message. In November, **No-No-Logic** (www.nonologic.com) is quirk on a grand scale and bids to fill nightclub **Sala Apolo** (p119) with Kraftwerk-inspired performance. **CCCB** (p88) hosts accessible electronica on a regular basis, while over in Poblenou, weekly minimalist performances at **NIU** (www.niubcn.com) are relaxing.

Lobby

C/Ribera 5 (93 319 38 55/www.lobby-bcn.com). Metro Barceloneta. **Open** 11am-8.30pm Mon-Sat. **Map** p75 C5 ❹

One of the new breed of multifunctional spaces devoted to a clued-up lifestyle concept, with designs from emerging talents and the newest offerings from larger brands. Although there are perfumes, homewares and magazines, Lobby's strongest suit is clothing: for the girls, there's Jaume Roca, Lilith and Pleats Please (by Issey Miyake), while the boys can choose from the likes of Final Home and Unity.

MTX Barcelona

C/Rec 32 (93 319 13 98/www.mertxe-hernandez.com). Metro Barceloneta. **Open** 11am-9pm Mon-Sat. **Map** p75 B4 ❺

Right now, nobody in Barcelona is hipper than local designer Mertxe Hernández. Her clothes have the distinction of being utterly different but immediately recognisable: colourful, multi-layered textiles, slashed and restructured.

Mujer

C/Carders 28 (93 315 15 31). Metro Jaume I. **Open** 10am-3pm, 5-8pm Mon-Fri; 11am-9pm Sat. Closed last 2wks Aug. **Map** p75 B3 ❻

Run by the energetic Lulu, Mujer is the local nerve centre for expat parents. It stocks imported funky baby gear from the likes of Cath Kidston or Twisted Twee and is the perfect place to pick up a tiny Metallica T-Shirt. There's also a range of maternity wear, baby accessories, books, toys and a chill-out space for playing and breastfeeding.

On Land

C/Princesa 25 (93 310 02 11/www.on-land.com). Metro Jaume I. **Open** 5-8.30pm Mon; 11am-2pm, 5-8.30pm Tue-Fri; 11am-8.30pm Sat. Closed 2wks Aug. **Map** p75 B4 ❼

This little oasis of urban cool has all you need to hold your head up high against the Barcelona hip squad: bags and wallets by Becksöndergaard and Can't Go Naked; cute dresses by Boba; elegant pencil skirts from Conni Kaminski; loose cotton trousers by IKKS and covetable T-shirts by Fresh From the Lab.

El Rei de la Màgia

C/Princesa 11 (93 319 39 20/www.el reidelamagia.com). Metro Jaume I. **Open** *Sept-June* 10am-2pm, 5-8pm Mon-Fri; 11am-2pm Sat. *July, Aug* 11am-2pm, 5-8pm Mon-Fri. **Map** p75 A4 ➌➑
Cut someone in half, make a rabbit disappear or try out any number of other professional-quality stage illusions at the beautiful old 'King of Magic.' Less ambitious tricksters can practise their sleight of hand with the huge range of whoopee cushions and the like.

Vila Viniteca

C/Agullers 7 (902 32 77 77/ www.vilaviniteca.es). Metro Jaume I. **Open** *Sept-June* 8.30am-8.30pm Mon-Sat. *July, Aug* 8.30am-8.30pm Mon-Fri; 8.30am-2pm Sat. **Map** p75 A5 ➌➒
This family-run business has built up a stock of more than 6,000 wines and spirits since 1932. Whether you want to blow €1,245 on a magnum of 2003 L'Ermita or just snag a €5 bottle of table wine, you'll find something to drink. The selection here is mostly Spanish and Catalan, but does cover international favourites. The new food shop next door at No.9 stocks fine cheeses, cured meats and oils.

Nightlife

Club Mix

C/Comerç 21 (93 319 46 96/www. clubmixbcn.com). Metro Jaume I. **Open** 9pm-3am Tue-Sun. **Map** p75 C4 ➍➊
With an interior by local tastemaker Silvia Prada, a fashionable postcode and a menu of delicate finger foods, Mix attracts a professional, stylish crowd who enjoy both an after-work cocktail and an after-dinner piss-up. DJs play funk, soul, world beats and rare groove.

Diobar

Diobar

C/Marquès de l'Argentera 27 (93 319 56 19). Metro Barceloneta. **Open** 11pm-3am Thur-Sat. **Map** p75 C5 ➍➊
The basement of a Greek restaurant is the unlikely setting for this cosy and wildly popular club. There's no plate throwing but instead, from Thursday to Saturday nights, it becomes a stone-walled temple of funk, soul and Latin beats as DJ Fred Spider hits the decks.

Arts & leisure

Aire de Barcelona

NEW *Passeig Picasso 22 (902 555 789/ www.airedebarcelona.com). Metro Arc de Triomf or Jaume I.* **Open** 10am-midnight daily. *Baths* (90 mins) €24; (incl 15-min massage) €35. **Map** p75 C4 ➍➋
These subterranean Arab baths are superbly relaxing, and offer a range of extra massages in addition to the basic package of hot and cold pools, jacuzzi, salt-water pool, hammam and relaxation zone. Entrance is offered every two hours from 10am and reservations are advisable. If you've left your swimsuit at home, you can borrow or buy one.

MACBA p88

Raval

For at least a hundred years, the Raval has been the city's forbidden core, its dark other. In the early 20th century, the area was notorious for its seedy theatres, brothels, anarchist groups and dosshouses. Gentrification has ensued in recent years, but, despite years of costly transformation, the old red-light district still retains a busy crew of prostitutes, transsexuals, drug addicts and poor labourers. Many of these unshiftable locals could have stepped straight from the pages of Jean Genet's *The Thief's Journal*, a chronicle of the time the writer spent here as a thieving, teenaged rent boy during the 1920s. The Raval is now one of the most ethnically diverse places in Europe, with more than 70 different nationalities calling it home. Shop signs appear in a babel of languages, plugging everything from halal meat to Bollywood films and cheap calls to South America.

Dominating the Upper Raval is the Plaça dels Àngels, where the 16th-century Convent dels Àngels houses a gigantic almshouse, the Casa de la Caritat, converted into a cultural complex housing the **MACBA** and the **CCCB**.

Over the years, the square has become unofficial home to the city's skateboarders, and the surrounding streets have filled with restaurants and boutiques. Beneath C/Hospital in the Plaça Sant Agustí lies one of the Raval's more arresting pieces of architecture, the unfinished 18th-century Església de Sant Agustí (no.2, no phone, Mass 11am, 1pm & 8pm Mon-Fri, 11am Sat, 11am, noon & 8pm Sun). The stone beams and jags protruding from its left flank (on C/Arc de Sant Agustí) and the undecorated sections of the Baroque façade show how suddenly work stopped when funding ran out.

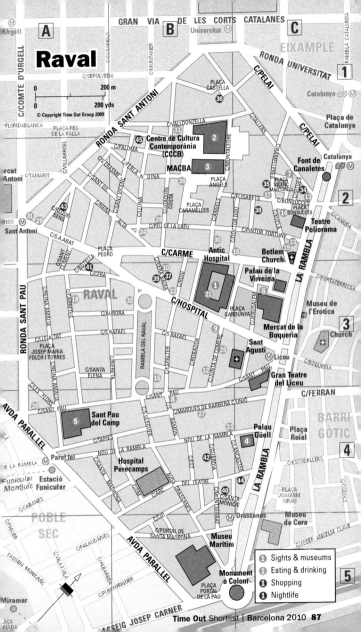

Raval

GRAN VIA DE LES CORTS CATALANES

EIXAMPLE

A   B   C

0   200 m
0   200 yds

© Copyright Time Out Group 2009

45 Centre de Cultura Contemporánia (CCCB)

MACBA

Antic Hospital

Betlem Church

Palau de la Virreina

Mercat de la Boqueria

Sant Agusti

Gran Teatre del Liceu

Teatre Poliorama

Font de Canaletes

RAVAL

Sant Pau del Camp

Hospital Perecamps

Palau Güell

Museu de l'Eròtica

Museu de Cera

Museu Marítim

Monument a Colóm

POBLE SEC

BARRI GÒTIC

● Sights & museums
● Eating & drinking
● Shopping
● Nightlife

MACBA

classical lecture theatre complete with revolving marble dissection table (open 10am-2pm Mon-Fri), and the entrance hall of the Casa de Convalescència, tiled with Baroque ceramic murals telling the story of St Paul. La Capella, the hospital chapel, has been converted to an exhibition space for contemporary art. The courtyard is a popular spot for reading or eating lunch.

CCCB (Centre de Cultura Contemporània de Barcelona)

C/Montalegre 5 (93 306 41 00/ www.cccb.org). Metro Catalunya. **Open** 11am-8pm Tue, Wed, Fri-Sun; 11am-10pm Thur. **Admission** 1 exhibition €4.50; €3.40 reductions & Wed. 2 exhibitions €6; €5.60 reductions & Wed. Free under-16s. Free 1st Wed of mth & 8-10pm Thur. **Map** p87 B2 **②**

Spain's largest cultural centre was opened in 1994 at the Casa de la Caritat, a former almshouse, built in 1802 on the site of a medieval monastery. The massive façade and part of the courtyard remain from the original building; the rest was rebuilt in dramatic contrast, all tilting glass and steel, by architects Piñon and Viaplana, known for the Maremàgnum shopping centre. The CCCB's exhibitions can lean toward heavy-handed didacticism, but there are occasional gems.

Event highlights 'The Century of Jazz' (until 18 Oct 2009); 'Between Metropolis and Postmetropolis' (14 Oct 2009-24 Feb 2010); 'World Press Photo' (10 Nov-Dec 2009).

MACBA (Museu d'Art Contemporani de Barcelona)

Plaça dels Àngels 1 (93 412 08 10/ www.macba.es). Metro Catalunya. **Open** *last wk in June-24 Sept* 11am-8pm Mon, Wed; 11am-midnight Thur, Fri; 10am-8pm Sat; 10am-3pm Sun. *last wk in Sept-23 June* 11am-7.30pm Mon, Wed-Fri; 10am-8pm Sat; 10am-3pm Sun. *Guided tours (Catalan/Spanish)*

Sights & museums

Antic Hospital de la Santa Creu & La Capella

C/Carme 47-C/Hospital 56 (no phone). Metro Liceu. **Open** 9am-8pm Mon-Fri; 9am-2pm Sat. *La Capella* (93 442 71 71) noon-2pm, 4-8pm Tue-Sat; 11am-2pm Sun. **Admission** free. **Map** p87 B3 **①**

There was a hospital on this site as early as 1024, but in the 15th century it expanded to centralise all the city's hospitals and sanatoriums. By the 1920s, it was hopelessly overstretched, and its medical facilities were moved uptown to the Hospital Sant Pau. One of the last patients was Gaudí, who died here in 1926; it was also where Picasso painted one of his first important pictures, *Dead Woman* (1903).

The buildings combine a 15th-century Gothic core with Baroque and classical additions. They're now given over to cultural institutions, among them the Catalan National Library, the Institute of Catalan Studies and the Royal Academy of Medicine, which hosts occasional concerts. Highlights include a neo-

On a mission

Bartomeu Marí takes over at the MACBA.

While its striking architecture receives many plaudits, many feel that the exhibitions at the MACBA (p88), Barcelona's contemporary art museum, can be inaccessible and overwhelming. Yet new director Bartomeu Marí, who stepped into the role in April 2008, says the gallery is more than fulfilling its 'public mission'.

What is the role of the MACBA?
We contribute to the growth of the cultural atmosphere of the city. The museum has a public mission comparable to schools. Our culture has a lack of intellectual relationship with the present and we are beginning a tradition of considering, thinking, presenting and dealing with it.

How would you like to see things improve in Barcelona?
Barcelona lacks postgraduate schools and training facilities for artists, artists-in-residence programmes and a solid gallery scene. There is not enough art criticism.

Why does the MACBA fail to draw in a large and diverse public?
You cannot compare the position of an institution like Tate Modern in London, the capital of a large country that attracts millions of tourists everyday, with Barcelona. Our audience grew 15 per cent last year [but] … it's not about numbers. We are not football stadiums. Our criterion is quality.

Is the MACBA sufficiently accessible and informative?
Of course! Art is a highly sophisticated code system. Exhibitions are a tool of communication.

Many shows seem set in a particular context: that of North America in the 1960s and '70s. Why?
It represents the beginning of our collection, [it was a time] when strong breaks with the traditions of art occurred. We are not MoMA; we don't have an encyclopaedic collection. There aren't enough works available to make that possible.

So what can we expect in 2010?
We're beginning to look at collaborations with institutions in Arab countries, a more diverse vocabulary for the presentation of art and site-specific commissions. In 2010, we start with a major retrospective of John Cage, then John Baldessari, [who is] a crucial player in the art scene of the late 20th century. At the end of the year we are looking at the 1980s, a decade when many changes took place.

6pm Wed, Sat; noon Sun. **Admission**
Permanent collection €3; €2 reductions.
Permanent & temporary exhibitions
€7.50; €6 reductions. *Temporary
exhibitions* €4; €3 reductions. Wed
€3.50. **Map** p87 B2 ❸

The real show at the MACBA is the
building itself, Richard Meier's cool ice-
berg of a museum sitting imperturbably
amid the ceaseless scrape and clatter of
skateboarders on the Plaça dels Àngels.
While the museum has fattened up its
holdings considerably since opening in
1995, the shows are often heavily political in concept and occasionally radical
to the point of inaccessibility, and
queues to enter are practically unheard
of. Perhaps aware of this, the MACBA's
new director, Bartomeu Marí (see box
p89), has expressed the desire to put the
thrill back into art.

The exhibits cover the last 50 years or
so; although there's no permanent collection as such, some of the works from the
museum's holdings are usually on display. The earlier pieces are strong on
artists such as Antonio Saura and
Tàpies, who were members of the Dau-
al-Set, a group of radical writers and
painters much influenced by Miró, who
kick-started the Catalan art movement
after the post-Civil War years of cultural apathy. Jean Dubuffet and Basque
sculptors Jorge Oteiza and Eduardo
Chillida also feature. Works from the last
40 years are more global, with the likes
of Joseph Beuys, Jean-Michel Basquiat,
AR Penck and photographer Jeff Wall.
Event highlights John Cage and
Experimental Art (23 Oct 2009-4 Jan
2010).

Palau Güell

*C/Nou de la Rambla 3 (93 317 39 74/
www.palauguell.cat). Metro Drassanes
or Liceu.* **Open** 10am-2.30pm Tue-Sat.
Admission free. **Map** p87 C4 ❹

A fortress-like edifice shoehorned into
a narrow six-storey sliver, the Palau
Güell was Gaudí's first major commis-
sion, begun in 1886 for textile baron
Eusebi Güell. After major structural

renovation, it has partially reopened to
the public, and is expected to fully
reopen in 2010. For the time being visitors can look around the subterranean
stables, with an exotic canopy of stone
palm fronds on the ceiling and the
ground floor. Here the vestibule has
ornate Mudéjar carved ceilings from
which the Güells could snoop on their
arriving guests through the jalousie
trellis-work; at the heart of the house
lies the spectacular six-storey hall complete with musicians' galleries and
topped by a dome covered in cobalt
honeycomb tiles.

Sant Pau del Camp

*C/Sant Pau 101 (93 441 00 01). Metro
Paral·lel.* **Open** *Visits* 5-8pm Mon;
10.30am-1.30pm, 5-8pm Tue-Fri. *Mass*
8pm Sat; noon Sun. **Admission** *Visits*
€2; €1 reductions. *Mass* free. No credit
cards. **Map** p87 A4 ❺

The name, St Paul in the Field, reflects
a time when the Raval was still coun-
tryside. In fact, this little Romanesque
church is over 1,000 years old; the date
carved on its most prestigious head-
stone – that of Count Guifré II Borrell,
son of Wilfred 'the Hairy' and inheritor
of all Barcelona and Girona – is AD
912. The church's impressive façade
includes sculptures of fantastical flora
and fauna along with human
grotesques. The tiny cloister is another highlight with its extraordinary
Visigoth capitals, triple-lobed arches
and central fountain.

Eating & drinking

Au Port de la Lune

NEW *Plaça Sant Galdric 1 (93 270 38
19). Metro Liceu.* **Open** 1.30-4pm Mon,
Tue, Thur; 1.30-4pm, 9-11.30pm Wed,
Fri, Sat. **€€€**. **French**. **Map** p87 C3 ❻

A tomato's toss from the Boqueria market is this sunny little French bistro,
chipped and battered in parts but ulti-
mately charming. The menu is a mix
of the delightful (oysters, cassoulet,
clafoutis) and the ever so slightly shab-

Elisabets p93

by, but it's difficult not to feel reassured by a blackboard that reads that 'there is no ketchup and no Coke, and there never will be'.

Bar Kasparo

Plaça Vicenç Martorell 4 (93 302 20 72). Metro Catalunya. **Open** *May-Aug* 9am-midnight Tue-Sat. *Sept-Apr* 9am-10pm Tue-Sat. Closed mid Dec-mid Jan. No credit cards. **Café**. Map p87 C2 ⑦
Still the best of the various café terraces now sitting on the edges of quiet, traffic-free Plaça Vicenç Martorell, Kasparo serves tapas, *bocadillos*, salads and a varying selection of more substantial dishes, available all day. There is no indoor seating, so this is more of a warm weather proposition.

Bar Marsella

C/Sant Pau 65 (93 442 72 63). Metro Liceu. **Open** 10pm-2.30am Mon-Thur; 10pm-3am Fri, Sat. No credit cards. **Bar**. Map p87 B4 ⑧
Opened in 1820 by a native of Marseilles, who may just have changed the course of Barcelona's artistic history by introducing absinthe, still

a mainstay of the bar's delights. Untapped 100-year-old bottles of the stuff sit in glass cabinets alongside old mirrors and William Morris curtains, probably covered in the same dust kicked up by Picasso and Gaudi.

Bar Mendizábal

C/Junta de Comerç 2 (no phone). Metro Liceu. **Open** 10am-midnight daily. No credit cards. **Café**. Map p87 B3 ⑨
Considered something of a classic, Bar Mendizábal has been around for decades, its multicoloured tiles and serving-hatch a feature in thousands of holiday snaps. Really it's little more than a hole in the wall, from which juices, sandwiches and soup are ordered, and carried to tables on the other side of the road.

Bar Resolis

C/Riera Baixa 22 (93 441 29 48). Metro Liceu. **Open** 1pm-2am Mon-Thur; 1pm-2.30am Fri, Sat. **€**. **Tapas**. Map p87 B3 ⑩
A favourite with traders from the vintage clothing shops on the pedestrianised C/Riera Baixa, Resolis blends a

trad look and run-of-the-mill tapas (tortilla, manchego cheese, prawns) with an immaculate selection of vinyl and some fanciful foodstuffs (like ceviche with oriental sauce). In the summer months, its serving-hatch ensures that the alley alongside it is rammed.

Baraka

C/Valldonzella 25 (93 304 10 61).
Metro Universitat. **Open** 2-11pm
Tue-Fri; 5-11pm Sat. Closed Aug.
Bar. Map p87 B1 ⑪

At the back of a beautiful old building converted into a health-food shop is this cosy little bar, where everything from the wine and beer to the milk used in the fair-trade coffee is organic and cheap – not a common combination. Should anything ail you, the amiable staff will make up an appropriate medicinal tea from the shop's stock of more than 100 herbs.

Biblioteca

C/Junta de Comerç 28 (93 412 62 21/
www.bibliotecarestaurant.com). Metro
Liceu. **Open** 8-11.30pm Mon-Fri; 1-4pm,
8-11.30pm Sat. Closed 2wks Aug. **€€**.
Mediterranean. Map p87 B3 ⑫

A tranquil, elegant space with beige, minimalist decor and a display of cookbooks; from Bocuse to Bourdain, they are all for sale, and their various influences collide in the menu. Increasingly, though, it draws from the Catalan culinary canon, with a good *esqueixada* (salt cod salad) or a reasonable onion *coca* (flat, crispy bread) with anchovies to start, followed by gamier mains that might include venison pie or pig's trotters stuffed with prunes.

Boadas

C/Tallers 1 (93 318 95 92). Metro
Catalunya. **Open** *Sept-June* noon-2am
Mon-Thur; noon-3am Fri, Sat. *July, Aug*
noon-3pm, 6pm-2am Mon-Thur; noon-3pm, 6pm-3am Fri, Sat. No credit cards.
Cocktails. Map p87 C2 ⑬

Set up in 1933 by Miguel Boadas, born to Catalan parents in Havana (where he became the first barman at the

legendary La Floridita), this classic cocktail bar has changed little since Hemingway used to come here. In a move to deter the hordes of rubber-necking tourists, they have instituted a smart dress code.

Buenas Migas

Plaça Bonsuccés 6 (93 318 37 08).
Metro Liceu. **Open** *June-Sept* 10am-midnight Mon-Thur, Sun; 10am-1am Fri, Sat. *Oct-May* 10am-11pm Mon-Thur, Sun; 10am-midnight Fri, Sat.
€€. Vegetarian. Map p87 C2 ⑭

A doggedly wholesome place, known for its red gingham and pine, and chewy spinach tart. The speciality, however, is tasty focaccia with various toppings, along with the usual high-fibre, low-fun cakes you expect to find in a vegetarian café. Its terrace sprawls across the wide pavement and street.

Cafè de les Delicies

Rambla del Raval 47 (93 441 57 14).
Metro Liceu. **Open** 10am-2am Mon,
Tue, Thur, Sun; 10am-3am Fri, Sat.
Closed 3wks Aug. No credit cards.
Café. Map p87 B3 ⑮

After an overhaul in the kitchen, the delightful Cafè de les Delicies is now serving breakfast, along with tapas and light dishes in its dining room at the back. Off the corridor there's a snug with armchairs, but otherwise the buzzing front bar is the place to be, with its theatre-set mezzanine, 1970s jukebox, shelves of books and reams of club flyers.

Dos Trece

C/Carme 40 (93 301 73 06/www.
dostrece.net). Metro Liceu. **Open**
9am-midnight Tue-Sun. **€€. Global.**
Map p87 C2 ⑯

Dos Trece has turned its cosy basement space into another dining room – this one with cushions and candles for postprandial lounging. Apart from a little fusion confusion (like ceviche with nachos) the food's not half bad for the price, and includes one of the few decent burgers to be had in Barcelona.

Elisabets

*C/Elisabets 2-4 (93 317 58 26). Metro
Catalunya.* **Open** 7am-11pm Mon-Sat.
Closed 3wks Aug. **€**. No credit cards.
Catalan. Map p87 C2 ⑰

Also open in the mornings for breakfast, and late at night for drinking at
the bar, Elisabets maintains a sociable
local feel. Dinner, served only on
Fridays, is actually a selection of tapas,
and otherwise only the set lunch or
myriad *bocadillos* are served. The
lunch deal is terrific value, with *osso
buco*, vegetable and chickpea stew,
baked cod with garlic and parsley, and
roast pork knuckle all making regular
appearances on the menu.

Las Fernández

*C/Carretas 11 (93 443 20 43). Metro
Paral·lel.* **Open** 9pm-1am Tue-Sun.
Closed 2wks Aug. **€**. **Spanish**.
Map p87 A3 ⑱

The inviting pillar-box red entrance
is a beacon of cheer on one of
Barcelona's less salubrious streets.
Inside, the three Fernández sisters
have created a bright and unpreten-
tious bar/restaurant that specialises in
wine and food from their native León.
Alongside *cecina* (dried venison),
gammon and sausages from the
region are lighter Mediterranean dishes and generous salads: think smoked
salmon with mustard and dill; pasta
filled with wild mushrooms; and sardines with a citrus *escabeche*.

Granja M Viader

*C/Xuclà 4-6 (93 318 34 86/www.
granjaviader.cat). Metro Liceu.*
Open 5-8.45pm Mon; 9am-1.45pm,
5-8.45pm Tue-Sat. Closed Aug. **Café**.
Map p87 C2 ⑲

The chocolate milk drink Cacaolat was
invented in this old *granja* in 1931, and
it is still on offer, along with strawberry and banana milkshakes, *orxata*
(tiger nut milk) and hot chocolate. It's
an evocative, charming place with century-old fittings and enamel adverts,
but the waiters refuse to be hurried.

Las Guindas

*C/Sant Pau 126 (mobile 670 437 709).
Metro Paral·lel.* **Open** 7pm-2.30am
Mon-Thur, Sun; 7pm-3am Fri, Sat.
No credit cards. **Bar**. Map p87 A4 ⑳

Las Guindas is a long narrow bar with
a crimson-hued retro look, edgy mural
and DJs fighting for turntable space to
show off their acquisitions of vinyl
from the 1950s to the '70s. Monday
night is rockabilly night, but the rest of
the week you're as likely to hear northern soul or boogaloo. For all this, Las
Guindas is refreshingly attitude-free.

El Jardí

*C/Hospital 56 (93 329 15 50). Metro
Liceu.* **Open** 10am-11pm Mon-Fri;
10am-midnight Sat. **€**. **Tapas**.
Map p87 B3 ㉑

The courtyard of the Gothic Antic
Hospital is a tranquil, tree-lined spot a
million miles from the hustle of
C/Hospital. Terrace café El Jardí actually has two separate bars – go to the
lesser known, further from the
entrance, for more chance of a table.
Breakfast pastries and all the usual
tapas are present and correct, along
with pasta dishes, quiches and salads.

Juicy Jones

*C/Hospital 74 (93 443 90 82). Metro
Liceu.* **Open** noon-11.30pm daily. **€**.
Vegetarian. Map p87 B3 ㉒

Alongside its two menus, one
European and one Indian, this colourful vegan restaurant has an inventive
list of juices and smoothies, salads and
filled baguettes. While its heart is in the
right place, it's mostly aimed at back-
packers and staffed, it would seem, by
somewhat clueless language-exchange
students. Bring a book.

London Bar

*C/Nou de la Rambla 34 (93 318 52 61).
Metro Liceu.* **Open** *Aug* 10.30am-3am
daily. *Sept-July* 8am-3am daily. **Bar**.
Map p87 B4 ㉓

Since it had its live music licence
revoked, this beloved classic, smoky

Pla dels Àngels

old bar has had to rely on the pool table or the occasional football match to entertain its patrons. The TV screen is hidden at the back, however, and easily avoided; there are plenty of other things to feast your eyes on, from the period posters to the graceful swirls of the turn-of-the-century woodwork.

Mam i Teca

C/Lluna 4 (93 441 33 35). Metro Sant Antoni. **Open** *1-4pm; 8.45pm-midnight Mon, Wed-Fri, Sun; 8.45pm-midnight Sat. Closed 2wks Aug.* **€€.** **Catalan.** Map p87 B2 ㉔

A bright little tapas restaurant with only three tables, so it pays to reserve. All the usual tapas, from anchovies to cured meats, are rigorously sourced, and complemented by superb daily specials such as organic *botifarra*, pork confit and asparagus with shrimp. The bar is worth mentioning for its superior vodka and tonic.

Organic

C/Junta de Comerç 11 (93 301 09 02/ www.antoniaorganickitchen.com). Metro Liceu. **Open** *12.30pm-midnight daily.* **€€.** **Vegetarian.** Map p87 B3 ㉕

The last word in refectory chic, Organic is better designed and lighter in spirit than the majority of the city's veggie spots. Friendly staff usher you inside and give you a rundown on options; an all-you-can-eat salad bar, a combined salad bar and main course, or the full whammy – salad, soup, main course and dessert. Beware the extras, drinks and so on, which can hitch up the prices.

Pla dels Àngels

C/Ferlandina 23 (93 329 40 47). Metro Universitat. **Open** *1.30-4pm, 9-11.30pm daily.* **€.** **Mediterranean.** Map p87 B2 ㉖

Appropriately, given its position opposite MACBA, Pla dels Àngels is a riot of colour and chimera, something that translates to its menu. The salads might include mango, yoghurt and mint oil, or radicchio, serrano ham and roast peppers, followed by a short list of pasta and gnocchi dishes and a couple of meat ones. The cheap set lunch includes two courses and a glass of wine.

The Quiet Man

C/Marqués de Barberà 11 (93 412 12 19). Metro Liceu. **Open** *6pm-2am*

Mon-Thur, Sun; 6pm-3am Fri, Sat. **Bar**. Map p87 B4 ㉗

One of the first and best of the city's many oirish pubs, the Quiet Man is a peaceful place with wooden floors and stalls that mostly eschews the beautiful game for occasional poetry readings and pool tournaments. There is Guinness (properly poured) and Murphy's, and you're as likely to see Catalans as you are homesick expats.

Ravalo

Plaça Emili Vendrell 1 (93 442 01 00). Metro Sant Antoni. **Open** 8pm-1am Tue-Sun. **€**. **Pizza**. Map p87 B2 ㉓

Perfect for fans of the thin and crispy, Ravalo's table-dwarfing pizzas take some beating, thanks to flour (and a chef) imported from Naples. Most of the pizzas come with the cornerstone toppings you'd expect in any pizzeria; less familiar offerings include the pizza soufflé, filled with ham, mushrooms and an eggy mousse (better than it sounds). The restaurant's terrace overlooking a quiet square is open year-round.

Sésamo

C/Sant Antoni Abat 52 (93 441 64 11). Metro Sant Antoni. **Open** 1-3.30pm, 8.30-11.30pm Mon, Wed-Sat; 8.30-11.30pm Sun. Closed Aug. **€€**. **Argentinian/vegetarian**. Map p87 A2 ㉙

Sésamo's head cook recently took up the reins of management, and revamped the menu a little: the front room now offers meaty Argentinian fare. However, despite the change, the back space continues to concentrate on excellent vegetarian cooking. Sésamo has never taken itself too seriously, and has always offered an interesting bunch of dishes – crunchy polenta with baked pumpkin, gorgonzola and radicchio; spicy curry with wild rice; and a selection of Japanese tapas – in a buzzing space.

Silenus

C/Àngels 8 (93 302 26 80). Metro Liceu. **Open** 1.30-4pm, 8.30-11.30pm

Mon-Thur; 1.30-4pm, 8.30pm-midnight Fri, Sat. **€€€**. **Mediterranean**. Map p87 B2 ㉚

Named after one of the drunken followers of Dionysus, Silenus is nonetheless all about restraint. Its quiet dining room has an air of scuffed elegance, with chipped and stained walls whereon the ghost of a clock is projected. The food too is artistically presented. It's not especially cheap, but the set lunch is generally a good bet, offering dishes from Caesar salad to crunchy gnocchi with creamed spinach or spicy *botifarra* with puréed potatoes.

Els Tres Tombs

Ronda Sant Antoni 2 (93 443 41 11). Metro Sant Antoni. **Open** 6am-2am daily. **€**. No credit cards. **Tapas**. Map p87 A2 ㉛

Not, perhaps, the most inspired tapas bar in town, with its overcooked patatas bravas, sweaty manchego and loos that leave a lot to be desired, but Els Tres Tombs is still a long-time favourite for its pavement terrace and proximity to the Sunday morning book market. The tres tombs in question are nothing more ghoulish than the 'three turns' of the area performed by a procession of men on horseback during the Festa dels Tres Tombs in January.

La Verònica

C/Rambla de Raval 2-4 (93 329 33 03). Metro Liceu. **Open** Sept-July 7pm-midnight Mon-Thur; 7pm-1am Fri; 1pm-1am Sat; noon-midnight Sun. *Aug* 7pm-midnight daily. **€€**. **Pizza**. Map p87 B3 ㉜

La Verònica's shortcomings (its huge popularity with young foreigners, the minuscule spacing between tables) are all but hidden by night, when candles add a cosy glow to the red, orange and yellow paintwork. Its pizzas are crisp, thin and healthy, and come with such toppings as smoked salmon, or apple, gorgonzola and mozzarella. Salads are inventive, and there is a short, reliable wine list.

BARCELONA BY AREA

La Xina

NEW *C/Pintor Fortuny 3 (93 342 96 28/www.grupotragaluz.com). Metro Catalunya.* **Open** 1-4pm, 8-11.30pm Mon-Fri; 1-4.30pm, 8pm-12.30am Sat, Sun. **€€**. **Chinese**. **Map** p87 C2 ㉝

La Xina's Shanghai chic owes much to Alan Yau's Hakkasan in London, with lacquered teak screens, satin and velvet seating and club lighting – nothing less than you'd expect from the team behind the Tragaluz restaurants. Straightforward Chinese food is hard to find in Barcelona, and La Xina does little to buck the trend, with its carpaccios and Madras curry, but there is decent dim sum, and plenty of wok dishes.

Shopping

Discos Castelló

C/Tallers 3, 7, 9 & 79 (93 302 59 46/www.discoscastello.es). Metro Catalunya. **Open** 10am-8.30pm Mon-Sat. **Map** p87 C2 ㉞

Discos Castelló is a home-grown cluster of small shops, each with a different speciality in music: No.3 is devoted to classical; the largest shop, at No.7, covers pretty much everything; No.9 does hip hop, rock and alternative pop, plus T-shirts and accessories; and No.79 is best for jazz, 1970s pop, electronica and ethnic music.

Free

C/Ramelleres 5 (93 301 61 15). Metro Catalunya. **Open** 11am-8.30pm Mon-Sat. **Map** p87 C2 ㉟

A skate emporium that has grown exponentially to cater for Barcelona's expanding population of enthusiasts. For boys, there's casualwear from Stüssy, Carhartt et al; girls get plenty of Compobella and Loreak Mendian. The requisite chunky or retro footwear comes courtesy of Vans and Etnies.

Holala! Ibiza

Plaça Castella 2 (93 302 05 93/www.holala-ibiza.com). **Open** 11am-9pm Mon-Sat. **Map** p87 B1 ㊱

The profusion of vintage clothing stores in the Raval now includes Holala! Ibiza, a spacious, browse-worthy store with the air of a funky street market. Obligatory sections dedicated to army surplus and Wrangler are garnished with a more original array of puffy ballroom gowns, chintzy shirts and how-does-this-stay-on? hats, all in good nic. **Other locations** Vintage Store Riera Baixa 11, Raval, 93 441 99 94; Hype Outlet C/Tallers 73, Raval, 93 412 23 07.

Lailo

C/Riera Baixa 20 (93 441 37 49). Metro Liceu or Sant Antoni. **Open** 11am-2pm, 5-8pm Mon-Sat. Closed 1wk end Aug. **Map** p87 B3 ㊲

Lailo stands out from the second-hand crowd by the quality of its stock. If you want something for a one-off occasion, you can hire everything from the tuxedos to the coming-out gowns.

Still Light

C/Notariat 8 (93 317 68 83/www.comitebarcelona.com). **Open** noon-3pm; 4-8.30pm Mon-Sat. Closed 2wks Aug. **Map** p87 C2 ㊳

Scandinavian sense and sensibility combine in this mid-priced downtown boutique, run by Finn, Roope Alho. Cecilia Sörensen does hand-printed shirts and blouses, local Txell Miras does the cute suits in cream and charcoal, and Danish brand Wood Wood tops it off with sleek, practical jackets.

Le Swing

C/Riera Baixa 13 (93 324 84 02). Metro Liceu or Sant Antoni. **Open** 10.30am-2.30pm, 4.30-8.30pm Mon-Sat. **Map** p87 B3 ㊴

Today's second-hand is known as vintage, and thrift is not on the agenda. Fervent worshippers of Pierre Cardin, YSL, Dior, Kenzo and other fashion deities scour all corners of the sartorial stratosphere and deliver their booty back to this little powder puff of a boutique. The odd Zara number and other mere mortal brands creep in as well.

Nightlife

Bar Pastis

C/Santa Mònica 4 (93 318 79 80/
www.barpastis.com). Metro Drassanes.
Open 7.30pm-2am Tue-Thur, Sun;
7.30pm-3am Fri, Sat. **Map** p87 B4 ⓭
This quintessentially Gallic bar once
served pastis to visiting sailors and
denizens of the Barrio Chino under-
world. It still has a louche feel: floor-to-
ceiling clippings and oil paintings, Piaf
on the stereo, paper cranes swaying
from the ceiling. But Ajuntament
crackdowns have put an end to live
shows, and the owner of 29 years has
put it up for sale. Interested?

Big Bang

C/Botella 7 (93 443 28 13/www.
bigbangbcn.net). Metro Liceu or Sant
Antoni. **Open** *Bar* 9.30pm-2.30am Tue-
Thur, Sun; 10.15pm-3am Fri, Sat. *Gigs*
around 10pm-1am Fri, Sat. *Jam session*
10.30pm-1am Sun. No credit cards.
Map p87 A2/3 ⓭
Big Bang is decked out like a New York
jazz club, circa 1930, with the low-lit
smokiness and bar stool seating that
implies. The diner-style tiled floor
leads from the bar to the tiny stage,
where groups of talented musicians
play swing, rock 'n' roll, bebop and
every other vintage genre that should
never have gone out of style. Bring
your Stetson and just a few euros for
beer; shows are almost always free.

La Concha

C/Guàrdia 14 (no phone). Metro
Drassanes. **Open** 5pm-2.30am Mon-
Thur, Sun; 5pm-3am Fri, Sat. No credit
cards. **Map** p87 B4 ⓭
Papered with posters of vintage Spanish
sexpot Sara Montiel and filled with
hookah smoke, La Concha is a gem of
dusty fabulousness that stands in direct
contrast to all the slick and pretentious
glamour of most of the newer late-night
bars. It's under Moroccan ownership
and there are plans to introduce tea and
baklava in the afternoon.

Jazz Sí Club

C/Requesens 2 (93 329 00 20/
www.tallerdemusics.com). Metro Sant
Antoni. **Open** 7.45-10.30pm Tue; 8.30-
11pm Mon, Wed-Sat; 6.30-10pm Sun.
No credit cards. **Map** p87 A2 ⓭
Tucked into a Raval side street, with
cheap shows every night and cheap bar
grub, this truly authentic place is well
worth seeking out. Since it functions as
both a venue for known-in-the-scene
locals and an auditorium for students
of the music school across the street,
it's packed to the brim with students,
teachers, music lovers and players.
Nights vary between jazz, flamenco
and Cuban, and there are jam sessions
on Tuesdays and Saturdays.

Moog

C/Arc del Teatre 3 (93 301 72 82/
www.masimas.com). Metro Drassanes.
Open midnight-5am Mon-Thur, Sun;
midnight-6am Fri, Sat. **Map** p87 C4 ⓭
Moog's an odd club: long, narrow and
enclosed, with the air conditioner
pumping; it's a bit like partying on an
aeroplane. The two floors are rather
hilariously divided along gender lines:
girls shake to pop and 1980s upstairs,
while there's non-stop hard house and
techno downstairs for the boys. It's
packed seven days a week, and Angel
Molina, Laurent Garnier and Jeff Mills
have all played here.

La Paloma

C/Tigre 27 (93 301 68 97/93 317 79
94). Metro Universitat. **Map** p87 B2 ⓭
This extraordinary dancehall is currently closed as it fights noise complaints, but the owners hope to reopen
the doors some time in 2009. Arrive
early and you'll see older *barcelonins* in
full eveningwear elegantly circling the
dancefloor. Take a seat in one of the
plush balconies to admire the chandeliers and belle époque fittings. Once the
foxtrot and tango have finished, DJs
mix anything from funk and Latin to
electro and acid. But phone first: no one
knows when or how this battle will end.

Gehry's Fish

Barceloneta & the Ports

From industrial slum to leisure port, Barcelona's shoreline transformation is the result of two decades of development, which started in preparation for the 1992 Olympics and just kept on going. The seafront got a second blast of wind in its sails from the 2004 Fòrum event, which spawned a huge new swimming and watersports area, resculpted beaches and a park. The final grand project at the far end of Barcelona's waterfront is a state-of-the-art marine zoo with four different ecosystems. Despite fierce protest from environmentalists, it's due to open in 2010.

Running between the still-traditional fishing neighbourhood of Barceloneta and the palm-lined promenade alongside the Port Vell, Passeig Joan de Borbó leads to the Nova Bocana development, which is currently under construction. The complex will combine high-end leisure facilities and offices and is dominated by Ricardo Bofill's Hotel Vela, a towering sail-shaped luxury hotel slowly rising under a sheath of scaffolding. This marks the beginning of Barcelona's seven kilometres of beach.

At the far end of the Passeig Marítim, the gateway to the Port Olímpic is heralded by the twin skyscrapers of the Hotel Arts and the Torre Mapfre, and Frank Gehry's shimmering copper Fish sculpture. Behind it is the Vila Olímpica, the Olympic Village created for the games in 1992. It provided parks, a cinema, four beaches, a leisure marina and accommodation for 15,000 athletes. These days, however, the low population density and lack of cafés and shops leaves it devoid of Mediterranean charm. The wide empty boulevards do, however, lend themselves to sculpture, including a jagged pergola on Avda Icària by Enric Miralles and Carme Pinós.

Sights & museums

Monument a Colom

Plaça Portal de la Pau (93 302 52 24). Metro Drassanes. **Open** *June-Sept* 9am-8.30pm daily. *Oct-May* 9am-8pm daily. **Admission** €2.50; €1.50 reductions; free under-4s. Map p100 A3 ❶

Inspired by Nelson's Column, and complete with eight majestic lions, the Christopher Columbus monument was designed for the Universal Exhibition of 1888. Positioned at the base of La Rambla, the monument allegedly marks the spot where Columbus docked in 1493 after his discovery of the Americas, and the carvings illustrate the key moments in his voyages. Columbus's white hair comes courtesy of the city pigeons, so take appropriate cover if you decide to take the tiny lift up inside the column to the vertiginous viewing platform.

Museu d'Història de Catalunya

Plaça Pau Vila 3 (93 225 47 00/www. mhcat.net). Metro Barceloneta. **Open** 10am-7pm Tue, Thur-Sat; 10am-8pm Wed; 10am-2.30pm Sun. **Admission** *All exhibitions* €5; €4 reductions; free under-7s. *Temporary exhibitions* €3; €2 reductions; free under-7s; free to all 1st Sun of mth. **Map** p100 C3 ❷

The Catalan History Museum spans the Lower Paleolithic era right up to Jordi Pujol's proclamation as President of the Generalitat in 1980. It offers a virtual chronology of the region's past, through two floors of text, film, animated models and reproductions of everything from a medieval shoemaker's shop to a 1960s bar. Hands-on activities, such as trying to lift a knight's armour or irrigating lettuces with a Moorish water wheel, add a

little pzazz to the rather dry early history; to exit the exhibition, visitors walk over a huge 3-D map of Catalonia. Every section has a decent introduction in English; the reception desk can offer in-depth English-language museum guides free of charge, and the English website is also very complete. Excellent temporary exhibitions typically examine recent aspects of regional politics and history, while the huge rooftop café terrace has unbeatable views over the city and marina.

Museu Marítim

Avda Drassanes (93 342 99 20/ www.museumaritimbarcelona.com). Metro Drassanes. **Open** 10am-7pm daily. **Admission** €6.50; €5.20 reductions; free under-7s. *Temporary exhibitions vary. Combined ticket with Las Golondrinas (35mins)* €9.60; €7.40 reductions; free under-4s. *(1hr 30mins)* €14.40; €5.50 reductions; free under-4s. **Map** p100 A2 ❸

Even if you can't tell a caravel from a catamaran, the excellent Maritime Museum is well worth a visit, as the soaring arches and vaults of vast shipyards represent one the most perfectly preserved examples of civil Gothic architecture in Spain. In medieval times, the shipyards sat right on the water's edge and were used to dry-dock, repair and build vessels for the royal fleets. The finest of these was Don Juan de Austria's galley, from which he commanded the fleet at Lepanto that defeated the Ottoman navy: a full-scale replica is the mainstay of the collection. With the aid of an audio guide, the maps, mastheads, nautical instruments, multimedia displays and models show you how shipbuilding and navigation techniques have developed over the years. Admission also covers the beautiful 1917 Santa Eulàlia schooner docked nearby in the Moll de la Fusta.

Event highlights The Marítim During the War (until 30 Sept 2009); Transition to Democracy (until 31 Oct 2009).

BARCELONA BY AREA

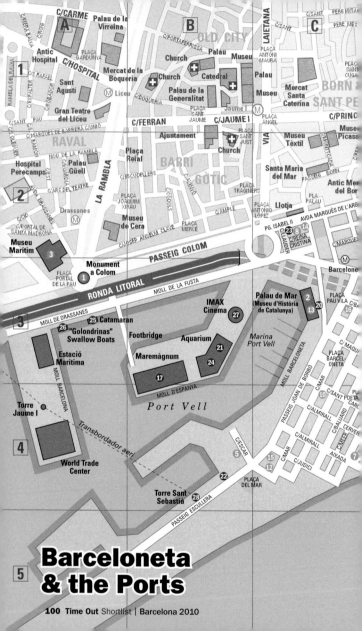

Barceloneta & the Ports

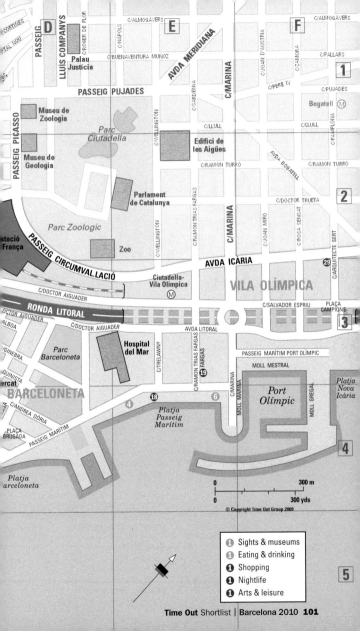

Museu d'Història de Catalunya p99

Eating & drinking

Agua

Passeig Marítim 30 (93 225 12 72/ www.aguadeltragaluz.com). Metro Barceloneta/bus 45, 57, 59, 157. **Open** *1-3.45pm, 8-11.30pm Mon-Thur, Sun; 1-4.30pm, 8pm-12.30am Fri, Sat.* **€€€.** **Mediterranean**. Map p101 E4 **4**

Agua's main draw is its large terrace overlooking the beach, but the relaxed dining room is usually buzzing. The menu rarely changes, but regulars never tire of the competently executed monkfish tail with *sofregit*, the risotto with partridge, and fresh pasta with juicy prawns. Scrummy puddings include marron glacé mousse and sour apple sorbet. Book ahead, especially during summer and at weekends.

Bar Colombo

C/Escar 4 (93 225 02 00). Metro Barceloneta. **Open** *noon-3am daily. Closed 2wks Jan-Feb. No credit cards.* **Bar**. Map p100 B4 **5**

Deck-shod yachties and monied locals stroll by all day, oblivious to this unassuming little bar and its sunny terrace overlooking the port. In fact, nobody

seems to notice it; odd, given its fantastic location and generous portions of *patatas bravas*. The only drawback is the nerve-jangling techno that occasionally fetches up on the stereo.

Bestial

C/Ramón Trias Fargas 2-4 (93 224 04 07/www.grupotragaluz.com). Metro Barceloneta. **Open** *1-4pm, 8-11.30pm daily.* **€€€. Italian**. Map p101 E4 **6**

A peerless spot for alfresco seaside dining, with tiered wooden decking and ancient olive trees. Bestial's dining room is also a stylish affair, with black-clad waiters sashaying along sleek runways, their trays held high. The food is modern Italian: mini-pizzas, rocket salad with parma ham and a lightly poached egg, tuna with black olive risotto and all the puddings you'd hope to find – panna cotta, tiramisu and limoncello sorbet. At weekends, a DJ takes to the decks, and drinks are served until 2am.

Can Majó

C/Almirall Aixada 23 (93 221 54 55). Metro Barceloneta. **Open** *1-4pm, 8-11.30pm Tue-Sat; 1-4pm Sun.* **€€€. Seafood**. Map p100 C4 **7**

BARCELONA BY AREA

Famous for its fresh-from-the-nets selection of oysters, scallops, Galician clams, whelks and just about any other mollusc you care to mention. While the menu reads much as you'd expect for a Barceloneta seafood restaurant, with plates of shellfish or (exemplary) fish soup to start, followed by rich paellas and exquisitely tasty *fideuà*, the quality is a cut above the norm. Sit inside the dapper green and yellow dining room, or within the periwinkle blue picket fence, overlooking the sea.

Can Paixano

C/Reina Cristina 7 (93 310 08 39/ www.canpaixano.com). Metro Barceloneta. **Open** 9am-10.30pm Mon-Sat. Closed 3wks Aug-Sept. No credit cards. **Bar**. **Map** p100 C2 ❽
The 'Champagne Bar', as it's invariably known, has a huge following among young Catalans and legions of foreigners who think they discovered it first. It can be impossible to talk, get your order heard or move your elbows, and yet it's always mobbed for its age-old look and atmosphere, dirt-cheap bottles of house cava and (literally) obligatory sausage butties.

Can Ramonet

C/Maquinista 17 (93 319 30 64). Metro Barceloneta. **Open** noon-midnight daily. Closed 2wks Jan. €€€. **Seafood**. **Map** p101 D3 ❾
Tucked away in the barrio of Barceloneta, this quaint, rose-coloured space with two quiet terraces is mostly overlooked by tourists and, consequently, it suffers none of the drop in standards of some of those paella joints on the seafront. Spectacular displays of fresh seafood show what's on offer that day, but it's also worth sampling the velvety fish soup and the generous paellas.
Other locations C/Carbonell 5 (93 268 33 13).

Can Solé

C/Sant Carles 4 (93 221 50 12/ www.cansole.cat). Metro Barceloneta.

Holiday reads

Barceloneta's new tourist-orientated 'beach libraries'.

In this era of travelling light, with fripperies from just-in-case hiking boots and any toiletry fancier than soap removed from suitcases everywhere, Ken Follett and his ilk have understandably taken a bit of a knock. Given the choice between 500g of Noah Gordon and a change of clothes, most people will plump for the latter.

Keen to improve the lot of their international visitors, and bolster the attractions of Barcelona's somewhat artificial shoreline at the same time, the people at the city council have set up two '*biblioplatges*' – beach libraries – for the use of tourists, who merely need to provide valid ID. The libraries stock around 200 novels, in various languages, along with kids' books, magazines and a selection of international newspapers.

Running alongside these services, and also incalculably useful for visitors with kids and small baggage allowances is the '*ludoplatja*', which lends buckets and spades, sand moulds, watering cans and the like. The adults, meanwhile, can help themselves to volley balls and nets, beach boules and frisbees courtesy of the '*esportplatja*'.

The services run daily from 11am to 7pm from the Centre de la Platja underneath the boardwalk below the Hospital del Mar in July and August, and from the Bac de Roda breakwater from July to September.
■ www.bcn.cat/platges

BARCELONA BY AREA

Kaiku

Open 1.30-4pm, 8-11pm Tue-Sat; 1.30-4pm Sun. Closed 2wks Aug. **€€€**. **Seafood**. Map p100 C4 ⑩
Portly, jovial waiters have been charming moneyed regulars for over a hundred years at Can Solé. Over time, many of these diners have added to the framed photos, sketches and paintings that line the sky-blue walls. What continues to lure them is the freshest shellfish (share a plate of *chipirones* to start) and fillets of wild turbot, lobster stews and sticky paellas. Beware the steeply priced extras (coffee, cover).

La Cova Fumada
C/Baluard 56 (93 221 40 61). Metro Barceloneta. **Open** 9am-3pm Mon-Wed; 9am-3pm, 6-8.15pm Thur, Fri; 9am-1pm Sat. Closed Aug. No credit cards. **€**. **Tapas**. Map p100 C4 ⑪
An authentic family-run *bodega*, hugely popular with local workers, where you'll need to arrive early for a cramped and possibly shared table. Said to be the birthplace of the spicy potato *bomba*, La Cova Fumada also turns out a great tomato and onion salad, delicious chickpeas with *morcilla* (black pudding) and unbeatable marinated sardines.

Kaiku
Plaça del Mar 1 (93 221 90 82). Metro Barceloneta. **Open** 1-3.30pm Tue-Sun. Closed 3wks Aug & 1wk Dec. **€€€**. **Seafood**. Map p100 C4 ⑫
With its simple look, missable façade and paper tablecloths, Kaiku looks a world apart from the upmarket seafood restaurants that pepper this *barrio*, but its dishes are in fact sophisticated takes on the seaside classics. A salad starter comes with shavings of foie gras or red fruit vinaigrette, and paella is given a rich and earthy spin with wild mushrooms. Book ahead, particularly for a terrace table.

La Miranda del Museu
Plaça Pau Vila 3 (93 221 17 47). Metro Barceloneta. **Open** 10am-7pm Tue;

10am-8pm Wed; 10am-7pm, 9-11pm Thur-Sat; 10am-5pm Sun. **Café**. Map p100 C3 ⑬
There's no need to buy a ticket to the Museu d'Història de Catalunya to make the most of this little-known rooftop museum café with fabulous views. The set lunches don't break any ground gastronomically, but are reasonable enough, or you can take coffee and a croissant to its vast terrace and watch the boats bobbing in the harbour.

Set Portes

Passeig Isabel II 14 (93 319 30 33/ www.7portes.com). Metro Barceloneta. **Open** 1pm-1am daily. €€€. **Seafood**. Map p100 C2 ⑭
The eponymous seven doors open on to as many dining salons, all kitted out in elegant 19th-century decor. Long-aproned waiters bring regional dishes, served in enormous portions, including a stewy fish *zarzuela* with half a lobster, a different paella daily (shellfish, for example, or rabbit and snails), and a wide array of fresh seafood or heavier dishes such as herbed black-bean stew with pork sausage, and *orujo* sorbet to finish. Reservations are available only for certain tables; without one, get there early or expect a long wait outside.

El Suquet de l'Almirall

Passeig Joan de Borbó 65 (93 221 62 33). Metro Barceloneta. **Open** 1-4pm, 8.30-11pm Tue-Sat; 1-4pm Sun. Closed 2wks Aug. €€€. **Seafood**. Map p100 C4 ⑮
One of the famous beachfront *xiringuitos* that was moved and refurbished in time for the 1992 Olympics, El Suquet remains a friendly, family-run concern, despite the smart decor and mid-scale business lunchers. The fishy favourites range from *xató* salad to *arròs negre* and include a variety of set menus, such as the 'blind' selection of tapas, a gargantuan taster menu and, most popular, the pica-pica, which includes roast red peppers with anchovies, a bowl of steamed cockles and clams, and a heap of *fideuà* with lobster.

El Vaso de Oro

C/Balboa 6 (93 319 30 98). Metro Barceloneta. **Open** 9am-midnight daily. Closed Sept. No credit cards. €€. **Tapas**. Map p100 C3 ⑯
The enormous popularity of this long, narrow cruise ship-style bar tells you everything you need to know about the tapas, but it also means that he who hesitates is lost when it comes to ordering. Elbow out a space and demand, loudly, *chorizitos*, *patatas bravas*, *solomillo* (cubed steak) or *atún* (tuna, which here comes spicy). The beer (its storage, handling and pouring) is also a point of great pride.

Shopping

Maremàgnum

Moll d'Espanya (93 225 81 00/ www.maremagnum.es). Metro Drassanes. **Open** 10am-10pm daily. Map p100 B3 ⑰
When Viaplana and Piñon's black-mirrored shopping and leisure centre opened in 1995, it was the place to hang out. After years of declining popularity, it's ditched most of the bars and taken a step upmarket: residents now include the likes of chocolate shop Xocoa, Calvin Klein and boudoirish Lollipops, which deals in Parisian accessories. All the high-street staples are present (Mango, H&M) and the ground floor focuses on the family market, with sweets, children's clothes and a Barça shop. There's also a handful of tapas restaurants.

Nightlife

CDLC

Passeig Marítim 32 (93 224 04 70/ www.cdlcbarcelona.com). Metro Ciutadella-Vila Olímpica. **Open** noon-2.30am daily. Map p101 E4 ⑱
Carpe Diem Lounge Club, to give the venue its full name, remains at the forefront of Barcelona's splash-the-cash, see-and-be-seen celeb circuit – the white beds flanking the dancefloor, guarded by a clipboarded hostess, are

perfect for showing everyone who's the daddy. Alternatively, for those not celebrating recently signed, six-figure record deals, funky house and a busy terrace provide an opportunity for mere mortals (and models) to mingle and discuss who's going to finance their next drink and, secondly, how to get chatting to whichever member of the Barça team has just walked in.

Club Catwalk

C/Ramón Trias Fargas s/n (93 221 61 61/www.clubcatwalk.net). Metro Ciutadella-Vila Olímpica. **Open** midnight-6am Thur-Sun. **Map** p101 E3 ⑲
Maybe it's the name or maybe it's the location, but most of the Catwalk queue seems to think they're headed straight for the VIP room – that's crisp white collars and gold for the boys and short, short skirts for the girls. Inside it's suitably snazzy; upstairs there's R&B and hip hop, but the main house room is where most of the action is, with everything from electro-house to minimal beats.

Le Kasbah

Plaça Pau Vilà (Palau del Mar) (93 238 07 22/www.ottozutz.com). Metro Barceloneta. **Open** 11pm-3am daily. **Map** p100 C3 ⑳
A white awning over terrace tables heralds the entrance to this decidedly louche bar behind the Palau de Mar. Inside, a North African harem look seduces a young and up-for-it mix of tourists and students on to its plush cushions for a cocktail or two before they depart for other venues. But as the night progresses, so does the music, from chill-out early in the night to full-on boogie after midnight, when it gets packed.

Mondo

Edifici IMAX, Moll d'Espanya (93 221 39 11/www.mondobcn.com). Metro Barceloneta or Drassanes. **Open** 11.30pm-3.30am Wed-Sat. **Map** p100 B3 ㉑
Arrive by yacht or Jaguar – anything less might not get you past the door.

Upscale dining alongside amazing views of the port precede late-night caviar and champagne house parties with DJs from Hed Kandi and Hôtel Costes. Multiple intimate VIP rooms provide privacy, pleasure and prestige.

Red Lounge Bar

Passeig Joan de Borbó 78 (mobile 626 561 309/www.redloungebcn.com). Metro Barceloneta. **Open** 8pm-3am daily. **Map** p100 B4 ㉒
Good news for those missing the legendary Café Royale: DJ Fred Guzzo is the man in charge at this bar, blending funk, latin and rare groove for a mix of music aficionados and glossy-haired uptown kids drawn to the high-class harem look. Nurse Saturday's hangover at the Sunday lounge party: nothing like tapas, beers and beach views to calm the regrets of the night before.

Sala Monasterio

Passeig Isabel II 4 (mobile 609 780 405/www.salamonasterio.com). Metro Barceloneta. **Open** 9.30pm-2.30am Mon-Thur, Sun; 9.30pm-3am Fri, Sat. No credit cards. **Map** p100 C2 ㉓
Its entrance is easily missed; go in through the bar at street level and descend to this low-ceilinged, bare-brick cavern to hear all nature of jamming and live music on a great sound system. On Mondays there are singer-songwriters, rock jams on Tuesdays, Wednesday sees Brazilian music, and Thursday blues jams. Weekends vary.

Arts & leisure

L'Aquàrium

Moll d'Espanya, Port Vell (93 221 74 74/www.aquariumbcn.com). Metro Barceloneta. **Open** Oct-May 9.30am-9pm Mon-Fri; 9.30am-9.30pm Sat, Sun. *June, Sept* 9.30am-9.30pm daily. *July, Aug* 9.30am-11pm daily. **Admission** €16.50; €11-€13 reductions; free under-4s. **Map** p100 B3 ㉔
The main draw here is the Oceanari, a giant shark-infested tank traversed via

a glass tunnel on a slow-moving conveyor belt, but naturally other aquaria house shoals of kaleidoscopic fish where kids can play 'hunt Nemo'. The upstairs section is devoted to children: for preschoolers, Explora! has 50 knobs-and-whistles style activities, such as turning a crank to see how ducks' feet move underwater or climbing inside a mini-submarine, though much of the equipment is looking a bit the worse for wear. Older children should head to Planet Aqua – an extraordinary split-level circular space with Humboldt penguins.

Catamaran Orsom

Portal de la Pau, Port de Barcelona (93 441 05 37/www.barcelona-orsom.com). Metro Drassanes. **Sailings** (approx 1hr 20mins; call to confirm times) mid Mar-Oct noon-8pm. **Tickets** €12.50-€14.90; €6.50-€9.50 reductions; free under-4s. No credit cards. **Map** p100 A3 ㉕
This 23m (75ft) sail catamaran is the largest in Barcelona. Departing from the jetty just by the Monument a Colom, it chugs up to 80 seafarers round the Nova Bocana harbour area, before unfurling its sails and peacefully gliding across the bay. There are 8pm jazz cruises from June to September; or, if you don't want to have to fight for the trampoline sun deck, it can be chartered for private trips.

Las Golondrinas

Moll de Drassanes (93 442 31 06/ www.lasgolondrinas.com). Metro Drassanes. **Tickets** €5.50-€11.50; free under-4s. **Map** p100 A3 ㉖
Since the 1888 World Exhibition, the 'swallow boats' have chugged around the harbour, giving passengers a bosun's eye-view of Barcelona's changing seascape. The traditional double-decker pleasure boats serve the shorter port tour (boats depart around every 40 minutes) while the more powerful catamarans tour as far as the Port Fòrum. The new Cine Mar tours (€25) on Friday and Saturday at 10pm show black and white films from the silent era with an authentic live piano accompaniment.

IMAX Port Vell

Moll d'Espanya, Port Vell (93 225 11 11/www.imaxportvell.com). Metro Barceloneta or Drassanes. **Tickets** €8-€12. **Map** p100 B3 ㉗
The predictable programming lets down the IMAX experience, and only if you're very lucky will you catch anything that's not about sharks, dinosaurs or adventure sports. If these rock your boat, however, you're in for a treat. Note that not all films are 3-D; check the website to see which is which.

Transbordador Aeri

Torre de Sant Sebastià, Barceloneta (93 441 48 20). Metro Barceloneta. **Open** *Mid June-mid Sept* 11am-8pm daily. *Mid Sept-mid June* 10.45am-7pm daily. **Tickets** €9 single; €12.50 return; free under-6s. No credit cards. **Map** p100 B4 ㉘
These rather battered cable cars do not appear to have been touched – except for the installation of lifts – since they were built for the 1929 Expo. They provide sky-high views over Barcelona on their grinding, squeaking path from the Sant Sebastià tower at the very far end of Passeig Joan de Borbó to the Jaume I tower in front of the World Trade Center; the final leg ends at the Miramar lookout point on Montjuïc. Go late to avoid the long queues.

Yelmo Icària Cineplex

C/Salvador Espriú 61, Vila Olímpica (information 93 221 75 85/tickets 902 22 09 22/www.yelmocineplex.es). Metro Ciutadella-Vila Olímpica. **Tickets** Mon €5.50. Tue-Sun €7; €5.50 before 3pm & reductions. **Map** p101 F3 ㉙
A vast multiplex, which has all the atmosphere of the near permanently empty shopping mall that surrounds it, but what it lacks in charm, it makes up for in choice, with 15 screens offering Hollywood blockbusters and mainstream foreign and Spanish releases. Weekends are seat-specific, so queues tend to be slow-moving; it's worth booking your seat online before you go.

CaixaForum p111

Montjuïc & Poble Sec

Maybe it was all those years of living within its walls, but the people of Barcelona seem to prefer to huddle and jostle amid the city's streets than high above the town on the hill gazing down over the city. The spectacular views came to the world's attention during the 1992 Olympic Games, but few bother to climb up for some fresh air on Tibidabo and Montjuïc, the city's remarkably underused hills.

In a city with as few parks as Barcelona, the hills of Montjuïc offer a precious green lung, along with some outstanding museums and galleries. Scattered over the landward side are buildings from the 1992 Olympic Games; facing the sea are a lighthouse and an enormous cemetery. At the top of the hill, all but invisible from below, is the heavily fortified Castell de Montjuïc, a dark and brooding symbol of the centuries Catalonia spent under Castilian rule (see p47 Route with a View).

Poble Sec, the name of the neighbourhood between Montjuïc and the Avda Paral·lel, actually means 'dry village'; it was 1894 before the thousands of poor workers who lived on the flanks of the hill celebrated the installation of the area's first water fountain (which is still standing today in C/Margarit). These days, Poble Sec is a friendly, working-class area of quiet, relaxed streets and leafy squares. The name Paral·lel derives from the fact that the avenue coincides exactly with latitude 41° 44' N, one of Ildefons Cerdà's more eccentric conceits. This was the prime centre of Barcelona nightlife during the first half of the 20th century, and was full of theatres, nightclubs and music halls. A statue on the corner adjoining C/Nou de la Rambla commemorates Raquel Meller, a legendary star of the street who went on to equal celebrity around the world. She now stands outside Barcelona's notorious live-porn venue, the Bagdad.

Montjuïc

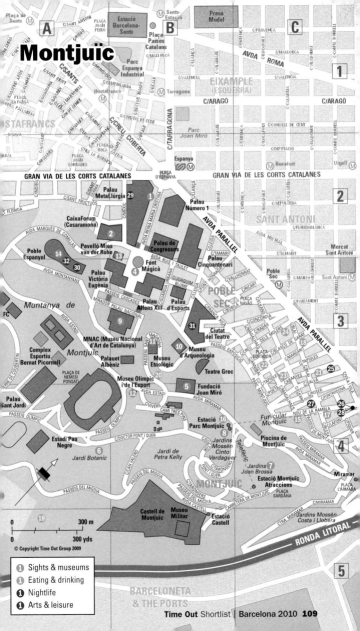

Légende:
- 1 Sights & museums
- 2 Eating & drinking
- 3 Nightlife
- 4 Arts & leisure

© Copyright Time Out Group 2009

CaixaForum

Sights & museums

Bus Montjuïc Turístic

*Torres Venecianas, Plaça d'Espanya
(93 415 60 20). Metro Espanya.*
Open *June, Oct* 10am-9.20pm Sat,
Sun. *July-Sept* 10am-9.20pm daily.
Day pass €3; €2 reductions.
No credit cards. **Map** p109 B2 ❶
An open-top tourist bus. There are two
routes: the blue line runs via Plaça
Espanya, the red one via Portal de la
Pau, near the Monument a Colom; they
coincide at the Olympic stadium and
the castle. Tickets are valid for both
routes. Buses pass every 40 minutes.

CaixaForum

*Casaramona, Avda Marquès de Comillas
6-8 (93 476 86 00/www.fundacio.la
caixa.es). Metro Espanya.* **Open** 10am-
8pm Mon-Fri, Sun; 10am-10pm Sat.
Admission free. **Map** p109 A/B2 ❷
One of the masterpieces of industrial
Modernisme, this red-brick former textile factory was designed by Puig i
Cadafalch in 1911. It spent most of the
last century in a sorry state, acting
briefly as a police barracks and then
falling into dereliction. Fundació La
Caixa, the charitable arm of Catalonia's
largest savings bank, bought it and set
about the reconstruction. The original
brick volume was supported, while the
ground below was excavated to house
a strikingly modern entrance plaza by
Arata Isozaki, a Sol LeWitt mural, an
auditorium, a bookshop and a library.
In addition to the permanent contemporary art collection, there are three
impressive spaces for temporary exhibitions – often among the most interesting shows to be found in the city.
Event highlights Joseph Beuys (until 31
Dec 2009).

Cementiri Sud-Oest

*C/Mare de Déu de Port 54-58 (93 223
16 83). Bus 38.* **Open** 9am-5pm daily.
Admission free. **Map** p109 A4 ❸
Designed by Leandro Albareda in
1880, this enormous necropolis rests at
the side of the motorway out of town,
and is a daily reminder to commuters
of their own mortality. The dead were
originally placed in four sections: one
for Catholics, one for Protestants, one for
non-Christians and a fourth for aborted
foetuses. It now stretches over the
south-west corner of the mountain,
with family tombs stacked five or six
storeys high. Many, especially those
belonging to the gypsy community, are
a riot of colour and flowers. The Fossar
de la Pedrera park memorialises those
fallen from the International Brigades
and the Catalan martyrs from the Civil
War. There is also a Holocaust memor-
ial and a mausoleum to the former president of the Generalitat Lluís Companys.

Font Màgica de Montjuïc

*Plaça Carles Buïgas 1 (93 316 10 00).
Metro Espanya.* **Shows** *May-Sept* every
30 mins 9.30-11pm Thur-Sun. *Oct-Apr*
every 30 mins 7-8.30pm Fri, Sat.
Map p109 B3 ❹
Still using its original plumbing, the
'magic fountain' works its wonders
with 3,600 pieces of tubing and more
than 4,500 light bulbs. On summer
evenings after nightfall, you can see a
pastel-coloured array of founts swell
and dance to music ranging from the
1812 *Overture* to Freddie Mercury and
Montserrat Caballé's *Barcelona*. A new
piece sees the fountain choreographed
to soundtracks from films, including
Blade Runner, *Gladiator* and *Lord
of the Rings*.

Fundació Joan Miró

*Parc de Montjuïc s/n (93 443 94 70/
http://fundaciomiro-bcn.org). Metro
Paral·lel then Funicular de Montjuïc;
or Bus 61.* **Open** *July-Sept* 10am-
8pm Tue, Wed, Fri, Sat; 10am-9.30pm
Thur; 10am-2.30pm Sun. *Oct-June*
10am-7pm Tue, Wed, Fri, Sat; 10am-
9.30pm Thur; 10am-2.30pm Sun.
Guided tours *Temporary exhibitions*
11.30pm Sat. *Permanent exhibition*
11.30pm Sun. **Admission** *All
exhibitions* €8; €6 reductions.

Cementiri Sud-Oest p111

Temporary exhibitions €4; €3 reductions; free under-14s. **Map** p109 B4 ⑤
The building, designed by Josep Lluís Sert, is approachable, light and airy. Its white walls and arches house a collection of more than 225 paintings, 150 sculptures and all of Miró's graphic works, plus some 5,000 drawings. The permanent collection, highlighting Miró's trademark use of primary colours and simplified organic forms symbolising stars, the moon, birds and women, occupies the second half of the space. On the way to the sculpture gallery is Alexander Calder's rebuilt Mercury Fountain, originally on display at the Spanish Republic's pavilion at the 1937 Paris Fair. In other works, Miró is portrayed as a cubist (*Street in Pedralbes*, 1917), naive (*Portrait of a Young Girl*, 1919) and surrealist (*Man and Woman in Front of a Pile of Excrement*, 1935). In the upper galleries, large, black-outlined paintings from Miró's final period precede a room of works with political themes. Outside

is a small sculpture garden with work by contemporary Catalan artists.

Jardí Botànic

C/Doctor Font i Quer (93 426 49 35/ www.jardibotanic.bcn.cat). Metro Espanya/bus 50, 55, 61. **Open** *Jan, Nov-Dec 10am-5pm daily. Feb-Mar, Oct 10am-6pm daily. Apr-May, Sept 10am-7pm daily. June-Aug 10am-8pm daily.* **Admission** €3.50; €1.70 reductions; free under-16s and last Sun of month. No credit cards. **Map** p109 A4 ⑥
After the original 1930s botanical garden was disturbed by the construction for the Olympics, the only solution was to build an entirely new replacement. This opened in 1999, housing plants from seven global regions with a climate similar to that of the Western Mediterranean. Everything about the futuristic design, from the angular concrete pathways to the raw sheet steel banking (and even the design of the bins), is the antithesis of the naturalistic, Gertrude Jekyll-inspired gardens of

England. It is meticulously kept, with all plants being tagged in Latin, Catalan, Spanish and English along with their date of planting, and features wonderful views across the city.

Jardins de Joan Brossa

*Plaça Dante (93 205 99 12/www.
bcn.cat/parcsijardins). Metro Paral·lel,
then funicular.* **Open** *Dec-Feb* 10am-
6pm daily; *Mar, Nov* 10am-7pm daily;
Apr, Oct 10am-8pm daily; *May-Sept*
10am-9pm daily. **Admission** free.
Map p109 C4 ❼

Set in five hectares of the former fairground, Montjuïc's latest park is part-forest, with 40 tree species, and part-urban playground. As well as a climbing frame, there are various wooden creations designed for children, allowing them to play tunes and pump water.

Jardins Mossèn Costa i Llobera

*Ctra de Miramar 1. Metro Paral·lel, then
funicular.* **Open** 10am-sunset daily.
Admission free. **Map** p109 B4 ❽

The port side of Montjuïc is protected from the cold north wind, creating a microclimate that's two degrees centigrade warmer than the rest of the city, – ideal conditions for 800 species of the world's cacti. This extraordinary collection has been closed to the public for some time while funding for essential maintenance is sought.

MNAC (Museu Nacional d'Art de Catalunya)

*Palau Nacional, Parc de Montjuïc
(93 622 03 76/www.mnac.cat). Metro
Espanya.* **Open** 10am-7pm Tue-Sat;
10am-2.30pm Sun. **Admission** (*valid
2 days) Permanent exhibitions* €8.50;
€6 reductions. *Temporary exhibitions*
€3.50-€5.50. *Combined ticket with Poble
Espanyol* €12. Free over-65s, under-14s
and 1st Sun of mth. **Map** p109 B3 ❾

'One museum, a thousand years of art' is the slogan of the National Museum, and the collection provides a dizzying overview of Catalan art from the 12th to the 20th centuries. In recent years, the museum has added an extra floor to absorb the holdings of the section of the Thyssen-Bornemisza collection previously kept in the Pedralbes convent, along with the mainly Modernista holdings from the former Museum of Modern Art in Ciutadella park, a fine photography section, coins and the bequest of Francesc Cambó, founder of the autonomist Lliga Regionalista, a regionalist conservative party.

The highlight of the museum, however, is still the Romanesque collection. As art historians realised that scores of solitary tenth-century churches in the Pyrenees were falling into ruin – and with them were disintegrating extraordinary Romanesque mural paintings that had served to instruct villagers in the basics of the faith – the laborious task was begun of removing the murals from the church apses. The display here features 21 mural sections in loose chronological order.

A highlight is the tremendous *Crist de Taüll* from the 12th-century church of Sant Climent de Taüll. The Gothic collection is also excellent and starts with some late 13th-century frescoes, which were discovered in 1961 and 1997 when two palaces in the city were being renovated. There are carvings and paintings from local churches, including works by the indisputable Catalan masters of the Golden Age, Bernat Martorell and Jaume Huguet. The highlight of the Thyssen collection is Fra Angelico's *Madonna of Humility* (c1430), while the Cambó bequest contains some wonderful Old Masters. Also unmissable is the Modernista collection: it includes Ramon Casas' mural of himself and Pere Romeu on a tandem – which decorated the café frequented by Picasso, Els Quatre Gats (p65). The rich collection of decorative arts includes original furniture from Modernista houses.

BARCELONA BY AREA

Bar Seco p116

Museu d'Arqueologia de Catalunya

Passeig de Santa Madrona 39-41 (93 423 21 49/93 423 65 77/www. mac.cat). Metro Poble Sec. **Open** 9.30am-7pm Tue-Sat; 10am-2.30pm Sun. **Admission** €3; €2.10 reductions; free under-16s. **Map** p109 B3 ⑩

The time frame for this archaeological collection starts with the Palaeolithic period, and there are relics of Greek, Punic, Roman and Visigothic colonisers, up to the early Middle Ages. A massive Roman sarcophagus is carved with scenes of the rape of Persephone, and an immense statue of Aesculapius, the god of medicine, towers over one room. A few galleries are dedicated to the Mallorcan Talayotic cave culture, and there is an exemplary display on the Iberians – the pre-Hellenic, pre-Roman inhabitants of south-eastern Spain. An Iberian skull with a nail driven through it effectively demonstrates a typical method of execution from that time. The display ends with the marvellous, jewel-studded headpiece of a Visigoth king. One of the best-loved pieces, naturally, is an alarmingly erect Priapus, found during building work in Sants in 1848 and kept under wraps 'for moral reasons' until 1986.

Museu Etnològic

Passeig de Santa Madrona s/n (93 424 68 07/www.museuetnologic.bcn.cat). Metro Poble Sec. **Open** *June-Sept* 10am-6pm Tue-Sat; 11am-3pm Sun. *Oct-June* 10am-7pm Tue, Thur, Sat; 10am-2pm Wed, Fri-Sun. **Admission** €3.50; €1.70 reductions; free under-16s and 1st Sun of mth. No credit cards. **Map** p109 B3 ⑪

The Ethnology Museum houses a vast collection of items, from Australian Aboriginal boomerangs to rugs and jewellery from Afghanistan, although by far the most comprehensive collections are from Catalonia. Of the displays upstairs, most outstanding are the Moroccan, Japanese and Philippine exhibits, though there are also some interesting pre-Columbian finds. The attempts to arrange the pieces themat-

Perhaps more entertaining are the interactive displays, such as one that compares your effort at the long jump with that of the pros.

Pavelló Mies van der Rohe

Avda Marquès de Comillas (93 423 40 16/www.miesbcn.com). Metro Espanya. **Open** 10am-8pm daily. **Admission** €4; €2 reductions; free under-18s. **Map** p109 B2 ⑬

Mies van der Rohe built the Pavelló Alemany (German Pavilion) for the 1929 Universal Exhibition not as a gallery but as a simple reception space, sparsely furnished by his trademark 'Barcelona Chair'. The pavilion was a founding monument of modern, rationalist architecture, with its flowing floor plan and a revolutionary use of materials. Although the original pavilion was demolished after the exhibition, a fine replica was built on the same site in 1986, the simplicity of its design setting off the warm tones of the marble and expressive Georg Kolbe sculpture in the pond.

ically, however, are not altogether successful: a potentially fascinating exhibition called 'Taboos', for instance, turned out to be a rather limp look at nudity in different cultures.

Museu Olímpic i de l'Esport

Avda Estadi 60 (93 292 53 79/ www.fundaciobarcelonaolimpica.es). Bus 50, 55, 61. **Open** *Apr-Sept* 10am-8pm Mon, Wed-Sat; 10am-2.30pm Sun. *Oct-Mar* 10am-6pm Mon, Wed-Sat; 10am-2.30pm Sun. **Admission** €4; €2.50 reductions; free under-14s. **Map** p109 B4 ⑫

Opened in 2007 in a new building across from the stadium, the Olympic and Sports Museum gives an overview of the Games (and, indeed, all games) from ancient Greece onwards. As well as photos and film footage of great sporting moments and heroes, there is an array of memorabilia (Ronaldinho's boots, Mika Häkkinen's Mercedes), along with a collection of opening ceremony costumes and Olympic torches.

Poble Espanyol

Avda Marquès de Comillas (93 325 78 66/www.poble-espanyol.com). Metro Espanya. **Open** *Village & restaurants* 9am-8pm Mon; 9am-2am Tue-Thur; 9am-4am Fri; 9am-5am Sat; 9am-midnight Sun. *Shops Dec-May* 10am-6pm daily. *June-Aug* 10am-8pm daily. *Sept-Nov* 10am-7pm daily. **Admission** €8; €5-€6 reductions; *family ticket* €20; free under-4s. *Combined ticket with MNAC* €12. **Map** p109 A2 ⑭

Built for the 1929 Universal Exhibition and designed by the Modernista architect Puig i Cadafalch, this composite Spanish village is charming and kitsch by turns, depending on your taste, and features reproductions of traditional buildings and squares from every region in Spain. The cylindrical towers at the entrance are copies from the walled city of Ávila, and lead on to a Castilian main square, a tiny whitewashed street from Arcos de la Frontera in Andalucía, the 16th-century House of Chains from Toledo, and so on. There are numerous bars and restaurants, a flamenco tablao and more than 60 shops selling Spanish crafts.

Refugi 307

C/Nou de la Rambla 169 (93 256 21 22/ www.museuhistoria.bcn.cat). Metro Paral·lel. **Open** *Guided tour, by appointment only* 11am, noon (Catalan), 1pm (Spanish) Sat, Sun. **Admission** €2. No credit cards. **Map** p109 C4 ⓯

About 1,500 Barcelona civilians were killed during the air bombings of the Civil War, a fact that the government has long silenced. As Poble Sec particularly suffered the effects of bombing, a large air-raid shelter was built partially into the mountain at the top of C/Nou de la Rambla – one of some 1,200 in the entire city. Now converted into a museum, it is worth a visit. The tour takes about 90mins.

Telefèric de Montjuïc (cable car)

Estació Funicular, Avda Miramar (93 318 70 74/www.tmb.net). Metro Paral·lel then Funicular. **Open** *Nov-Mar* 10am-6pm daily. *Apr-May, Oct* 10am-7pm daily. *June-Sept* 10am-9pm daily. **Tickets** *one way* €5.70, €4.50 reductions; *return* €7.90, €6 reductions; free under-4s. No credit cards. **Map** p109 B4 ⓰

The rebuilt system has eight-person cable cars that soar from the funicular all the way up to the castle. In the summer months, the Picnic al Cel offers the chance to enjoy a vertiginous dining experience.

Eating & drinking

Bar Seco

Passeig Montjuïc 74 (93 329 63 74). Metro Paral·lel. **Open** 9am-1am Tue-Thur; 9am-2.30am Fri, Sat. Closed 2wks Aug. No credit cards. **Bar**. **Map** p109 C4 ⓱

La Bella Napoli

The 'Dry Bar' is, in fact, anything but, and its ethical, friendly choices range from local beers and organic wines to fairtrade Brazilian cachaça. Despite a quiet location, it has already gathered a following for the quality of its Italian-Spanish vegetarian dishes and tapas, its fresh milkshakes and a heavenly home-made chocolate and almond cake.

La Bella Napoli

C/Margarit 12 (93 442 50 56). Metro Paral·lel. **Open** 8.30pm-midnight Tue; 1.30-3.45pm, 8.30pm-midnight Wed-Sun. **$$**. **Italian**. **Map** p109 C3 ⓭

La Bella Napoli's welcoming Neapolitan waiters can talk you through the long list of antipasti and pasta dishes, while you can't go wrong with the crispy baked pizzas – such as the Sofia Loren, complete with provolone, basil, bresaola, cherry tomatoes, rocket and parmesan. Beer is Moretti, the wine list all-Italian; in fact the only thing lacking authenticity is the catalogue of pre-made ice-cream desserts. There is own-made tiramisu, but you have to ask.

La Caseta del Migdia

Mirador del Migdia, Passeig del Migdia (mobile 617 956 572). Bus 55 or funicular, then 10min walk. Follow signs to Mirador de Montjuïc. **Open** *June-Sept* 8pm-2.30am Thur-Sat; noon-1am Sun. *Oct-May* noon-7pm Sat, Sun. No credit cards. **Bar. Map** p109 A5 ⑲

Completely alfresco, high up in a clearing among the pine trees, this is a magical space, scattered with deckchairs, hammocks and candlelit tables. DJs spinning funk, rare groove and lounge alternate surreally with a faltering string quartet; food is pizza and other munchies. To find it, follow the Camí del Mar footpath south around the castle, and be aware that it's much cooler up here than in town.

La Font del Gat

Passeig Santa Madrona 28 (93 289 04 04). Funicular Parc Montjuïc/bus 55. **Open** 1-4pm Tue-Sun. Closed 3wks Aug. **$$. Catalan. Map** p109 B3 ⑳

A welcome watering hole perched high on Montjuïc between the Miró paintings and ethnological museums. The small, informal-looking restaurant has a surprisingly sophisticated menu: ravioli with truffles and wild mushrooms, for example, or foie gras with Modena caramel. However, most come for the set lunch: start with scrambled egg served with Catalan sausage and peppers or a salad, follow it with baked cod or chicken with pine nuts and basil, and finish with fruit or a simple dessert. For tables outside, you pay a surcharge.

Quimet i Quimet

C/Poeta Cabanyes 25 (93 442 31 42). Metro Paral·lel. **Open** noon-4pm, 7-10.30pm Mon-Fri; noon-4pm Sat. Closed Aug. **$$. Tapas. Map** p109 C3 ㉑

Packed to the rafters with dusty bottles of wine, this classic but minuscule bar makes up for its lack of space with great tapas. The specialities are *conservas* (shellfish preserved in tins), which aren't always to non-Spanish tastes, but the *montaditos* (sculpted tapas served on bread) are spectacular. Try salmon sashimi with cream cheese, honey and soy, or cod, passata and black olive pâté. Get there early for any chance of a table.

La Soleá

Plaça del Sortidor 14 (93 441 01 24).
Metro Poble Sec. **Open** noon-midnight
Tue-Sat; noon-4.30pm Sun. **$**. No credit
cards. **Global**. Map p109 C3 ㉒

An unassuming but jolly neighbourhood joint, with a sunny terrace on the
Plaça del Sortidor. There's barely a
continent that isn't represented on the
menu, which holds houmous, tabouleh
and goat's-cheese salad plus juicy
burgers served with roquefort or
mushrooms, smoky tandoori chicken,
Mexican tacos, vegetable samosas and
slabs of Argentine beef. Between 4pm
and 8.30pm, the kitchen is officially
closed, but simple platters of cold
hams, cheeses and so on are served.

Tapioles 53

C/Tapioles 53 (93 329 22 38/
www.tapioles53.com). Metro Paral·lel
or Poble Sec. **Open** 9-11pm Tue-Sat.
Closed Aug. **$$$**. **Mediterranean**.
Map p109 C3 ㉓

Tucked down a residential Poble Sec
street, behind a doorbell and slatted
blinds, Tapioles is both elegant and
homely, with accomplished but unpre-
tentious food. Its menu changes daily
but has included gnocchi with goat's
cheese and sage butter; boeuf bour-
guignon; fresh pasta with baby broad
beans and artichokes; rose-water rice
pudding with pomegranate, or ginger
and mascarpone cheesecake. The
freshest produce is bought according
to demand, so booking is obligatory.

Tinta Roja

C/Creu dels Molers 17 (93 443 32 43/
www.tintaroja.net). Metro Poble Sec.
Open *Bar* 8.30pm-2am Thur; 8pm-
3am Fri, Sat; 7pm-1am Sun. Closed
2wks Aug. No credit cards. **Bar**.
Map p109 C3 ㉔

This smooth, mysterious bar was
once a dairy farm, but these days it's
an atmospheric spot for a late-night
drink. Push through the depths of
the bar and you'll be transported to a
Buenos Aires-style bordello/theatre/

circus/cabaret with plush red velvet
sofas, smoochy niches and an ancient
ticket booth.

Nightlife

Barcelona Rouge

C/Poeta Cabanyes 21 (93 442 49 85).
Metro Paral·lel. **Open** 7pm-1am Tue,
Wed, Sun; 7pm-3am Thur-Sat. No
credit cards. Map P109 C3 ㉕

This is a pretty place done up with
throw rugs, vintage lamps that don't
do a whole lot (the lighting concept is
the uncomplicated 'dark') and dusty
sofas. Later in the night it gets packed
with singing, decked-out thirtysome-
things who don't mind getting tipsy
in a place where it costs a fair bit of
coin to do so. There are occasional live
shows (normally Sundays).

La [2]

C/Nou de la Rambla 111-113 (93
441 40 01/www.sala-apolo.com).
Metro Paral·lel. **Open** *Concerts*
9.30pm daily. *Club* 12.30am-6am Fri,
Sat. Map p109 C4 ㉖

La [2] has excellent sounds, an intimate
layout and the only hip flamenco night
in the city (which runs on Mondays
from May to September). The music is
reliably good, with performances by
more cultish artists than those that
play next door. Punters can stay on for
indie-rock club Nitsa.

Maumau

C/Fontrodona 33 (93 441 80 15/
www.maumaunderground.com). Metro
Paral·lel. **Open** 11pm-2.30am Thur;
11pm-3am Fri, Sat; 7pm-midnight Sun.
No credit cards. Map p109 C4 ㉗

Ring the bell by the anonymous grey
door. Inside, a large warehouse space
is humanised with colourful projec-
tions, Ikea-style sofas and scatter
cushions, as well as a friendly, laid-
back crowd. DJ Wakanda schools pun-
ters in the finer points of deep house,
jazz, funk or whatever other music
takes his fancy.

Sala Apolo

C/Nou de la Rambla 111-113
(93 441 40 01/www.sala-apolo.com).
Metro Paral.lel. **Open** *Concerts* 9.30pm
daily. *Club* 12.30am-6am Wed-Sat.
Map p109 C4 ㉓
Sala Apolo, one of Barcelona's most
popular clubs, is a 1940s dancehall,
which means a great atmosphere but
bad acoustics. Live acts range from
Toots & the Maytals to Killing Joke,
but note that buying tickets for the
band doesn't provide admission to the
club night: you'll need to re-enter for
that, and pay an extra charge. On
Wednesdays, the DJs offer African and
Latin rhythms; on Thursdays, it's funk,
Brazilian, hip hop and reggae; and
Fridays and Saturdays are an extrav-
aganza of bleeping electronica.

Sala Instinto

C/México 7 (93 424 83 31/www.
salainstinto.com). Metro Espanya.
Open midnight-6am Wed-Sat;
9pm-4am Sun. No credit cards.
Map p109 B2 ㉙
Sessions in this packed, eclectic club
run from soul and funk to world and
house music, and the crowd varies
according to the music: Thursday's is
young and beer-swilling (checking out
hip hop on a work night); Friday's is
dreadlocked (taking in reggae and jun-
gle sounds); and Saturday's is change-
able (check the website, as the DJ
schedule varies). It's not for glamour
queens – the shoes are as low-key as the
vibe – but if it's the music that makes
the party, then it's worth the trip.

La Terrrazza

Poble Espanyol, Avda Marquès de
Comillas s/n (93 272 49 80/www.
laterrrazza.com). Metro Espanya.
Open *May-mid Oct* midnight-6am
Thur-Sat. No credit cards. **Map**
p109 A2 ㉚
Gorgeous, glamorous, popular (with
the young, hair-gel-and-heels brigade),
La Terrrazza is a nightclub that's the
stuff of Hollywood dreams. Here, you
can wander through the night-time
silence of Poble Espanyol to the starry
patio that's the dancefloor for one of
the more surreal experiences you can
have with a highly priced gin & tonic
in your hand. Gazebos, lookouts and
erotic paintings add to the magic of it
all. So what if the music is mostly
crowd-pleasing house tunes, with the
occasional big-name DJ, but no one
truly fabulous? That's not what you
came here for.

Arts & leisure

Mercat de les Flors

Plaça Margarida Xirgú, C/Lleida 59,
Poble Sec (93 426 18 75/www.mercat
flors.org). Metro Poble Sec. **Box office**
1hr before show. No credit cards.
Map p109 B3 ㉛
British theatre director Peter Brook is
credited with transforming this former
flower market into a venue for the
performing arts in 1985, when he
was looking for a place to stage
his legendary production of the
Mahabharata. After decades of diffuse
programming, the Mercat has finally
focused in on national and international contemporary dance, and offers a
strong programme that experiments
with unusual formats and mixes in
new technologies and live music.

El Tablao de Carmen

Poble Espanyol, Avda Marquès de
Comillas, Montjuic (93 325 68 95/
www.tablaodecarmen.com). Metro
Espanya. **Open** 7pm-midnight Tue-
Sun. *Shows* 7.45pm, 10pm Tue-Sun.
Map p109 A3 ㉜
This rather sanitised version of the fla-
menco tablao sits in faux-Andalucían
surroundings in the Poble Espanyol.
You'll find both stars and new young
talent, displaying the various styles of
flamenco singing, dancing and music.
It's advisable to book (up to a week
ahead in summer). The admission
charge includes entry to the Poble
Espanyol after 7pm.

Passeig de Gràcia

Eixample

With its showstopping Modernista architecture, elegant boutiques and cutting-edge restaurants, the Eixample forms the crucible for Barcelona's image as a city of design. Its extraordinary waffle-iron street layout was designed as an extendible matrix for future growth, gradually coming to connect Barcelona with outlying villages in Europe's first expansive work of urban planning. The period of construction coincided with Barcelona's golden age of architecture: the city's bourgeoisie employed Gaudí, Puig i Cadafalch, Domènech i Montaner and the like to build them ever more daring townhouses in an orgy of avant-garde one-upmanship.

Most of the sites of interest for visitors are within a few blocks of the grand central boulevard of Passeig de Gràcia, which ascends directly from the city's central square of Plaça Catalunya. Incorporating some of

Barcelona's finest Modernista gems, it is the showpiece of the Quadrat D'Or (Golden District) – a square mile of open-air museum between C/Muntaner and C/Roger de Flor that contains 150 protected buildings.

A particularly striking Modernista masterpiece is Puig i Cadafalch's 1901 Palau Macaya at Passeig de Sant Joan 108. Other buildings of interest include the tiled Mercat de la Concepció on C/Aragó, designed by Rovira i Trias, and the turret-topped Casa de les Punxes, another by the prolific Puig i Cadafalch, which combines elements of Nordic Gothic with Spanish plateresque. Further down C/Roger de Llúria, the Casa Thomas and the Palau Montaner were both designed by Lluís Domènech i Montaner, while on C/Casp, stands one of Gaudí's lesser-known works, the Casa Calvet. Look right to see the egg-topped Plaça de Braus Monumental

(C/Marina 749), but the city's last active bullring is now mainly frequented by tour buses from the Costa Brava; out of season, it hosts tatty travelling circuses.

Sights & museums

Casa Amatller

Passeig de Gràcia 41 (93 487 72 17/ www.amatller.org). Metro Passeig de Gràcia. **Open** 10am-8.30pm daily. **Admission** free; guided tour €5; reductions €2.50. **Map** p122 C3 ❶

Built for the chocolate baron Antoni Àmatller, this playful building is one of Puig i Cadafalch's finest creations. Inspired by 17th-century Dutch townhouses, it has a distinctive stepped Flemish pediment with a ceramic façade incorporating lively sculptures by Eusebi Arnau. These include chocolatiers at work, almond trees and blossoms (after the family name) and Sant Jordi slaying the dragon. See box p124.

Casa Àsia

Avda Diagonal 373 (93 238 73 37/ www.casaasia.org). Metro Diagonal. **Open** *Exhibitions* 10am-8pm Mon-Sat; 10am-2pm Sun. *Library* 10am-8pm Mon-Fri; 10am-2pm Sat. *Café* 10am-9pm Mon-Fri. **Admission** free. **Map** p123 D2 ❷

This cultural centre for Asia and the Asian Pacific is housed in the jaw-droppingly ornate Palau Baró de Quadras, designed by Puig i Cadafalch. The centre's underlying function is to promote Asian culture in Barcelona by means of language courses, international conferences, cinema cycles (often subtitled in English) and excellent temporary exhibits covering anything from modern Chinese abstract art to Iranian graphics. It also houses an oriental café on the ground floor.

Casa Batlló

Passeig de Gràcia 43 (93 216 03 06/ www.casabatllo.cat). Metro Passeig de Gràcia. **Open** 9am-8pm daily. **Admission** €17.50; €14 reductions; free under-7s. **Map** p122 C3 ❸

Gaudí and his long-time collaborator Josep Maria Jujol took an ordinary apartment block and remodelled it inside and out for textile tycoon Josep Batlló between 1902 and 1906. The result was one of the most impressive and admired of all Gaudí's creations, although opinions differ on what the building's remarkable façade represents, particularly its polychrome shimmering walls, sinister skeletal balconies and scaly humpbacked roof. Some say it's the spirit of carnival, others a Costa Brava cove. But the most popular theory takes into account Gaudí's deep patriotism, claiming that it depicts Sant Jordi and the dragon: the cross on top being the knight's lance, the roof the dragon's back, and the balconies below the skulls and bones of its hapless victims.

Fundació Antoni Tàpies

C/Aragó 255 (93 487 03 15/www.fundaciotapies.org). Metro Passeig de Gràcia. **Open** 10am-8pm Tue-Sun. **Admission** €6; €4 reductions; free under-16s. **Map** p122 C3 ❹

Eixample

Choc value

A new tour that highlights a sweet side of the city's history.

The Belgians and the Swiss may get all the kudos, but Europe has Spain to thank for chocolate. Cocoa made its way from South America via the *conquistadores*, and it was the Spanish court that first popularised the spicy Aztec drink. Barcelona, which had important trade links with the Americas, became the centre of a burgeoning chocolate industry. The **Casa Amatller** (p121) on the Passeig de Gràcia was one of many mansions paid for by chocolate, thanks to the Amatller family business, established in 1797.

New guided tours of the mansion offer a fascinating glimpse into the Modernista movement, the Amatller family, and the world of the Catalan bourgeoisie at the end of the 19th century. The tours begin in the opulent, neo-Gothic vestibule on the ground floor, where the guide puts the house in its historical context. Wealthy industrialist Antoni Amatller, grandson to the founders of the chocolate-making firm, bought a mansion on the newly fashionable Passeig de Gràcia and commissioned hot young architect, Josep Puig i Cadafalch, to remodel it into a showpiece home. The result is a heady fusion of neo-medieval styles and the popular craft techniques such as tiling, ironwork and woodwork celebrated by the Modernista movement.

The tour picks out delightful details like a greedy stone monkey gobbling a bar of chocolate under the main staircase, and provides amusing anecdotes, including the story of Amatller's motor car: early motor cars did not have a reverse gear and so a special turntable was built inside the hall to turn the car around. The visit continues in Amatller's top-floor photography studio with a 30-minute slide show, fleshing out the family history and its local context, and includes a selection of beautiful photographs depicting the mansion just after its completion in 1900. In a few years (theoretically by 2013) visitors will be able to see Amatller's sumptuous first-floor apartment, which is being restored to look exactly as it did at the turn of the 20th century. A cup of thick hot chocolate awaits at the end of the tour, served in the former kitchen (now an exhibition space).

Antoni Tàpies exploded on to the art scene in the 1950s, when he began to incorporate wastepaper, mud and rags into his paintings, eventually moving on to whole pieces of furniture, running water and girders. As Barcelona's most celebrated living artist, his trademark abstract expressionism graces everything from wine bottle labels to theatre posters. The artist set up the Tàpies Foundation in 1984, and crowned the building with a glorious tangle of aluminium piping and ragged metal netting (*Núvol i Cadira*, or Cloud and Chair). The building is one of the earliest examples of Modernisme to combine exposed brick and iron and is now a cultural centre and museum dedicated to the man himself.

Fundació Joan Brossa

C/Provença 318 (93 467 69 52/www. fundacio-joan-brossa.org). Metro Diagonal or Verdaguer. **Open** 10am-2pm, 3-7pm Mon-Fri. Closed Aug. **Admission** free. **Map** p123 D3 ➎
This polymathic artist (1919-98) left his fingerprints all over his home city, not only in physical sculptures such as the letters spelling 'Barcino' by the cathedral or the Illusory Clock outside the Teatre Poliorama on La Rambla, but also in his vast legacy of poems, theatre plays, tireless campaigning for the Catalan language and the Espai Brossa theatrical space in the Born. The foundation's permanent collection fills three white rooms with some 35 of Brossa's visual and object poems along with posters, manuscripts, books and photographs, plus screenings of some of his short films.

Fundació Suñol

Passeig de Gràcia 98 (93 496 10 32/ www.fundaciosunol.org). Metro Diagonal. **Open** 4-8pm Mon-Wed, Fri, Sat. **Admission** €5; €2.50 reductions. No credit cards. **Map** p123 D2 ➏
The foundation's two floors house the contemporary art collection of busi-

nessman Josep Suñol. At any one time, 100 works of painting, sculpture or photography are on show, shuffled every six months from an archive of 1,200 pieces amassed over 35 years. Catalan and Spanish artists (Picasso, Miró and Pablo Gargallo) predominate, augmented by international big names Warhol, Giacometti and Man Ray.

Fundación Alorda Derksen

C/Aragó 314 (93 272 62 50/www. fundacionad.com). Metro Girona or Passeig de Gràcia. **Open** 10am-1pm, 4-7pm Wed, Fri; 10am-2pm, 4-8pm Sat. Closed Aug. **Admission** €5; €3 reductions. No credit cards. **Map** p123 D3 ➐
Manuel Alorda and his wife Hanneke Derksen opened this impressive contemporary art gallery in 2008. Some pieces in the inaugural exhibition came from their private collection but, as a patron of Tate Modern and the MACBA, Alorda's connections have

Casa Batlló p121

Sagrada Família p129

allowed him to borrow high-profile works of art that have never before been seen in Barcelona. These include works from Damien Hirst's *Butterfly* series and photorealist paintings based on the birth of Hirst's son. Catalan conceptual artist Jaume Plensa's body sculpture of metal letter 'cells' also impresses.

Fundación Francisco Godia

C/Diputació 250 (93 272 31 80/www. fundacionfgodia.org). Metro Passeig de Gràcia. **Open** 10am-8pm Mon, Wed-Sun. Closed Aug. **Admission** €4.50; €2.10 reductions; free under-5s. **Map** p122 C4 ❽
Transplanted in late 2008 from a first-floor flat to the Casa Garriga Nogués – a Modernista masterpiece in its own right – this vast private art collection now covers two floors of exhibition space. Godia was a Formula 1 driver for Maserati in the 1950s who funnelled his considerable fortune into an impressive array of medieval religious art, historic Spanish ceramics, sculpture and modern painting. The permanent collection largely consists of medieval sculptures and paintings, including Alejo de Vahía's *Pietà*, a Luca Giordano, and some outstanding Romanesque sculptures. The inaugural temporary exhibition on the ground floor has a more modern flavour, with pieces by Eduardo Chillida, Picasso, Antoni Tàpies and Joan Miró.

Hospital de la Santa Creu i Sant Pau

C/Sant Antoni María Claret 167 (93 291 90 00/www.santpau.cat). Metro Hospital de Sant Pau. **Open** Call for details. **Map** p123 F2 ❾
When part of the roof of the gynaecology department collapsed in 2004, it was clear that the restoration of Domènech i Montaner's century-old Modernista 'garden city' hospital was unavoidable. In spring 2009, the last of the departments were transferred to the

modern Nou Sant Pau building and the old complex ceased to function as a hospital, although there are tentative plans to turn part of it into a museum of Modernisme. Renovations will take another decade or so, but the complex will remain open to visitors. A UNESCO World Heritage Site, the hospital consists of 20 pavilions abundantly adorned with the Byzantine, Gothic and Moorish flourishes that characterise the architect's style, all set in peaceful gardens. The public enjoy free access to the grounds, and guided tours (€5; €2.50 reductions) in English are held daily at 10.15am and 12.15pm.

Museu de Carrosses Fúnebres

C/Sancho de Avila 2 (93 484 17 10). Metro Marina. **Open** 10am-1pm, 4-6pm Mon-Fri; 10am-1pm Sat, Sun (check in advance). **Admission** free. **Map** p123 F5 ⑩

This obscure and macabre museum is hard to find – ask at the reception desk of the Ajuntament's funeral service and, eventually, a security guard will take you down to a silent and shuddersome basement housing the world's largest collection of funeral carriages and hearses dating from the 18th century through to the 1950s.

Museu de la Música

L'Auditori, C/Padilla 155 (93 256 36 50/www.museumusica.bcn.cat). Metro Glòries. **Open** 11am-9pm Mon, Wed-Fri; 10am-7pm Sat, Sun. **Admission** €4; €3 reductions; free under-16s. **Map** p123 F5 ⑪

The Music Museum comprises over 1,600 instruments, presented like precious jewels on red velvet in glass cases, along with multimedia displays, interactive exhibits and musical paraphernalia. Spanning ancient civilisations to the modern day, instruments from all corners of the globe are represented; the museum's world-class collection of guitars from the 17th century is a high note.

Museu del Perfum

Passeig de Gràcia 39 (93 216 01 21/ www.museudelperfum.com). Metro Passeig de Gràcia. **Open** 10.30am-7.30 Mon-Fri; 10.30am-1.30pm Sat. **Admission** €5; €3 reductions. No credit cards. **Map** p122 C4 ⑫

In the back room of the Regia perfumery sits this collection of nearly 5,000 scent bottles, cosmetic flasks and related objects. You'll find all manner of unguent containers, from a predynastic Egyptian tube of black eye make-up to Edwardian atomisers and a prized double-flask pouch that belonged to Marie Antoinette. Rare bottles, among them a garish Dali creation for Schiaparelli, are displayed in the second chamber.

Museu Egipci de Barcelona

C/València 284 (93 488 01 88/ www.museuegipci.com). Metro Passeig de Gràcia. **Open** 10am-8pm Mon-Sat; 10am-2pm Sun. **Admission** €11; €8 reductions; free under-5s. **Map** p123 D3 ⑬

One of the finest collections of Ancient Egyptian artefacts in Europe, this collection is owned by prominent Egyptologist Jordi Clos and spans 3,000 years of Nile-drenched culture. The exhibits include religious statuary – such as the massive baboon heads used to decorate temples – everyday copper mirrors and alabaster headrests, and some really rather moving infant sarcophagi. Outstanding pieces include some painstakingly matched fragments from the Sixth Dynasty Tomb of Iny, mummified cats, baby crocodiles and falcons, and a 5,000-year-old bed.

Parc de l'Estació del Nord

C/Nàpols (no phone). Metro Arc de Triomf. **Open** 10am-sunset daily. **Admission** free. **Map** p123 F5 ⑭

Otherwise known as Parc Sol i Ombra (meaning 'Sun and Shadow'), this small park is home to three pieces of landscape art in blue and white ceramic by

BARCELONA BY AREA

The man with the plan

The Year of Cerdà.

The demolition of Barcelona's medieval walls in the 1850s coincided with huge economic expansion, and the cultural reawakening of the Catalan Renaixença. The seeds of the city's audacious urban planning were sown, and a showground for Modernisme was created.

The man behind the spread of the city up to Gràcia and other outlying towns was engineer **Ildefons Cerdà** (1815-75), a radical concerned with the poor condition of workers' housing in the Old City.

With its love of straight lines and grids, Cerdà's plan was closely related to the visionary rationalist ideas of its time. His central aim was to alleviate overpopulation while encouraging social equality through using quadrangular blocks, built only on two sides, to a limited height, and with a garden. Each district would be of 20 blocks, with all community necessities. This idealised use of space was rarely achieved, however, with private developers disregarding Cerdà's restrictions.

In time, though, the interplay between the Eixample's straight lines and the disorderly tangle of the older city became a key part of Barcelona's identity. From summer 2009 to summer 2010, L'Any Cerdà (Year of Cerdà), there will be 12 months of exhibitions and activities acknowledging his unique contribution to the city.

New York sculptor Beverly Pepper. Along with a pair of incongruous white stone entrance walls, *Espiral Arbrat* (*Tree Spiral*) is a spiral bench set under the cool shade of lime-flower trees, while *Cel Caigut* (*Fallen Sky*) is a 7m-high (23ft) ridge rising from the grass. The colourful tile work recalls Gaudí's trencadís smashed-tile technique.

Parc Joan Miró (Parc de l'Escorxador)

C/Tarragona (no phone). Metro Espanya. **Open** 10am-sunset daily. **Map** p122 A3 ⑮
Covering an area the size of four city blocks, the old slaughterhouse (*escorxador*), demolished in 1979, provided a much-needed park, although there's little greenery. Palms and pines are dwarfed by Miró's sculpture *Dona i Ocell* (*Woman and Bird*) getting its feet wet in a rather grim cement lake; there's a playground for small children.

La Pedrera (Casa Milà)

Passeig de Gràcia 92-C/Provença 261-265 (93 484 59 00/www.caixa catalunya.cat/obrasocial). Metro Diagonal. **Open** *Jan, Dec* 9am-6.30pm daily. *Feb-Nov* 9am-8pm daily. **Admission** €8; €4.50 reductions; free under-12s. **Map** p123 D3 ⑯
Gaudí's Casa Milà apartment block (known as La Pedrera, or 'the stone quarry') has no straight lines and is a stupendous feat of architecture, the culmination of Gaudí's experimental attempts to recreate natural forms with bricks and mortar (not to mention ceramics and even smashed-up cava bottles). Now a UNESCO World Heritage Site, its marine feel is completed by Jujol's tangled balconies, doors of twisted kelp ribbon, seafoamy ceilings and interior patios as blue as a mermaid's cave. It is supported entirely by pillars, without a single master wall, allowing great swathes of natural light to come in through the vast asymmetrical windows of the façade.

La Pedrera houses an art gallery showing eminent international artists, while the upstairs is dedicated to giving visitors a finer appreciation of Gaudí the architect. Visit a reconstructed Modernista flat on the fourth floor, with a sumptuous bedroom suite by Gaspar Homar, while an exhibition offering an overview of Gaudí's career is located in the attic, framed by parabolic arches worthy of a Gothic cathedral. Best of all is the roof of the building with its trencadís-covered ventilation shafts: their heads are shaped like the helmets of medieval knights, which led the poet Pere Gimferrer to dub the spot 'the garden of warriors'.

Sagrada Família

C/Mallorca 401 (93 207 30 31/ www.sagradafamilia.org). Metro Sagrada Família. **Open** *Mar-Sept* 9am-8pm daily. *Oct-Feb* 9am-6pm daily. **Admission** €8; €5 reductions; €3 8-10 years; free under-8s. *Lift to spires* €2. **Map** p123 F3 ⑰

The Temple Expiatori de la Sagrada Família manages to be both Europe's most fascinating building site and Barcelona's most emblematic creation. In the 1930s, anarchists managed to destroy Gaudí's intricate plans and models for the building by setting fire to them, which means that the ongoing work is a matter of conjecture and considerable controversy; the putative completion date of 2020 is looking increasingly optimistic.

Gaudí, buried beneath the nave of the Sagrada Família, dedicated more than 40 years of his life to the project, the last 14 exclusively, and the crypt, the apse and the nativity façade, all of which were completed in his lifetime, are the most beautiful elements of the church. The latter, facing C/Marina, looks at first glance as though some careless giant has poured candlewax over a Gothic cathedral, but closer inspection reveals that every protuberance is an intricate sculpture of flora, fauna or a human figure, combining to form an astonishingly moving stone tapestry depicting scenes from Christ's life. The other completed façade, the Passion, which faces C/Sardenya, is more austere, with vast diagonal columns in the shape of bones and haunting sculptures by Josep Maria Subirachs. Japanese sculptor Etsuro Sotoo has chosen to adhere more faithfully to Gaudí's intentions, and has fashioned six more modest musicians at the rear of the temple, as well as the exuberantly coloured bowls of fruit to the left of the nativity façade.

Eating & drinking

Alkimia

C/Indústria 79 (93 207 61 15). Metro Joanic or Sagrada Família. **Open** 1.30-3.30pm, 8.30-11pm Mon-Fri. Closed 3wks Aug. €€€€. **Catalan**. **Map** p123 F2 ⑱

Chef Jordi Vilà is hugely respected, and turns out complex dishes that play with Spanish classics – for instance, liquid *pa amb tomàquet* with fuet sausage, wild rice with crayfish and strips of tuna on a bed of foamed mustard. There is also an enviably stocked wine cellar. What is lacking, however, is a great deal of warmth in either the minimalist dining room or from the occasionally tight-lipped waiting staff.

Bar Mut

C/Pau Claris 192 (93 217 43 38). Metro Diagonal. **Open** 9am-midnight Mon-Fri; 11.30am-midnight Sat, Sun. €. **Tapas**. **Map** p123 D2 ⑲

Bar Mut has an ineffably Gallic feel, with its etched glass, bronze fittings, chanteuses on the sound system, and Paris prices. The tapas are undeniably superior, however: try everything from a carpaccio of scallops and sea urchin to fried eggs with foie gras. Come early in the morning for breakfast dishes such as haricot beans with wild mushrooms and *morcilla*. *Formidable*.

Bar Mut p129

La Bodegueta

Rambla de Catalunya 100 (93 215 48 94). Metro Diagonal. **Open** *Sept-July* 8am-2am Mon-Sat; 6.30pm-1am Sun. *Aug* 7pm-1am daily. €€. **Tapas**. No credit cards. **Map** p122 C3 ⑳

This delightful old bodega, with a pretty tiled floor, is unreconstructed, dusty and welcoming, supplying students, businessmen and anyone in between with reasonably priced wine, vermouth on tap and prime-quality tapas. The emphasis is on locally sourced products (try Montserrat tomatoes with tuna), and old favourites such as *patatas bravas*.

Café del Centre

C/Girona 69 (93 488 11 01). Metro Girona. **Open** 8am-11.30pm Mon-Fri. Closed Aug. **Café. Map** p123 D4 ㉑

Possibly the only café of its type left in the Eixample, with a delightfully dusty air, Modernista wooden banquettes, walls stained with the nicotine of ages and marble tables sitting on a chipped chequered floor that almost certainly dates back to the bar's opening in 1873. It's still in the hands of the same family, whose youngest members' attempts to instigate change haven't progressed much beyond a list of fruit teas.

Casa Calvet

C/Casp 48 (93 412 40 12). Metro Urquinaona. **Open** 1-3.30pm, 8.30-11pm Mon-Sat. Closed 2wks Aug. €€€€. **Catalan. Map** p123 D4 ㉒

One of Gaudí's more understated buildings from the outside, Casa Calvet has an interior full of glorious detail in the carpentry, stained glass and tiles. The food is up to par, with surprising combinations almost always hitting the mark: sole with pistachio sauce and sautéed aubergine; scallops with black olive tapenade and wild mushroom croquettes, and roast beef with apple sauce and truffled potatoes. Puddings are superb – try goat's cheese cream with pistachio and beetroot ice-cream.

Cinc Sentits

C/Aribau 58 (93 323 94 90/www.cinc sentits.com). Metro Passeig de Gràcia or Universitat. **Open** 1.30-3.30pm, 8.30-11.15pm Tue-Sat. Closed 2wks Aug. €€€€. **Catalan. Map** p122 B3 ㉓

notable lack of stuffiness: the barmen welcome all comers and the music is more trip hop than rat pack.

Fast Good

C/Balmes 127 (93 452 23 74/www. fast-good.com). Metro Diagonal/FCG Provença. **Open** 12.30pm-midnight daily. Closed Aug. €. **Fast food.** **Map** p122 C3 ㉕
Ferran Adrià's take on fast food is meant for people of taste in a hurry. There are great-quality burgers (garnished with mint and tarragon, say, or roquefort, rocket and sundried tomato), along with panini, various ethnic takes on roast chicken and a sublime fry-up – eggs with jamón ibérico and chips fried in olive oil. There's a good range of salads, while fresh fruit juices and yoghurt shakes are more in evidence than diet coke. Eat in or take away.

Talented chef Jordi Artal shows respect for the classics (flat *coca* bread with foie gras and crispy leeks, duck magret with apple), while adding a personal touch to dishes such as Palamós prawn in *ajoblanco* (garlic soup) with cherries and an ice-cream made from their stones. Save room for the artisanal Catalan cheeses. After a long wait, Cinc Sentits has finally received a well-deserved Michelin star, so be prepared to book.

Dry Martini

C/Aribau 162-166 (93 217 50 72). FGC Provença. **Open** *Sept-July* 1pm-2.30am Mon-Thur; 1pm-3am Fri; 6.30pm-3am Sat; 6pm-2.30am Sun. *Aug* 6.30pm-2.30am Mon-Thur, Sun; 6.30pm-3am Fri, Sat. **Cocktails.** **Map** p122 B2 ㉔
A shrine to the eponymous cocktail, which is honoured in Martini-related artwork and served in a hundred forms. All the trappings of a trad cocktail bar are here (bow-tied staff, leather banquettes, drinking antiques and wooden cabinets displaying a century's worth of bottles) but there's a

Fonda Gaig

NEW *C/Còrsega 200 (93 453 20 20/ www.fondagaig.com). Metro Hospital-Clinic.* **Open** 1.30-3.30pm, 9-11.30pm Tue-Sat; 1.30-3.30pm Sun. €€€€. **Catalan.** **Map** p122 B2 ㉖
It's currently all the rage for Barcelona's top chefs to set up more affordable offshoots and this one is under the guiding hand of Carles Gaig. The Fonda Gaig schtick, like that at Petit Comitè (p133), is a return to grandmotherly Catalan basics, and the favourite dish here is the *canelons* – hearty, steaming tubes of pasta filled with shredded beef and topped with a fragrant béchamel. The dining rooms are smart, modern and wonderfully comfortable.

Gresca

NEW *C/Provença 230 (93 451 61 93/www.gresca.net). Metro Diagonal/ FGC Provença.* **Open** 1.30-3.30pm, 8.30-10.30pm Mon-Fri; 8.30-10.30pm Sat. Closed 2wks Aug. €€€€. **Modern European.** **Map** p122 C3 ㉗
A potentially great new restaurant let down by a dining room rendered clamorous by a steel floor. The lighting is

BARCELONA BY AREA

Gresca p131

also a bit spotty and unforgiving, but sympathetic, if harried, service and excellent food go some way towards smoothing what, with luck, are teething troubles. There is a classy wine list, but the real highlights are dishes such as foamed egg on a bed of *jamón ibérico*, fennel and courgette, or puddings like the coca bread with roquefort and lychee and apple sorbet.

Inopia

C/Tamarit 104 (93 424 52 31/ www.barinopia.com). Metro Poble Sec. **Open** 7-11pm Mon-Fri; 1-3.30pm, 7-11pm Sat. Closed Aug. **€€. Tapas.** Map p122 A5 ㉘
Being brother (and pastry chef) to infamous chef Ferran Adrià has proved both a curse and a blessing for Albert Adrià. On the one hand, his traditional tapas bar has been rammed since it opened; on the other, its glaringly bright, old-school look and approach has disappointed those expecting El Bulli-style culinary fireworks. If classic tapas – *patatas bravas*, Russian salad, croquettes and tripe – are to your liking, however, Inopia certainly does them better than anywhere.

Manairó

C/Diputació 424 (93 231 00 57/www. manairo.com). Metro Monumental. **Open** 1.30-4pm, 8.30-11pm Mon-Sat. **€€€€. Catalan.** Map p123 F4 ㉙
If you're curious to try postmodern haute cuisine (we're talking offal rather than the latest fancies from the Blumenthal school), Manairó is the place to start. Its divine tasting menu takes in small portions of Catalan specialities such as *cap i pota* (a stew of calves' head and feet) and langoustine with *botifarra* sausage and cod tripe, rendering them so delicately that the most squeamish diner will be seduced.

Moo

C/Rosselló 265 (93 445 40 00/www. hotelomm.es). Metro Diagonal. **Open** 1.30-3.45pm, 8.30-10.45pm Mon-Sat. Closed Aug. **€€€€. Catalan.** Map p123 D2 ㉚
The tables at Moo are as desirable as the rooms in its parent, Hotel Omm. Inventive cooking, overlooked by the celebrated Roca brothers, is designed as half portions, the better to experience the full range, from sea bass with lemongrass to suckling pig with a sharp Granny Smith purée. Particular wines

(from a list of 500) are suggested to go with every course, with many dishes even built around them: finish, for example, with 'Sauternes', the wine's bouquet perfectly rendered in mango ice-cream, saffron custard and grapefruit jelly.

Noti

C/Roger de Llúria 35 (93 342 66 73/ www.noti-universal.com). Metro Passeig de Gràcia or Urquinaona. **Open** 1.30-4pm, 8.30pm-midnight Mon-Fri; 8.30pm-midnight Sat. €€€.
Mediterranean. Map p123 D4 ③①
Housed in the former offices of *El Noticiero* newspaper, which won awards for the design, Noti pulls in a glamorous selection of the great and the good for its globetrotting range of dishes. Centrally positioned tables surrounded by reflective glass and gold panelling make celebrity-spotting unavoidable, but other reasons for coming here include steak tartare, squid stuffed with pigs' trotters and a good selection of French cheeses.

Petit Comité

NEW *Ptge de la Concepció 13 (93 550 06 20/www.petitcomite.cat). Metro Diagonal.* **Open** 1pm-1am daily.
€€€€. **Catalan**. Map p122 C3 ③②
Said to be the mentor of über-chef Ferran Adrià, Fermi Puig has enjoyed years of quiet success with the mon-eyed classes in his restaurant Drolma, at the Hotel Majestic. This bistro, aimed at a less élite public, serves more affordable versions of the Catalan classics – *suquet* (fish and potato stew), pig's trotters with spinach and pine nuts, and so on. Be warned; portions are tapas-size and need to be ordered as such, so this is not a cheap option.

Saüc

Ptge Lluis Pellicer 12 (93 321 01 89/ www.saucrestaurant.com). Metro Hospital-Clínic. **Open** 1.30-3.30pm, 8.30-10.30pm Tue-Sat. Closed 3wks Aug & 1wk Jan. €€€€. **Catalan**.
Map p122 B2 ③③

Top-notch but unstuffy, Saüc (which means 'elderberry') is overlooked by the section of international media crazy for 'Spain is the new France' restaurant stories. This may be down to chef Xavier Franco's focus on precise, imaginative cooking, without the tricksy, experimental approach of some of his peers. There's the odd nod to fashion (cherry gazpacho, liquorice in the puddings), but otherwise a rigorous approach to sourcing and tradition is evident in dishes such as terrine of *cap i pota* with chickpea cream, and sturgeon caviar from the Vall d'Aran.

Stush & Teng

NEW *C/Rosselló 209 (93 368 93 93). FGC Provença.* **Open** 8am-4pm, 6pm-2am Mon-Sat. €€€. **Jamaican**.
Map p122 C2 ③④
Spain's first and only Jamaican restaurant is not quite what you might expect – forget ackee and patties, or rather forget the traditional renderings of them, and welcome a brave new world of double-skinned perforated walls, white leather sofas, reggae videos in the toilets, sexy little amuses bouches and sophisticated takes on jerk chicken and goat curry, alongside seafood carpaccio with lime mojo sauce and duck magret with vanilla and barley.

Tapaç24

C/Diputació 269 (93 488 09 77/ www.carlesabellan.com). Metro Passeig de Gràcia. **Open** 9am-midnight Mon-Sat. €€. **Tapas**. Map p123 D4 ③⑤
A new venture from chef Carles Abellan of Comerç 24 fame (p79), this is an ostensibly old-school tapas bar; but among the lentils with chorizo or ham croquettes you'll find playful snacks more familiar to his many fans. The McFoie Burger is an exercise in fast-food heaven, as is the Bikini – a small version of his signature take on the ham and cheese toasty, this one with truffle.

BARCELONA BY AREA

Tragaluz

Ptge de la Concepció 5 (93 487 01 96/ www.grupotragaluz.com). Metro Diagonal. **Open** *Sept-July* 1.30-4pm, 8.30pm-midnight daily. *Aug 11* 1.30-4pm, 8.30-midnight Mon-Fri; 8.30pm-midnight Sat.* **€€€. Mediterranean. Map** p122 C3 ㊱

The stylish flagship for this extraordinarily successful restaurant group has weathered the city's culinary revolution well and is still covering new ground in Mediterranean creativity. It doesn't come cheap – the wine mark-up is particularly hard to swallow – but there's no faulting monkfish tail in a sweet tomato *sofrito* with black olive oil or cherry *consommé* for dessert.

Ty-Bihan

Ptge Lluis Pellicer 13 (93 410 90 02). Metro Hospital Clínic. **Open** 1.30-3.30pm Mon; 1.30-3.30pm, 8.30-11.30pm Tue-Fri; 8.30-11.30pm Sat. Closed Aug. **€€. Crêperie. Map** p122 B2 ㊲

A small restaurant and centre for all things Breton, with live music on Wednesday nights. There's a blend of specialities of the region with Spanish produce in starters such as *andouille* sausage and *membrillo* (quince jelly), but from there on in it's French all the way. Try *galettes*, or scrumptious little blinis (with jam and cream). The Petite menu will take care of *les enfants*, with Breton cider for the grown-ups.

Windsor

C/Còrsega 286 (93 415 84 83/www. restaurantwindsor.com). Metro Diagonal. **Open** 1-4pm, 8.30-11pm Mon-Fri; 8.30-11pm Sat. Closed Aug. **€€€€. Catalan. Map** p122 C2 ㊳

Despite a smart but drab dining room, which attracts a preponderance of business-trippers, Windsor nevertheless serves some of the most creative and uplifting food around. Most dishes are based on Catalan cuisine – pigs' trotters stuffed with *cap i pota*, squab risotto – while others have a lighter, Mediterranean feel.

Xix Bar

C/Rocafort 19 (93 423 43 14/www. xixbar.com). Metro Poble Sec. **Open** 6.30pm-1.30am Mon-Thur; 6.30pm-3am Fri, Sat. **Cocktails. Map** p122 A5 ㊴

Xix (pronounced 'chicks', and a play on the street number, among other things) is an unconventional cocktail bar in the candlelit surroundings of a prettily tiled former *granja* (milk bar). It's dead cosy and just a little bit scruffy, which makes the list of 20 brands of gin all the more unexpected.

Shopping

Altaïr

Gran Via de les Corts Catalanes 616 (93 342 71 71/www.altair.es). Metro Universitat. **Open** 10am-2pm, 4.30-8.30pm Mon-Fri; 10am-3pm, 4-8.30pm Sat. **Map** p122 C4 ㊵

This is the largest travel bookshop in Europe; expect everything from guides to free eating in Barcelona and academic tomes on geolinguistics, to handbooks on successful outdoor sex and CDs of tribal music. Also stocks the usual maps for hikers, travel guidebooks, multilingual dictionaries, travel diaries and equipment such as mosquito nets.

Camper

C/Pelai 13-37 (93 302 41 24/www. camper.com). Metro Catalunya. **Open** 10am-10pm Mon-Sat. **Map** p122 C5 ㊶

Mallorca-based Camper has sexed up its ladies' lines in recent years with high heels (albeit rubbery ones) and girly straps. Of course, it still has its classic round-toed and clod-heeled classics, and the guys still have their iconic bowling shoes.

Casa del Llibre

C/Passeig de Gràcia 62 (93 272 34 80/ www.casadellibro.com). Metro Passeig de Gràcia. **Open** 9.30am-9.30pm Mon-Sat. **Map** p123 D3 ㊷

Part of a well-established Spanish chain, this bookstore offers a diverse assortment of titles that includes some

English-language fiction. Glossy, Barcelona-themed coffee-table tomes with good gift potential sit by the front right-hand entrance.

Colmado Quilez

Rambla Catalunya 63 (93 215 23 56). Metro Passeig de Gràcia. **Open** *Jan-mid Oct* 9am-2pm, 4.30-8.30pm Mon-Fri; 9am-2pm Sat. *Mid Oct-Dec* 9am-2pm, 4.30-8.30pm Mon-Sat. **Map** p122 C3 ➍➌

Colmados – old-school grocery stores – are relics of the time before the invasion of the supermarkets. This is one of the few surviving examples in the Modernista Eixample, with floor-to-ceiling shelves stacked full of gourmet treats: local preserved funghi in cute mushroom-shaped bottles (Delicias del Bosque), and the store's own-label caviar, cava, saffron and anchovies.

El Corte Inglés

Plaça Catalunya 14 (93 306 38 00/ www.elcorteingles.es). Metro Catalunya. **Open** 10am-10pm Mon-Sat. **Map** p123 D5 ➍➍

The mother ship of Spanish retail. This department store is the place for toiletries and cosmetics, fashion and homewares. It also houses a supermarket and a gourmet food hall in the basement, plus services from key cutting to currency exchange; on the top floor, there's a restaurant with great views (but service station-style food). The Portal de l'Àngel branch stocks CDs, DVDs, books, electronic equipment, stationery and sports gear.

Du Pareil au Même

Rambla Catalunya 95 (93 487 14 49/ www.dupareilaumeme.com). Metro Diagonal/FGC Provença. **Open** 10am-8.30pm Mon-Sat. **Map** p122 C3 ➍➎

This French chain stocks everything a pint-sized fashionista might need, though the girls do a bit better than the boys. Newborns to 14-year-olds are served with a covetable range of funky and well-designed clothes at great prices.

Els Encants

C/Dos de Maig 177-187, Plaça de les Glòries (93 246 30 30/www.encants bcn.com). Metro Glòries. **Open** 9am-6pm Mon, Wed, Fri, Sat. *Auctions* 7-9am Mon, Wed, Fri. No credit cards. **Map** p123 F4 ➍➏

The new location of this open-air flea market has been up in the air for years, but the Ajuntament has finally decided on the central plaza of the remodelled Sant Antoni market. It should open in 2012; until then, the market remains a crazy and chaotic antidote to the Glòries shopping mall next door, with teetering piles of everything from old horseshoes and Barça memorabilia to electrical gadgets, religious relics and ancient schoolbooks.

For furniture at a decent price, join the commercial buyers at the auctions from 7am, or arrive at noon, when unsold stuff drops in price. Don't forget to check out the vast warehouses on the market's outskirts, where you may find a bargain among the junk. Avoid Saturdays, when the crowds and the prices increase, and watch out for pickpockets.

Escribà

Gran Via de les Corts Catalanes 546 (93 454 75 35/www.escriba.es). Metro Urgell. **Open** 8am-3pm, 5-9pm Mon-Fri; 8am-9pm Sat, 8am-3pm Sun. **Map** p122 B4 ➍➐

Antoni Escribà, the 'Mozart of Chocolate', died in 2004, but his legacy lives on. His team produces jaw-dropping creations for Easter, from a chocolate Grand Canyon to a life-size model of Michelangelo's *David*. Smaller miracles include cherry liqueur encased in red chocolate lips. The Rambla branch (La Rambla 83, 93 301 60 27) is situated in a pretty Modernista building.

FNAC

El Triangle, Plaça Catalunya 4 (93 344 18 00/www.fnac.es). Metro Catalunya. **Open** 10am-10pm Mon-Sat. **Map** p122 C5 ➍➑

BARCELONA BY AREA

This French multimedia superstore supplies info and entertainment in all possible formats. The ground floor stocks magazines, along with a small café, ticket desk and a travel agent. Above are two floors of CDs, DVDs, computers, stereos, cameras and books in various languages.

Imaginarium

Passeig de Gràcia 103 (902 21 42 15/ www.imaginarium.es). Metro Diagonal. **Open** *9am-9pm Mon-Sat.* **Map** p123 D2 ⓐ

As well as the racks of excellent toys that made Imaginarium famous, the three-floor flagship of Spain's biggest toy chain has a hairdresser's, shoe department, computer zone, a multilingual book department, a play area and reading corner. Expect craft activities, balloon-bending and puppet shows, while the top floor Saborea restaurant has organic food.

Jamonísimo

C/Provença 85 (93 439 08 47/www. jamonisimo.com). Metro Hospital Clínic.

Open *Sept-July* 5-9pm Mon; 9.30am-2.30pm, 5-9pm Tue-Fri; 9.30am-2.30pm, 5.30-9pm Sat. *Aug* 9.30am-2.30pm, 5-9pm Mon-Fri; 9.30am-2.30pm Sat. **Map** p122 A3 ⓐ

This is where Alain Ducasse, Joël Robuchon and Ferran Adrià buy their ham: simply the best available acorn-fed Iberian hams, made by artisans who control the entire process from breeding to curing. The dedicated and passionate salesmen are also happy to talk you through the purchase of *jamón* paraphernalia, such as leg holders and knives, and there are tables where you can try a 'plate of three textures' or divine ham croquettes matched with great Spanish wines.

Jordi Labanda

C/Rosselló 232 (93 496 14 03/www. jordilabanda.com). Metro Diagonal. **Open** *10am-8.30pm Mon-Sat.* **Map** p122 C2 ⓐ

After years of drawing beautiful people in beautiful outfits, Barcelona's most successful illustrator launched his own fashion line. Labanda's shop is

Muxart

skirts, knitwear and stretchy tops. Unsold items end up at the Mango Outlet (C/Girona 37, 93 412 29 35).
Other locations Passeig de Gràcia 8-10 (93 412 15 99).

Muxart
C/Rosselló 230 (93 488 10 64/www. muxart.com). Metro Diagonal. **Open** 10am-2pm, 4.30-8.30pm Mon-Fri; 10am-2pm, 5-8.30pm Sat. **Map** p122 C2 54
Muxart sells shoes around which to build an outfit. The materials are refined, and the styles are sharp, avant-garde and blatantly designed to be seen – and heard. Lines for men and women are complemented by equally creative bags and accessories.

Santa Eulalia
Passeig de Gràcia 93 (93 215 06 74/ www.santaeulalia.com). Metro Diagonal. **Open** 10am-8.30pm Mon-Sat. **Map** p122 C3 55
Barcelona's oldest design house and a pioneer in the local catwalk scene, Santa Eulalia was founded in 1843 and remains a seriously upmarket proposition. The prêt-à-porter collection carries labels such as Balenciaga, Jimmy Choo and Stella McCartney. Services include bespoke tailoring and wedding wear for grooms. The C/Pau Casals branch is for men only.

Sephora
El Triangle, C/Pelai 13-37 (93 306 39 00/www.sephora.es). Metro Catalunya. **Open** 10am-10pm Mon-Sat. **Map** p122 C5 56
Sephora is your best bet for unfettered playing around with scents and make-up. Cosmetics and toiletries range from basic to high-end brands; there are also handy beauty tools, such as eyebrow tweezers and pencil sharpeners.

Vinçon
Passeig de Gràcia 96 (93 215 60 50/ www.vincon.com). Metro Diagonal. **Open** 10am-8.30pm Mon-Sat. **Map** p123 D2 57

an arrangement of blinding white and glossy black with off-kilter mirrors that complement the 1960s-inspired monochrome collections. The most popular items are the cartoon T-shirts.

Josep Font
C/Provença 304 (93 487 21 10/ www.josepfont.com). Metro Diagonal. **Open** *Sept-July* 10am-8.30pm Mon-Sat. *Aug* 10am-2pm, 4.30-8.30pm Mon-Sat. **Map** p123 D3 52
Font's romantic and feminine designs are dripping with ribbons and ruffles yet somehow never stray into Barbara Cartland territory. Look for cute 1950s-inspired shorts suits, floral maxi dresses and sumptuous materials, from shimmery silks to millefeuille chiffon.

Mango
Passeig de Gràcia 65 (93 215 75 30/ www.mango.es). Metro Passeig de Gràcia. **Open** 10am-9pm Mon-Sat. **Map** p122 C3 53
A small step up from Zara in quality and price, Mango's womenswear includes tailored trouser suits and

BARCELONA BY AREA

Keeping Barcelona's reputation as a city of cutting-edge design alive, the building itself is a monument to the history of local design: the upstairs furniture showroom is surrounded by Modernista glory (you get a peek at Gaudí's La Pedrera); downstairs in the kitchen, bathroom, garden and other departments, everything is black, minimalist and hip. Although its not cheap, almost everything you buy here is, or will be, a design classic, be it a Bonet armchair or a 'perfect' corkscrew.

Nightlife

Arena

Classic & Madre C/Diputació 233 VIP & Dandy Gran Via de les Corts Catalanes 593 (93 487 83 42/www. arenadisco.com). Metro Universitat. **Open** 12.30am-6am Mon-Sat; 7.30pm-5am Sun. No credit cards. **Map** p122 C4 ⑧

The four Arena clubs are still packing them in every week with a huge variety of gay punters. The USP is that you pay once, get your hand stamped and can then switch between all four clubs. Madre is the biggest and most full-on; VIP doesn't take itself too seriously and is popular with just about everyone; Classic is similarly mixed, if even cheesier; and, finally, Dandy bangs away with vintage chart hits.

City Hall

Rambla Catalunya 2-4 (93 317 21 77/ www.grupo-ottozutz.com). Metro Catalunya. **Open** 10.30pm-6am daily. **Map** p122 C4 ⑨

City Hall ain't big, but it is popular. The music is mixed, from deep house to electro rock, and there's an older post-(pre-?) work crowd joining the young, tanned and skinny to show the dancefloors some love. Outside, the terrace is a melting pot of tourists and locals, who rub shoulders under the watchful (and anti-pot-smoking) eye of the bouncer.

D-Boy

Ronda Sant Pere 19-21 (93 318 06 86/ www.matineegroup.com). Metro Urquinaona. **Open** midnight-6am Thur-Sat. No credit cards. **Map** p123 D5 ⑩

The much-loved Salvation recently reopened, after a €2m makeover and much fanfare, as D-Boy. With two spaces, one for house and another for deep house, and a huge darkroom, it's kept its megatron and go-gos, although its attitude and pricing policy could be said to exceed its actual charms.

Lotus Theatre

NEW C/Bailen 22 (902 627 987/ mobile 692 043 191/www.lotus theatre.info). Metro Arc de Triomf or Tetuan. **Open** midnight-5am Thur-Sun. No credit cards. **Map** p123 E4 ⑪

Formerly a strip club, this place was recently reborn as the city's hottest, biggest, most over-hyped nightspot. Its former incarnation hasn't been forgotten – the decor is dark glass, marble, mirrors and poles, the bar staff appear to be Playboy bunnies and dancers in full burlesque occasionally adorn the tabletops. Live salsa and funk shows on weekends are followed by DJs playing funk, hip hop, house and R&B.

Opium

C/Paris 193-197 (93 414 63 62/ www.opiumcinema.com). Metro Diagonal. **Open** 11.30pm-2.30am Tue-Thur, Sun; 11.30pm-3.30am Fri, Sat. Closed Aug. **Map** p122 C2 ⑫

Opium offers a break from the norm. For a start, the club is housed in a converted 1950s cinema, so the projections are actually watchable. There are three bars, plenty of comfortable seating and a small dancefloor; the very special get to sit on a heart-shaped cushion in the tiny VIP area. Somewhat inevitably, Opium has become the domain of Barcelona's monied classes.

La Pedrera de Nit

C/Provença 261-265 (93 484 59 00/ www.caixacatalunya.es/obrasocial).

Metro Diagonal. **Open** *July* 9-11.30pm Fri, Sat. Closed Aug-June. **Map** p123 D3 ❻❸

In July, the gorgeous and hallucinatory roof terrace of Gaudí's La Pedrera becomes a jazz club with a view. Spend a fine Friday or Saturday evening engaged in the apex of civilised revelry: sip cava, sway to live music and contemplate city life from above. Concerts are at 10pm; book well in advance as tickets sell fast.

Arts & leisure

L'Auditori

C/Lepant 150 (93 247 93 00/www. auditori.cat). Metro Marina. **Open** *Information* 8am-10pm daily. **Map** p123 F5 ❻❹

Designed by Rafael Moneo and directed by Joan Oller, L'Auditori offers something for everyone. The 2,400-seat Pau Casals hall, dedicated to the Catalan cellist, provides a stable home for city orchestra OBC, now under the baton of conductor Eiji Oue. Look out for the revered Jordi Savall in a superb series of early music concerts called El So Original, running from October to April. An intimate 600-seat chamber space incorporates contemporary and world music, while experimental and children's work is staged in a 400-seat space named after jazz pianist Tete Montoliu.

Casablanca-Gràcia

C/Girona 173-175 (93 459 03 26). Metro Verdaguer. **Tickets** Mon, Tue, Thur-Sun €6.50. Wed €4.80. No credit cards. **Map** p123 D2 ❻❺

Three screens show independent Spanish and European films; if none appeals, its sister cinema, the Kaplan, is just a short walk away (Passeig de Gràcia 115, 93 218 43 45).

Cinemes Méliès

C/Villarroel 102 (93 451 00 51/www. cinesmelies.net). Metro Urgell. **Tickets** *Mon* €3. *Tue-Sun* €4.50. No credit cards. **Map** p122 B4 ❻❻

The small, two-screen Cinemes Méliès is the closest that Barcelona comes to an art house theatre; idiosyncratic classics nestle alongside more recent films that aren't quite commercial enough for general release.

La FilmoTeca

Cinema Aquitania, Avda Sarrià 31-33 (93 410 75 90/http://cultura.gencat. net/filmo). Metro Hospital Clínic. Closed Aug. **Tickets** €2.70; €2 reductions; €18 for 10 films. **Map** p122 A2 ❻❼

Funded by the Catalan government, the Filmoteca can be a little dry, offering seasons of cinema's more recondite auteurs, alongside better-known classics. Books of 20 and 100 tickets bring down the price per film to a negligible amount. The 'Filmo' also runs an excellent library of film-related books, videos and magazines at Portal Santa Madrona 6-8 (93 316 27 80), just off La Rambla.

Renoir-Floridablanca

C/Floridablanca 135 (93 228 93 93/ www.cinesrenoir.com). Metro Sant Antoni. **Tickets** Mon €4.80. Tue-Fri €6.50. Sat, Sun €6.80. *Late show* Fri, Sat €4.80. **Map** p122 B5 ❻❽

This, the more central of the Renoir cinemas, screens up to eight independent, offbeat American, British and Spanish films per day, though programming tends towards the worthy.

Other locations Renoir-Les Corts, C/Eugeni d'Ors 12, Les Corts (93 490 43 05).

Teatre Nacional de Catalunya (TNC)

Plaça de les Arts 1 (93 306 57 00/ www.tnc.cat). Metro Glòries. **Map** p123 F4 ❻❾

The Generalitat-funded theatre designed by Ricardo Bofill boasts three performance spaces. Director Sergi Belbel has opted for a good mix of contemporary and classical pieces and incorporated a fine dance programme. Works by new writers are normally performed in the more experimental Sala Tallers.

Gràcia

Dissent has been a recurring feature in Gràcia's history: streets boast names such as Llibertat, Revolució and Fraternitat; and for the 64 years preceding the Civil War, there was a satirical political magazine called *La Campana de Gràcia*, named after the famous bell in Plaça Rius i Taulet. However, few vestiges of radicalism remain. Sure, the *okupa* squatter movement inhabits a relatively high number of buildings in the area, but the middle-class population has been waging an increasingly successful campaign to dislodge them.

Gràcia is both alternative and upmarket, and anything bigger than a shoebox costs a fortune to rent or buy, but for many, it's the only place to be in Barcelona. As a consequence it radiates a sort of global chic of sleek bars, yoga centres, shiatsu, acupuncture and every form of holistic medicine, as well as piercing and tattoo parlours, dotted among the antique shops and *jamonerías*. It really comes into its own for a few days in mid August, when its famous *festa major* grips the entire city.

The district's Modernista gem is one of Gaudí's earliest and most fascinating works, the Casa Vicens of 1883-88, hidden away in C/Carolines. The building is a private residence and not open to visitors, but the castellated red brickwork and colourful tiled exterior with Indian and Mudéjar influences should not be missed; notice too the spiky wrought-iron leaves on the gates.

Sights & museums

Fundació Foto Colectània
C/Julián Romea 6, D2 (93 217 16 26/ www.colectania.es). FGC Gràcia. **Open** 11am-2pm, 5-8.30pm Mon-Sat. Closed Sat in Aug. **Admission** free-€3, depending on exhibition. **Map** p142 B4 ●

Park Güell

This private foundation is dedicated to the promotion of the work of major Spanish and Portuguese photographers from the 1950s to the present day. It also has an extensive library of Spanish and Portuguese photography books and monographs.

Park Güell

C/Olot (Casa-Museu Gaudí 93 219 38 11). Metro Lessreps/bus 24, 25. **Open** *Park* 10am-sunset daily. *Museum* Apr-Sept 10am-7.45pm daily. Oct-Mar 10am-5.45pm daily. **Admission** *Park* free. *Museum* €4; €3 reductions; free under-9s. **Map** p143 F1 ②

Gaudí's brief for this spectacular project was to emulate the English garden cities so admired by his patron Eusebi Güell (hence the unusual spelling of 'park'): to lay out a self-contained suburb for the wealthy, but also to design the public areas. The idea never took off and the Güell family donated the park to the city in 1922.

It is a real fairy-tale place; the fantastical exuberance of Gaudí's imagination is breathtaking. The visitor was previously welcomed by two life-sized mechanical gazelles, although these were destroyed in the Civil War. The two gatehouses that do still remain were based on designs the architect made earlier for the opera *Hansel and Gretel*, one of them featuring a red and white mushroom for a roof. From here, walk up a splendid staircase flanked by multicoloured battlements, past the iconic mosaic lizard sculpture, to what would have been the main marketplace. Here, 100 palm-shaped pillars hold up a roof, reminiscent of the hypostyle hall at Luxor. On top of this structure you'll find the esplanade, a circular concourse surrounded by undulating benches in the form of a sea-serpent decorated with shattered tiles – a technique known as trencadís, which was actually perfected by Gaudí's overshadowed but talented assistant Josep Maria Jujol.

The park itself, now a UNESCO World Heritage Site, is magical, with twisted stone columns supporting curving colonnades or merging with the natural structure of the hillside. The park's peak is marked by a large cross and offers an amazing panorama of Barcelona and the sea beyond. Gaudí lived for a time in one of the two houses built on the site. It has since become the Casa-Museu Gaudí; guided tours, some of which are in English, are available. The best way to get to the park is on the 24 bus; if you go via Lesseps metro, be prepared for a steep uphill walk.

Eating & drinking

Bo

Plaça Rius i Taulet 11 (93 368 35 29). Metro Diagonal or Fontana. **Open** 10am-1am Mon-Thur; 10am-2.30am Fri-Sun. **€**. *Café.* **Map** p142 C4 ③

It claims to serve the best *patatas bravas* in Barcelona, but really we love Bo for its terrace on one of Gràcia's most lively and emblematic squares. Its reasonably original sandwiches, little terracotta dishes of *gambas al ajillo* or octopus, and the generously portioned tapas are also a boon.

Gràcia

The big squeeze

The global crisis has hit almost everybody, and tourists travelling with weak currencies such as the pound will feel the pinch. Here are a few tips for getting a little more out of your *céntims*:

■ In 2009, municipal museums extended free entry on the first Sunday of the month to free entry every Sunday, between 3 and 6pm.

■ Sales come between 7 January and early March, while summer sales are in July.

■ Free-entry contemporary art museums include: Fundació Joan Brossa (p125); CaixaForum (p111); Centre d'Art Santa Mònica (p57).

■ There is free museum entry across the board on 18 May for the Dia Internacional dels Museus. Many are also free on the night of the 17th for the new Nit dels Museus.

■ Particularly good-value set lunches are served at La Soleá (p118), Himali (p146), Kaiku (p104), Organic (p94) and Wushu (p81).

■ Longer-term visitors with a library card get discounts at cinemas, theatres and bookshops.

■ Unsold theatre tickets are on sale at a 30 to 50 per cent discount from the Tiquet 3 box office in the main tourist office underneath Plaça Catalunya up to three hours before the start of the show.

■ Sample cheap but top quality seafood by serving yourself at La Paradeta (p81).

■ Monday is discount day at most cinemas; exceptions are the Boliche and the Casablanca-Gràcia, which drop their prices on Wednesdays.

■ If you intend to use a lot of public transport, it can be cheaper to buy a travel card than the standard single ticket or T-10 carnet. TMB offers travel cards for 1-5 days that give unlimited access to all forms of public transport.

■ The Museu Frederic Marès (p58), the CCCB (p88) and the Parc del Laberint (p160) are discounted or free on Wednesdays.

■ Carrer Girona in the Eixample is packed with remainder stores and factory outlets, such as Mango Outlet at No.37.

■ Save your paella experience for Thursday lunchtime when it is a standard feature on set lunch menus.

Bodega Manolo

C/Torrent de les Flors 101 (93 284 43 77). Metro Joanic. **Open** 10am-5.30pm Tue, Wed; 10am-5.30pm, 9-11pm Thur, Fri; noon-5.30pm, 9-11pm Sat; noon-3pm Sun. Closed Aug. **€**. No credit cards. **Tapas**. **Map** p143 E3 ➍

A smoky but likeable old family *bodega* with a faded, peeling charm, barrels on the wall and rows of dusty bottles. Manolo specialises not only in reasonably priced wine, but in classy food: try the foie gras with port and apple, or a fresh anchovy salad with Greek yoghurt and tomato confit. Push through the bar to the dining room at the back.

Botafumeiro

C/Gran de Gràcia 81 (93 218 42 30/ www.botafumeiro.es). Metro Fontana. **Open** 1pm-1am daily. **€€€**. **Seafood**. **Map** p142 C4 ➎

The speciality at this vast Galician restaurant is seafood in every shape and form, served with military precision by a fleet of nautically clad waiters. The sole cooked in cava with prawns is superb, as are more humble dishes such as a cabbage and pork broth typical of the region. The platter of seafood (for two) is an excellent introduction to the various molluscs of the Spanish coastline. It can be hard to get a table at peak times, but the kitchen is open all day.

Cantina Machito

C/Torrijos 47 (93 217 34 14). Metro Fontana or Joanic. **Open** 1-4pm, 7pm-1.30am daily. **€€**. **Mexican**. **Map** p143 D3 ➏

Every day is Day of the Dead in this cheerily decked out little Mexican joint, with its tissue paper bunting and chaotic hubbub. The minuscule writing on the menu and low lighting make for some guesswork when placing your order, but the choices are standard enough – quesadillas, tacos, ceviche and enchiladas – with a couple of surprises, such as the tasting platter of insects. Service can be slow and the kitchen a

little heavy-handed with the sauces, but portions are huge and prices reasonable.

Envalira

Plaça del Sol 13 (93 218 58 13). Metro Fontana. **Open** 1.30-4pm, 9pm-midnight Tue-Sat; 1.30-5pm Sun. Closed Aug. **€€**. **Spanish**. **Map** p142 C4 ➐

Most regions of Spain are represented on the menu at this profoundly traditional restaurant, with a particular emphasis on Galicia (*caldeirada gallega* is a hearty fish stew, *lacón con grelos* is gammon with turnip tops and *tarta de Santiago* is an almond cake). The Basque oxtail stew is also very tasty. The dining room could do with a lick of paint and some subtlety in its lighting; arrive early for the more comfy leather banquettes at the front, and be sure to book ahead at weekends.

Flash Flash

C/Granada del Penedès 25 (93 237 09 90). FGC Gràcia. **Open** 1.30pm-1.30am daily. **Bar**. **Map** p142 B4 ➑

Opened back in 1970, this bar was a design sensation in its day, with its white leatherette banquettes and walls imprinted with silhouettes of a life-size frolicking, Twiggy-like model. They describe it as a *tortilleria*, with 60 or so tortilla variations available, alongside a list of child-friendly dishes and adult-friendly cocktails.

Gelateria Caffetteria Italiana

Plaça Revolució 2 (93 210 23 39). Metro Fontana or Joanic. **Open** 5pm-12.30am daily. Closed mid Dec-mid Jan. **€**. No credit cards. **Ice-cream**. **Map** p143 D4 ➒

Run by an Italian mother and daughter, Caffetteria Italiana is famous for its own-recipe dark chocolate ice-cream – of which it runs out every night. Other freshly made, additive-free flavours include fig, strawberry, peach: basically, whatever fruit happens to be in season. Prepare to queue on summer evenings.

BARCELONA BY AREA

The policy at Barcelona's only Iraqi restaurant is to have everything on the menu at the same price, so that the cost won't hold anybody back from ordering what they want. The menu is based on Arab 'staff of life' foods, such as yoghurt and rice. Best value is the huge taster menu, which includes great Lebanese wines, a variety of dips for your *riqaq* bread, bulgur wheat with aromatic roast meats and vegetables, sticky baklava and Arabic teas. Also good are the potato croquettes stuffed with minced meat, almonds and dried fruit.

La Nena
C/Ramón y Cajal 36 (93 285 14 76). Metro Fontana or Joanic. **Open** *Oct-July* 9am-10pm daily. *Aug, Sept* 9am-2pm, 4-10pm daily. Closed 3wks Aug. No credit cards. **Café**. **Map** p143 D4 ⑫
With whitewashed stone walls, piles of books and games, and a gaily painted table-and-chair set for children, La Nena is wonderfully cosy, or would be if the staff would only lighten up. The speciality is sugar and spice and all things nice; waffles, crêpes, hot chocolate, fresh juices and ice-cream. Savoury delights include sandwiches and toasted bread with various toppings. Note there is no alcohol.

Noise i Art
C/Topazi 26 (93 217 50 01). Metro Fontana. **Open** 6pm-2.30am Tue-Thur, Sun; 7pm-3am Fri, Sat. Closed 2wks end Aug, 1st wk Sept. **Map** p143 D3 ⑬
Colourful, pop art decor coupled with a chilled and convivial atmosphere makes this the perfect bar to sit and shoot the breeze. It's occasionally livened up with a flamenco session, and all the usual Gràcia food staples, such as houmous and tabbouleh, are served. We could live without the Madonna and Depeche Mode videos looping on a giant screen, but the large spirit measures do help.

Octubre
C/Julián Romea 18 (93 218 25 18). Metro Diagonal/FGC Gràcia. **Open**

Botafumeiro p145

Himali
C/Milà i Fontanals 68 (93 285 15 68). Metro Joanic. **Open** noon-4pm, 8pm-midnight Tue-Sun. **€**.
Nepalese. **Map** p143 D4 ⑩
A comic metaphor for modern-day Barcelona, Himali moved into what was a local boozer, but has retained the silhouettes of famous Catalans – Dali and Montserrat Caballé among them – on the windows, while inside there are Nepalese prayer flags and tourist posters of the Himalayas. The alien and impenetrable menu looks a bit daunting, but the waiters are useful with recommendations; or you could start with momo dumplings or Nepalese soup, followed by *mugliaco kukhura* (barbecued butter chicken in tomato sauce) or *khasi masala tarkari* (baked spicy lamb). All dishes include rice and nan bread.

Mesopotamia
C/Verdi 65 (93 237 15 63). Metro Fontana. **Open** 8.30pm-midnight Tue-Sat. Closed 2wks Dec. **€€**. No credit cards. **Iraqi**. **Map** p143 D3 ⑪

1.30-3.30pm, 9-11pm Mon-Fri; 9-11pm Sat. Closed Aug. **€€**. **Catalan**. Map p142 B4 ⑭

Time stands still in this quiet little spot, with its quaint old-fashioned decor, swathes of lace and brown table linen. Time often stands still, in fact, between placing an order and receiving any food, but this is all part of Octubre's sleepy charm. Also contributing to its appeal is a roll-call of reasonably priced, mainly Catalan dishes, like squid stuffed with meatballs on a bed of *samfaina*, and pig's trotter with fried cabbage and potato.

Restaurante Hofmann

C/Granada del Penedès 14-16 (93 218 71 65/www.hofmann-bcn.com). FCG Gràcia. **Open** 1.30-3pm, 9-11.15pm Mon-Fri. Closed Aug. **€€€**. **Global**. Map p142 B4 ⑮

Recently transplanted here from a space in its associated cookery school in the Born, Hofmann puts its pupils to good use in its top-class kitchens and dining room. The affordable lunch *menú* might start with a truffle salad, followed by bream in bacon or a rack of lamb with mustard sauce, but, as is the case with the à la carte menu, the puddings are really the high point. Artful constructions such as a jam jar and lid made of sugar and filled with red fruit, or a tarte tatin in a spun-sugar 'cage', are as delicious as they are clever.

San Kil

C/Legalitat 22 (93 284 41 79). Metro Fontana or Joanic. **Open** 1-4pm, 8.30pm-midnight Mon-Sat. Closed 2wks Aug. **€€**. **Korean**. Map p143 E3 ⑯

If you've never eaten Korean food before, it pays to gen up a bit before you head to this bright and spartan restaurant. *Panch'an* is the ideal starter for the beginner in this cuisine: four little dishes containing vegetable appetisers, one of which will be tangy *kimch'i* (fermented cabbage with chilli). Then try mouth-watering *pulgogi* – beef served sizzling at the table

and eaten rolled into lettuce leaves – and maybe *pibimbap* – rice with vegetables (and occasionally meat) topped with a fried egg. Finish up with a shot of soju rice wine.

Shojiro

C/Ros de Olano 11 (93 415 65 48). Metro Fontana. **Open** 1.30-3.30pm Mon, Tue; 1.30-3.30pm, 9-11.30pm Wed-Sat. Closed Aug. **€€**.
Japanese. Map p142 C4 ⑰

A curious but surprisingly successful mix of Catalan and Japanese applies to the decor as much as the food at Shojiro, with original mosaic flooring and dark-green paintwork setting off a clean feng-shuied look. There are only set meals on offer (drinks are all included in lunch). Dishes might include mackerel cooked with miso and white aubergine, followed by venison with wild mushrooms and black basil. Two puddings are also included in the price.

La Singular

C/Francisco Giner 50 (93 237 50 98). Metro Diagonal or Fontana. **Open** 1.30-4pm, 9pm-midnight Mon-Thur; 1.30-4pm, 9pm-1am Fri; 9pm-1am Sat. Closed last wk Aug & 1st wk Sept. **€€**.
Mediterranean. Map p142 C5 ⑱

While this is often described as a lesbian-friendly restaurant, in fact that's the least noteworthy thing about it, and all are made welcome. Most come here for the good-value set lunch (salads and light pasta dishes to start, followed by dishes such as roast beef carpaccio with red cabbage and onion) in snug surroundings of red walls with pale green woodwork and a tiny, leafy patio. It can get noisy when full; it's best to come early and beat the rush. Reservations are necessary for Friday and Saturday nights.

Sureny

Plaça de la Revolució 17 (93 213 75 56). Metro Fontana or Joanic. **Open** 8.30pm-midnight Tue-Thur, Sun; 8.30pm-1am Fri, Sat. Closed 2wks Apr, 2 wks Dec. **€€**. **Tapas**. Map p143 D4 ⑲

A well-kept gastronomic secret, Sureny boasts superb gourmet tapas and waiters who know what they're about. In addition to the usual run-of-the-mill tortilla 'n' calamares fare, look out for dishes such as tuna marinated in ginger and soy sauce, partridge, venison and other game when in season, and a sublime duck foie with redcurrant sauce.

Shopping

BCN Computers
C/Mozart 26 (93 217 61 66).
Metro Fontana. **Open** 10am-2pm, 4-8pm Mon-Fri. No credit cards.
Map p142 C5 ⑳
Everything for Macs and PCs: software in English, hardware and software installations, repairs for personal computers and laptops and ADSL support. There's English-speaking customer service and, unlike many local shops, staff offer a free evaluation of your computer's problems when you take it for repair.

Hibernian Books
C/Montseny 17 (93 217 47 96/ www.hibernian-books.com). Metro Fontana. **Open** 4-8.30pm Mon; 10.30am-8.30pm Tue-Sat. Closed 1wk Aug. No credit cards. **Map** p142 C4 ㉑
With its air of pleasantly dusty intellectualism, Hibernian feels like a proper British second-hand bookshop. There are books for all tastes, from bound early editions to classic Penguin paperbacks, biographies, cookbooks, poetry and plays – in all more than 30,000 titles. Part-exchange is possible here.

Kwatra
C/Gran de Gràcia 262 (93 237 66 37).
Metro Lesseps. **Open** 11am-2.30pm, 4-8.30pm Mon-Sat. **Map** p142 C2 ㉒
This is urban trainer heaven, with the latest models and limited-editions from Nike, 555DSL, Vans, Adidas, Diesel, Converse, Onitsuka Tiger, Quicksilver, Puma and Roxy. There's also a small but very covetable selection of bags and T-shirts from the same labels.

Nightlife

Bar Elèctric
Travessera de Gràcia 233 (no phone/ www.myspace.com/barelectricbcn).
Metro Joanic. **Open** 8pm-2am Tue-Thur, Sun; 8pm-3am Fri, Sat. Closed last wk July, 1st wk Aug. No credit cards. **Map** p143 E4 ㉓
Elèctric was the first bar in Gràcia to be connected to the mains (as local legend has it), yet this former bastion of modernity seems not to have changed since. An innocuous entry opens into a sprawling bohemian den that has an agenda as colourful as its clientele: theatre, puppetry and storytelling on weekdays, live music at night.

Gusto
C/Francisco Giner 24 (no phone).
Metro Diagonal. **Open** 10pm-2.30am Tue-Thur; 10pm-3am Fri, Sat. No credit cards. **Map** p142 C5 ㉔
Gusto doesn't fall in line with the neighbourhood's favoured shabby-chic aesthetic – it opts instead for a minimalist look, with sleek furnishings and a high-design interior that draws a quirky-hot clientele and DJs with crates of electro records. But it does have one bizarre feature to lure the alternative arts crowd that rules Gràcia: a back room with a floor that is, strangely, covered in sand.

Heliogabal
Ramón y Cajal 80 (no phone/ www.heliogabal.com). Metro Joanic.
Open 9pm-2.30am Mon-Thur, Sun; 9pm-3am Fri, Sat. *Concerts* 10pm. No credit cards. **Map** p143 D4 ㉕
Loved by habitués of the Gràcia arts scene, this low-key bar and performance venue is filled to bursting with cutie pies in cool T-shirts who just really adore live poetry. Events change nightly, running from live music to film screenings, art openings and readings, and programming focuses on local talents. On concert nights, arrive early for an 'at-least-I'm-not-standing' folding chair.

KGB

KGB

KGB

C/Alegre de Dalt 55 (93 210 59 06/ www.salakgb.net). Metro Joanic.
Open 1-6am Thur-Sat. No credit cards. **Map** p143 F3 ㉙
KGB is a cavern-like space that was, in its heyday, the rock 'n' roll disco barn capital of the city and *'un after'* where Sidecar heads would bolt at 6am on the weekend. It still remains loud, whether featuring concerts or DJ sessions. Thursday's concerts tend towards pop rock, which then continues for the DJ sessions, while the occasional weekend gigs vary but are followed by tech-house.

Vinilo

C/Matilde 2 (mobile 626 464 759/ http://vinilus.blogspot.com). Metro Fontana. **Open** 8pm-2.30am Mon-Thur, Sun; 7pm-3am Fri, Sat.
No credit cards. **Map** p142 C4 ㉗
Run by an affably hip family, Vinilo seems like an artist's den masquerading as a neighbourhood bar. The walls are papered with original prints and concert posters; a silent television plays 1980s cartoons on loop; the sandwiches are big and delicious and the beer selection certainly nothing to scoff at. But it's really the music that makes it: Sufjan Stevens, Coco Rosie, Leonard Cohen… You'll wish you lived here.

Arts & leisure

Verdi

C/Verdi 32, Gràcia (93 238 79 90/ www.cines-verdi.com). Metro Fontana. **Tickets** 1st screening daily €5. Mon €5. Tue-Sun €7.
Map p143 D3 ㉘
The five-screen Verdi and its four-screen annexe Verdi Park on the next street have transformed this corner of Gràcia, bringing with them vibrant bars and cheap eats for the crowds that flock to their diverse programme of independent, mainly European and Asian cinema. At peak times, chaos reigns; arrive early and make sure you don't mistake the line to enter for the ticket queue, which can stretch to Madrid on rainy Sundays.
Other locations Verdi Park, C/Torrijos 49 (93 238 79 90).

Other Districts

Sants & Les Corts

Sants, or at least the immediate environs of Estació de Sants, which is all that most visitors see of the area, stands as a monument to the worst of 1970s urban design. Just outside the station is the forbidding Plaça dels Països Catalans, a snarl of traffic around a roundabout whose centrepiece looks like a post-Miró bus shelter. However, for those with time to spare, Sants merits a few hours' investigation for historic, if not aesthetic, reasons. Most routes of interest start and end at the hub of the barri, Plaça de Sants, halfway up C/Sants high street, where Jorge Castillo's Ciclista statue is also to be found. Also worth checking out are the showy Modernista buildings at nos.12, 130, 145 and 151, all designed by local architect Modest Feu.

Another village engulfed by the expanding city in the 19th century, Les Corts ('cowsheds' or 'pigsties'), remains one of the most Catalan of

the city's *barris*, but the rows and rows of unlovely apartment blocks have stamped out almost any trace of its bucolic past. Something has been retained, however, in the Plaça de la Concòrdia, a quiet square dominated by a 40-metre (131-foot) bell tower. This is an anachronistic oasis housing the civic centre Can Deu, formerly a farmhouse and now home to a great bar hosting jazz acts every other Thursday. The area is much better known, though, for what happens every other weekend, when tens of thousands pour in to watch FC Barcelona, whose **Nou Camp** takes up much of the west of the barri.

Sights & museums

Parc de l'Espanya Industrial

Passeig de Antoni (no phone). Metro Sants-Estació. **Open** 10am-sunset daily. **Admission** free.
In the 1970s, the owners of the old textile factory announced their intention to

Torre de Collserola p152

use the land to build blocks of apartments. The neighbourhood's residents, though, put their collective foot down and insisted on a park, which was eventually laid out in 1985. The result is a puzzling space, with ten watchtowers overlooking a boating lake with a statue of Neptune in the middle, flanked by a stretch of mud used by dog walkers, but little greenery. By the entrance children can climb over Andrés Nagel's *Drac*, a massive black dragon sculpture.

Eating & drinking

Fragments Café

Plaça de la Concòrdia 12, Les Corts (93 419 96 13/www.fragmentscafe.com). Metro Les Corts or Maria Cristina. **Open** 10am-1am Tue, Wed, Sun; 10am-2am Thur-Sat. Closed 2wks Aug. $$$. **Tapas**.

A tapas bar with a classy look in the one remaining pocket of charm left in the neighbourhood of Les Corts. Sit on the tables in the square or the bar's own garden at the back (candlelit at night), and order some vermut (on tap here) and *gildas* (anchovies with chilli) before you so much as begin to peruse the menu. Later there are scrambled eggs with foie, juicy steaks, and homemade pasta.

La Parra

C/Joanot Martorell 3, Sants (93 332 51 34). Metro Hostafrancs. **Open** 8.30pm-12.30am Tue-Fri; 1.30-4.30pm, 8.30pm-12.30am Sat; 1.30-4.30pm Sun. Closed Aug. $$$. **Catalan**.

A charming converted 19th-century coaching inn with a shady vine-covered terrace. The open wood grill sizzles with various parts of goat, pig, rabbit and cow, as well as a few more off-piste items such as deer and even foal. Huge, oozing steaks are slapped on to wooden boards and accompanied by baked potatoes, calçots, grilled vegetables and *all i oli*, with jugs of local wines from the giant barrels.

Nightlife

Bikini

C/Déu i Mata 105, Les Corts (93 322 08 00/www.bikinibcn.com). Metro Les Corts or Maria Cristina. **Open** midnight-5am Wed-Sun.

Bikini lost some muscle in recent years, with the big-name stars it once booked replaced by little-knowns and ageing rockers. However, it has shown a few signs of new life lately, offering shows from the likes of Martha Wainwright and the Ting Tings. Divide your time between the rooms playing hip hop, pop, lounge or Latin sounds.

Arts & leisure

Nou Camp – FC Barcelona

Avda Arístides Maillol, access 9, Les Corts (93 496 36 00/08/www. fcbarcelona.com). Metro Collblanc, Les Corts or Maria Cristina. **Open** *Apr-mid Oct* 10am-8pm Mon-Sat; 10am-2.30pm Sun. *Mid Oct-Mar* 10am-6.30pm Mon-Sat; 10am-2.30pm Sun. **Admission** €8.50; €6.80 reductions; free under-5s. *Guided tour* €13; €10.40 reductions.

Nou Camp, where FC Barcelona has played since 1957, is one of football's great stadiums. If you can't get there on match day but love the team, it's worth visiting the club museum. The excellent

BARCELONA BY AREA

guided tour of the stadium takes you through the players' tunnel to the dugouts and then, via the away team's changing room, on to the President's box, where there is a replica of the European Cup, which the team won at Wembley in 1992 and again in Paris in 2006. The club museum commemorates those glory years. Last tour begins an hour before closing time.

Tibidabo & Collserola

Tibidabo is the dominant peak of the Collserola massif, with sweeping views of the whole of the Barcelona conurbation stretching out to the sea. The neo-Gothic Sagrat Cor church crowning the peak has become one of the city's most recognisable landmarks; it's clearly visible for miles around. At weekends, thousands of people head to the top of the hill in order to whoop and scream at the **funfair**.

Getting there on the **Tramvia Blau** (Blue Tram) and then the funicular railway is part of the fun; between the two is Plaça Doctor Andreu, a great place for an alfresco drink. For the best view of the city, either take a lift up Norman Foster's tower, the **Torre de Collserola**, or up to the mirador at the feet of Christ atop the Sagrat Cor.

The vast Parc de Collserola is more a series of forested hills than a park, its shady paths through holm oak and pine opening out to spectacular views. It's most easily reached by FGC train on the Terrassa-Sabadell line from Plaça Catalunya or Passeig de Gràcia, getting off at Baixador de Vallvidrera station.

Sights & museums

Tibidabo Funfair
Plaça del Tibidabo(93 211 79 42/ www.tibidabo.es). FGC Avda Tibidabo. **Open** varies (see website). Closed mid

Dec-mid Jan. **Admission** *Individual rides* €11-€14. *Unlimited rides* €24; €19 reductions; €7-€14 children under 1.2m (3ft 11in); free children under 90cm (2ft 11in).

This hilltop fairground, dating from 1889, is investing millions in getting itself bang up to date, with the terrifying freefall Pendulum, a new rollercoaster and a hot-air balloon style ride for smaller children. The many other attractions include a house of horrors, bumper cars and the emblematic Avió, the world's first popular flight simulator when it was built in 1928. Don't miss the antique mechanical puppets and contraptions at the Museu d'Autòmats, and there are hourly puppet shows at the Marionetàrium (from 1pm). At the weekends, there are circus parades at the end of the day and, in summer, street theatre.

Torre de Collserola
Ctra de Vallvidrera al Tibidabo (93 211 79 42/www.torredecollserola.com). FGC Peu Funicular then funicular. **Open** *Apr-June, Sept* 11am-2pm, 3.30-6pm Wed-Fri; 11am-2pm, 3.30-7pm Sat, Sun. *July, Aug* 11am-2pm, 3.30-7pm Wed-Fri;

Disseny Hub Barcelona/Museu de Ceràmica p154

11am-2pm, 3.30-8pm Sat, Sun. *Oct-Mar* 11am-2pm, 3.30-5pm Wed-Fri; 11am-2pm, 3.30-6pm Sat, Sun. **Admission** €5; reductions €4; free under-4s. Barcelona's most visible landmark, Norman Foster's communications tower, was built in 1992 to transmit images of the Olympics around the world. Those who don't suffer from vertigo attest to the wonderful views of Barcelona and the Mediterranean from the top.

Eating & drinking

La Venta

Plaça Doctor Andreu, Tibidabo (93 212 64 55/www.restaurantelaventa.com). FGC Avda Tibidabo, then Tramvia Blau. **Open** 1.30-3.15pm, 9-11.15pm Mon-Sat. **$$$. Mediterranean**.
La Venta's pretty Moorish-influenced interior plays second fiddle to the terrace during every season: shaded by day and uncovered by night in summer, sealed and warmed with a wood-burning stove in winter. Of the food, complex starters include lentil and spider crab salad, and sea urchins au gratin (a must). Simpler but high-qual-ity mains run from rack of lamb to delicate monkfish in filo pastry with pesto. Friendly service is a bonus.

Nightlife

Mirablau

Plaça Doctor Andreu 1, Tibidabo (93 418 58 79). FGC Avda Tibidabo then Tramvia Blau. **Open** 11am-4am Mon-Thur; 11am-5.30am Fri-Sun. **Admission** free.
It doesn't get any more uptown than this, geographically and socially. Located at the top of Tibidabo, this small bar is packed with the high rollers of Barcelona, from local footballers living on the hill to international businessmen on the company card. Watch out for the view and the artificial wind that sweeps through the tropical shrubbery outside.

Zona Alta

Zona Alta (the 'upper zone', or 'uptown') is the name given collectively to a series of smart neighbourhoods including Sant Gervasi, Sarrià and Pedralbes that

Tramvia Blau p156

stretch out across the lower reaches of the Collserola hills. The centre of Sarrià and the streets of old Pedralbes around the monastery retain a flavour of the sleepy country towns these once were.

Gaudí fans are rewarded by a trip up to the **Pavellons de la Finca Güell** at Avda Pedralbes 15; its extraordinary and rather frightening wrought-iron gate features a dragon into whose gaping mouth the foolhardy can fit their heads. Once inside the gardens, via the main gate on Avda Diagonal, look out for a delightful fountain designed by the master himself. Across near Putxet is Gaudí's relatively sober Col·legi de les Teresianes (C/Ganduxer 85-105), while up towards Tibidabo, just off Plaça Bonanova, rises his Gothic-influenced Torre Figueres or Bellesguard.

Sights & museums

CosmoCaixa

C/Teodor Roviralta 47-51 (93 212 60 50/www.fundacio.lacaixa.es). Bus 60/ FGC Avda Tibidabo then Tramvia Blau (see p152). **Open** 10am-8pm Tue-Sun.

Admission €3; €2 reductions; free under-7s. *Planetarium* €2; €1.50 reductions; free under-7s.

Said to be the biggest science museum in Europe, CosmoCaixa doesn't, perhaps, make the best use of its space. A glass-enclosed spiral ramp runs down an impressive six floors, but actually represents quite a long walk to reach the main collection five floors down. Here you'll find the Flooded Forest, a reproduction of a corner of Amazonia complete with flora and fauna, and the Geological Wall, along with temporary exhibitions. The Matter Room covers 'inert', 'living', 'intelligent' and 'civilised' matter, but, for all the fanfare made by the museum about taking exhibits out of glass cases and making scientific theories accessible, many of the displays still look dated.

On the plus side, the installations for children are excellent: the Planetarium pleases those aged five to eight, and the wonderful Clik (ages three to six) and Flash (seven to nine) introduce kids to science through games.

Disseny Hub Barcelona/ Museu de Ceràmica

NEW *Palau Reial de Pedralbes, Avda Diagonal 686 (93 256 34 65/*

www.dhub-bcn.cat/www.museuceramica.bcn.cat). Metro Palau Reial. **Open** 10am-6pm Tue-Sun. **Admission** €4.20; €2.40 reductions. Free under-16s & 3pm-6pm Sun. No credit cards.

In 2008, the Museu Tèxtil, previously located in the Born, joined the ceramic and decorative arts museums in the Palau Reial de Pedralbes, built in the 1920s and briefly used as a royal palace. The textile, decorative arts and, in the future, a graphic arts collection form the new design megamuseum, the Disseny Hub Barcelona, which will be relocated to the Plaça de les Glòries in the future.

The Textile Museum provides a chronological tour of clothing and fashion, from its oldest piece, a man's Coptic tunic from a seventh-century tomb, through to Karl Lagerfeld.

The Museum of Decorative Arts is informative and fun, and looks at the different styles informing the design of artefacts in Europe since the Middle Ages, from Romanesque to art deco and beyond. A second section is devoted to post-war Catalan design of objects as diverse as urinals and man-sized inflatable pens.

The Ceramics Museum is equally fascinating, showing how Moorish ceramic techniques from the 13th century were developed after the Reconquista with the addition of colours (especially blue and yellow) in centres such as Manises (in Valencia) and Barcelona. Upstairs is a display of 20th-century ceramics, with a room devoted to Miró and Picasso. Event highlights The Souvenir Effect (until 10 Jan 2010).

Monestir de Pedralbes

Baixada del Monestir 9 (93 256 21 22). FGC Reina Elisenda. **Open** *Apr-Sept* 10am-5pm Tue-Sat; 10am-8pm Sun. *Oct-Mar* 10am-2pm Mon-Sat; 10am-8pm Sun. **Admission** €6; €4 reductions; free under-16s & Sun 3pm-8pm.

In 1326, the widowed Queen Elisenda of Montcada used her inheritance to buy this land and build a convent for the Poor Clare order of nuns, which she soon joined. The result is a jewel of Gothic architecture with an understated single-nave church with fine stained-glass windows and a beautiful three-storey 14th-century cloister. The place was out of bounds to the general public until 1983, when the nuns, a closed order, opened it up as a museum in the mornings (when they escape to a nearby annexe). A fascinating insight into life in a medieval convent.

Parc de la Creueta del Coll

C/Mare de Déu del Coll (no phone). Metro Penitents. **Open** 10am-sunset daily. **Admission** free.

Created from a quarry in 1987 by Josep Martorell and David Mackay, the team that went on to design the Vila Olímpica, this park boasts a sizeable swimming pool complete with a 'desert island' and a sculpture by Eduardo Chillida: a 50-ton lump of curly granite suspended on cables, called *In Praise of Water*.

Pavellons de la Finca Güell

Avda Pedralbes 15 (93 317 76 52/ www.rutadelmodernisme.com). Metro Palau Reial. **Open** 10.50am-2pm Mon, Fri-Sun. *Tours in English* 10.15am, 12.15pm. **Admission** €5; €2.50 reductions. No credit cards.

Industrial textile businessman Eusebi Güell bought what is now Palau Reial in 1882 as a summer home, contracting Gaudí to remodel the entrance lodges and gardens for the estate. In 1883, they began to build what would be one of Gaudí's first projects in Barcelona for the Güell family.

The Porta del Drac (Dragon's Gate) used to be the private entrance for the Güell family, and was connected to the Güell home in Barcelona by a private, walled road. The Pavellons must be visited with a guide, and tours are offered in Spanish and English. Really though, it isn't much of a tour, lasting for about 25 minutes with a look at nothing more than the gate and the stables.

Tramvia Blau

Avda Tibidabo (Plaça Kennedy) to Plaça Doctor Andreu (93 318 70 74/ www.tramvia.org/tramviablau). FGC Avda Tibidabo. **Open** *Mid June-mid Sept* 10am-8pm daily. *Mid Sept-mid June* 10am-6pm Sat. Frequency 20mins. **Tickets** €2.30 single; €3.50 return. No credit cards.

Barcelonins and tourists have been clanking 1,225m (4,000ft) up Avda Tibidabo in the 'blue trams' since 1902. In the winter months, when the tram only operates on weekends, a rather more prosaic bus (no.195) takes you up (or you can walk it in 15 minutes).

Eating & drinking

Artkuisine

C/Madrazo 137, Sant Gervasi (93 202 31 46/www.artkuisine.blogspot.com). FGC Sant Gervasi. **Open** *Sept-June* 1.30-3.45pm Mon; 1.30-3.45pm, 8.30-11.45pm Tue-Sat. *July* 1.30-3.45pm, 8.30-11.45pm Mon-Sat. *Closed 3wks Aug.* **$$$$. Mediterranean**.

Artkuisine's French credentials do not leap out sporting berets and strings of onions. Instead, they make themselves known in other, more subtle ways: the buttermilk Regency furniture, the charming and soigné waiting staff, and the classical approach underpinning the chef's wilder flights of fancy. Who would have thought, for example, that cocoa and banana compôte would complement oxtail stew, or that tonka bean and vanilla ice-cream would work with tarte tatin? The French, apparently.

Hisop

Passatge Marimon 9, Sant Gervasi (93 241 32 33/www.hisop.com). Metro Hospital Clínic or Diagonal. **Open** 1.30-3.30pm, 8.30-11pm Mon-Fri; 9-11pm Sat. *Closed 3wks Aug.* **$$$$. Mediterranean**.

Run by two young, enthusiastic and talented chefs, Hisop aims to bring serious dining to the non-expense-account masses by keeping its prices on the low side and its service approachable. The €52 tasting menu is a popular choice among diners, with dishes that vary according to the season but often include its rich 'monkfish royale' (served with its liver, a cocoa-based sauce and tiny pearls of saffron) and a pistachio soufflé with Kaffir lime ice-cream and rocket 'soup'.

Shopping

Pedralbes Centre

Avda Diagonal 609-615, Pedralbes (93 410 68 21/www.pedralbescentre.com). Metro Maria Cristina. **Open** 10.30am-9pm Mon-Sat.

The mall's focus is on upmarket clothes, accessories and homewares, with plenty of local names such as Elena Miró, Majoral jewellers and Luis Guirau in among the likes of Hello Kitty and Timberland. The cafés and restaurants appeal to ladies who lunch, with salad buffets and gourmet tapas. In winter, the mall's plaza is transformed into an ice rink.

Nightlife

Elephant

Passeig dels Til·lers 1, Pedralbes (93 334 02 58/www.elephantbcn.com). Metro Palau Reial. **Open** 11.30pm-5am Thur-Sat.

If you have a Porsche and a model girlfriend, this is where you meet your peers. Housed in an old mansion, Elephant is as elegant and hi-design as its customers. The big attraction is the outdoor bar and terrace dancefloor – though the low-key, low-volume (due to the neighbours' complaints) house music doesn't inspire much hands-in-the-air action.

Luz de Gas

C/Muntaner 246 (93 209 77 11/ www.luzdegas.com). FGC Muntaner. **Open** *Club* 1-5.30am daily. *Gigs* 11.30am daily.

This lovingly renovated old music hall, garnished with chandeliers and

Fòrum

classical friezes, is a mainstay on the live music scene and one classy joint. In between visits from international artists and benefits for local causes, you'll find nightly residencies: blues on Mondays, Dixieland jazz on Tuesdays, disco on Wednesdays, pop-rock on Thursdays, soul on Fridays and vintage and Spanish rock on weekends.

Sala BeCool

Plaça Joan Llongueras (93 362 04 13/ www.salabecool.com). Metro Hospital Clinic. **Open** *Gigs* 10pm Thur-Sat. *Club* midnight-5am Thur; 1am-6am Fri, Sat. The latest from Berlin's minimal electro scene reaches Barcelona via this uptown concert hall. After the live shows by local rock stars or international indie success stories, a packed and music-loving crowd throbs to sophisticated electronica and its bizarre attendant visuals. Upstairs, in the Red Room, DJs playing indie pop-rock provide an alternative to the pounding beats of the main room.

Arts & leisure

Boliche

Avda Diagonal 508 (93 218 17 88). Metro Diagonal/FGC Provença.

Tickets Mon, Tue, Thur €6.70; Wed €5.50; Fri-Sun €7. No credit cards. This comfortable four-screen cinema has recently made the move from dubbed films and now shows crowd-pleasers in their original languages.

Poblenou

In its industrial heyday, Poblenou was known as 'little Manchester' due to the concentration of cotton mills. The old mills and other factories are now being bulldozed or remodelled as the district is rebranded as a technology and business district, snappily tagged 22@, which will exist side by side with the garages, exhaust fitters, wheel balancers and car washes that are a feature of the *barrio*.

Work is about to begin on remodelling the ghastly, traffic-choked Plaça de les Glòries, partly to open up the land around the hugely phallic **Torre Agbar**, and to form a gateway to the Diagonal Mar area and the new commercial and leisure area on the shoreline, known as the **Fòrum**, after the event in 2004 for which it was

Hey Mr DJ

Over the last ten years, **Javier Estalella**, or **DJ Buenavista**, has carved a niche for himself spinning a contagious 'Barcelona brand' of energetic pop. These days he has a residency at the Pop Bar: a small club within Poblenou macroclub **Razzmatazz** (p159).

What's your style?
Anything melodic: house, electro, rock 'n' roll; records and CDs, or just with the laptop and 'Final Scratch'.

Is the much-hailed Barcelona nightlife all hype?
We have a unique geographical position and so we combine European influences, but there is a lack of funding, which makes it hard for new groups to tour. Also, rehearsal space is expensive.

The city seems to be full of mega-clubs.
The only really big club here is Razz, which is hard to fill with clubbers, but which has great facilities for live music and DJs.

What's the Barcelona sound?
Astrud and Hidrogenesse, on the Astrohungaro label, who sing in Catalan. But mostly the Barcelona brand is a melodic, chaotic pop.

What about the public?
There's a resurgence of 'clubkiddismo' – the teeny-techno boom of the 1990s – but this has mashed into a quality blend of rock 'n' roll, electronica, hip hop and punk, with a dress code to match. It makes me feel old.

Where does anyone over 25 go?
Pop Bar attracts hipsters, an older crowd and a gay crowd. Fellini (p70) and Sala Apolo (p119) have a twenty- and thirtysomething crowd. Moog (p97) or sometimes Lotus (p138) can be a mix of 30s and up. The Matinee group caters to a similar mixed gay/straight crowd; it's Ibiza-esque.

Is the recent council clampdown on clubs justified?
It has done well to close illegal clubs with insufficient security and crappy-quality drinks. But closing a venue like La Paloma (p97) is like closing the Liceu opera house. There's a problem with noise, but they should give funding to soundproof. Also, grants should be given to all local music, not just to groups who sing in Catalan. That doesn't promote the language at all; it just limits the audience.

created. The tower, designed by French architect Jean Nouvel and owned by the Catalan water board, has been a bold and controversial project; it's not unlike London's famed Gherkin. Nouvel has also designed the new, walled Parc Central del Poblenou, one of a number of highly designed gardens in Barcelona, which features giant plants, an island, a cratered lunar landscape and a perfumed garden.

Eating & drinking

Els Pescadors

Plaça Prim 1, Poblenou (93 225 20 18/ www.elspescadors.com). Metro Poblenou. **Open** 1-3.45pm, 8pm-midnight daily. **$$$$. Seafood**.
In a forgotten, almost rustic square of Poblenou lies this first-rate fish restaurant, with tables under a canopy formed by two huge and ancient ombú trees. Suspend your disbelief with the crunchy sardine skeletons that arrive as an aperitif (trust us, they're delicious), and move on to tasty fried chipirones, followed by cod and pepper paella or creamy rice with prawns and smoked cheese. Desserts include the likes of strawberry gelatine 'spaghetti' in a citric soup.

Shopping

Barcelona Glòries

Avda Diagonal 208 (93 486 04 04/ www.lesglories.com). Metro Glòries. **Open** *Shops* 10am-10pm Mon-Sat.
Since opening in 1995, this mall, office and leisure centre has become a focus of local life. There are more than 220 shops, including a Carrefour supermarket, an H&M, a Mango and a Disney Store, facing on to a large, café-filled square decorated with jets of coloured water.

Diagonal Mar

Avda Diagonal 3, Poblenou (93 567 76 37/www.diagonalmar.com). Metro El Maresme-Forum. **Open** 10am-10pm Mon-Sat.

This three-level mall at the sea end of Avda Diagonal has an airy marine theme and a sea-facing roof terrace filled with cafés and restaurants. As well as major anchors, such as an Alcampo supermarket, Zara and FNAC, there's a particular emphasis on children's clothes and toy shops, plus plenty of smaller global brands (like Miss Sixty).

Nightlife

Razzmatazz

C/Almogàvers 122 (93 320 82 00/ www.salarazzmatazz.com). Metro Bogatell or Marina. **Concerts** 9.30pm Mon-Sun.
This monstrous club's five distinct spaces form the night-time playground of seemingly all young Barcelona. There's indie rock in Razz Club, tech-house in the Loft, techno pop in Lolita, electro pop in the Pop Bar and electro rock in the Rex Room. Live music runs from Arctic Monkeys to Banarama.

Torre Agbar p157

Horta

Horta was once a picturesque little village that still remains aloof from the city that swallowed it in 1904. Originally a collection of farms (its name means 'market garden'), the *barrio* is still peppered with old farmhouses, such as Can Mariner on C/Horta, dating back to 1050, and the medieval Can Cortada at the end of C/Campoamor, which is now a huge restaurant located in beautiful grounds. An abundant water supply also made Horta the place where much of the city's laundry was done: a whole community of *bugaderes* (washerwomen) lived and worked in lovely C/Aiguafreda, where you can still see their wells and open-air stone washtubs.

The Vall d'Hebron is a leafy area located just above Horta in the Collserola foothills. Here, formerly private estates have been put to public use; among them are the chateau-like Palauet de les Heures, now a university building. The area was one of the city's four major venues for the Olympics and is rich in sporting facilities, including public football pitches, tennis courts, and cycling and archery facilities at the Velòdrom. It's also home to one of Barcelona's major concert venues. Around these environs there are several striking examples of street sculpture, including Claes Oldenburg's *Matches* and Joan Brossa's *Visual Poem* (in the shape of the letter 'A').

Sights & museums

Parc del Laberint

C/Germans Desvalls, Passeig Vall d'Hebron (010/www.bcn.cat/parcsi jardins). Metro Mundet. **Open** 10am-sunset daily. **Admission** €2.05; €1.30 reductions; free under-5s, over-65s. Free Wed, Sun.

In 1791, the Desvalls family, owners of this marvellously leafy estate, hired Italian architect Domenico Bagutti to design gardens set around a cypress maze, with a romantic stream and a waterfall. The mansion may be gone (replaced with a 19th-century building), but the gardens are remarkably intact, shaded in the summer by oaks, laurels and an ancient sequoia. Best of all, the maze, an ingenious puzzle that intrigues those brave enough to try it, is still in use. Nearby stone tables provide a handy picnic site. On paying days, last entry is one hour before sunset.

Eating & drinking

Can Travi Nou

C/Jorge Manrique s/n, Parc de la Vall de Hebron, Horta (93 428 03 01/ www.gruptravi.com). Metro Horta or Montbau. **Open** 1.30-4pm, 8.30-11pm Mon-Sat; 1.30-4pm Sun. **$$$**. **Catalan**. An ancient rambling farmhouse clad in bougainvillea and perched high above the city, Can Travi Nou offers wonderfully rustic dining rooms with roaring log fires in winter, while in summer the action moves out to a covered terrace in a bosky, candlelit garden. The food is hearty, traditional Catalan cuisine though it's a little expensive for what it is; Can Travi Nou is really all about location, location, location.

L'Esquinica

Passeig Fabra i Puig 296, Horta (93 358 25 19). Metro Virrei Amat or Vilapicina. **Open** 8am-midnight Tue-Sat; 8am-4pm Sun. Closed last 2wks Aug. No credit cards.
Think of it not as a trek, but as a quest; queues outside are testament to the great value tapas. On especially busy nights you'll be asked to take a number, supermarket-style. Waiters will advise first-timers to start with *chocos* (creamy squid rings), *patatas bravas* with *all i oli*, *llonganissa* sausage and *tigres* (stuffed mussels). After which the world is your oyster, cockle or clam.

Essentials

Barceló Raval p168

Hotels

The economic downturn, or *'la crisis'* as the Spanish have it, has its flipside. The city's popularity during the last decade and a half has seen hotel prices reach excruciating levels. But thanks to the slowdown, hoteliers have had to rethink drastically, and while there are still plenty of luxury options for those who can afford it, creativity in the mid-range is starting to boom, with rooms ranging between €80 and €150 a night.

High season runs year round and finding somewhere to lay your head at short notice can be tough. Hotels generally require you to guarantee your booking with credit-card details or a deposit; it's worth calling a few days before arrival to reconfirm the booking (get it in writing if you can; many readers have reported problems) and check the cancellation policy. Often you will lose the first night. *Hostales* are more laid-back and don't always ask for a deposit.

To be sure of a room with natural light or a view, ask for an outside room (*habitació/habitación exterior*), which will usually face the street. Many of Barcelona's buildings are built around a central airshaft, and the inside rooms (*habitació/habitación interior*) around them can be quite gloomy, albeit quieter. However, in some cases (especially in the Eixample), these inward-facing rooms look on to large, open-air patios or gardens, which benefit from being quiet and having a view.

Apartment rentals

Short-term apartment rental is a rapidly expanding market. Some firms rent out their own flats, while others act as intermediaries between apartment owners and visitors, taking a cut of the rents.

When renting, it pays to use a little common sense. Check the small print (payment methods, deposits, cancellation fees) and exactly what is included (cleaning, towels and so on) before booking. Note that apartments offered for rental tend to be very small.

Some of the many websites offering flats include: www.rent thesun.com, www.inside-bcn.com, www.oh-barcelona.com, www.barcelona-home.com, www.destinationbcn.com, www.rentaflatinbarcelona.com, and www.friendlyrentals.com.

Barri Gòtic & La Rambla

Bonic B&B

NEW *C/Josep Anselm Clavé 9, 1º-4ª (mobile 626 05 34 34/www.bonic-barcelona.com). Metro Drassanes.* €€.
Bonic is painted in daisy-fresh colours with sunlight streaming through the windows and has meticulously restored original features, such as ornately tiled floors. The gregarious Fernando does all he can to make you feel at home. Free newspapers and magazines, tea, coffee and water, and flowers in the three immaculate, communal bathrooms all add up to an experience that raises the budget bar considerably.

Duc de la Victòria

C/Duc 15 (93 270 34 10/www.nh-hotels.com). Metro Catalunya. €€.
The trusty NH chain has high standards of comfort and service, and this good-value downtown branch is thankfully no exception to the rule. The rooms, with a blue-and-beige colour scheme, may not be very exciting, but the superior quality beds ensure a sound night's sleep. Note the street has changed name from Duc de la Victòria.

H1898

La Rambla 109 (93 552 95 52/ www.nnhotels.es). Metro Catalunya or Liceu. €€€.

ESSENTIALS

100%
BARCELONA

Best rate guarantee www.grandhotelcentral.co

GRAND HOTEL **CENTRA**

Via Laietana 30, 08003 BARCELONA. Tel. (34) 93 295 79 00 info@grandhotelcentral

All aboard

With real-estate prices through the roof, global crisis notwithstanding, hoteliers are increasingly looking out to sea. Sweden has its Salt & Sill, Dubai has the retired QE2, and never one to be outdone, Barcelona too has its very own super-duper 'yacht hotel'.

The **Sunborn Barcelona** docked in the Port Fòrum in the summer of 2009, and is the second such project for Finnish-owned Sunborn International (the first is in Finland, the next is scheduled for London). It's been granted a 25-year licence in Barcelona, the hope being that it will attract well-heeled pleasure-seekers to the Distrito 22@, a futuristic neighbourhood of skyscrapers and technology businesses that has so far failed to excite the leisure traveller.

That could all change, however, as this imposing vessel takes its place among the gin palaces and pleasure craft of the newly built quayside. Fuelled by solar energy provided by the extraordinary photovoltaic pergola that dominates the complex, the Sunborn is built over six floors with 180 suites each, boasting private terraces and vast picture windows on to the big blue, sleek wooden floors and lots of pearl-coloured leather. An infinity pool will crown the rooftop, along with a spa and sports facilities, and a Michelin-starred chef is currently being sought to head up the main restaurant, all at the cool cost of €152 million.

■ www.sunborninternational.com

A dapper luxury hotel in a 19th-century building, the former Philippine Tobacco Company headquarters. Rooms are candy-striped; one floor is all perky green and white, another is red and white, and so on. The more expensive rooms have wooden-decked terraces, while some of the suites have private plunge pools. There's also a rooftop deck with navy-tiled pool and luxurious four-poster day beds.

Hostal Fontanella
Via Laietana 71, 2º (93 317 59 43/ www.hostalfontanella.com). Metro Urquinaona. **€**.
The splendid Modernista lift lends a somewhat unjustified aura of grandeur to this simply furnished 11-room *hostal*. The downside of the Fontanella's central location on a busy thoroughfare is that outward-facing rooms are abuzz with the sound of traffic. But it's a clean and comfy, and double-glazing helps.

Hotel Barcelona Catedral
NEW *C/Capellans 4 (93 304 22 55/ www.barcelonacatedral.com). Metro Jaume I.* **€€€**.
This newcomer to the city's heart is modern and relaxed, with a lobby that doubles as a funky lounge and cocktail bar. Rooms, while not particularly exciting, are bright and comfortable, with vast bathrooms and king-size beds. A garden terrace and a rooftop deck with pool are added pluses.

Hotel Duquesa de Cardona
Passeig Colom 12 (93 268 90 90/ www.hduquesadecardona.com). Metro Drassanes or Jaume I. **€€**.
This elegantly restored 16th-century palace retains many original features and is furnished with natural materials – wood, leather, silk and stone – complemented by a soft colour scheme. Deluxe rooms and junior suites on the higher floors have views out across the harbour. Guests can sunbathe and lunch on the roof terrace and then cool off in the mosaic-tiled plunge pool.

ESSENTIALS

Hotel Medinaceli

Plaça del Duc de Medinaceli 8 (93 481 77 25/www.gargallo-hotels.com). Metro Drassanes. €€€.
Rooms in this restored palace are done out in soothing rusty shades. Some of the bathrooms have jacuzzi baths, while others come with massage showers. Repro versions of the sofa Dalí created, inspired by Mae West's lips, decorate the lobby, to match the crimson velvet thrones in the courtyard. Rooms overlooking the street can be noisy.

Hotel Le Meridien Barcelona

La Rambla 111 (93 318 62 00/ www.barcelona.lemeridien.com). Metro Liceu. €€€€.
After a €23-million refurb, Le Meridien has maintained its conservative look, opting for classy hardwood floors, polished marble and leather furnishings, along with Egyptian cotton bedlinen, rain showers and plasma-screen TVs. However, at this price you'd expect more facilities: a rooftop pool, perhaps, or at least a decked terrace.

Hotel Neri

C/Sant Sever 5 (93 304 06 55/www.hotelneri.com). Metro Jaume I. €€€€.
Arguably the sexiest boutique in town, in a former 18th-century palace. The lobby-cum-library teams flagstone floors with red velvet chaises longues and lashings of gold leaf, though rooms are more understated. Natural materials and rustic finishes stand in stylish contrast to lavish satins, sharp design and high-tech perks (hi-fis, plasma-screen TVs). There's a lush rooftop garden.

Hotel Petit Palace Opera Garden

C/Boqueria 10 (93 302 00 92/ www.hthoteles.com). Metro Liceu. €€€.
The rooms are white and futuristic, with a different zingy colour on each floor and opera scores printed on the walls above the beds. Lamps and chairs lend a 1960s air, so pack your kinky boots and groovy flares to enjoy your stay to the full. Some bathrooms have massage showers, others jacuzzi baths. Only breakfast is served in the chic dining room. There's a little-known public garden at the back; a real luxury in this densely packed area.

Pensió Alamar

C/Comtessa de Sobradiel 1, 1º-2ª (93 302 50 12/www.pensioalamar.com). Metro Jaume I or Liceu. €.
A basic, but tasteful family-run *hostal*. Beds are new and excellent quality, and windows are double-glazed to keep noise to a minimum. The downside is that 12 rooms share two bathrooms. There are discounts for longer stays, and larger rooms for families. Single travellers are made welcome, with no supplement for occupying a double, and guests can do their laundry and cook in a well-equipped kitchen.

Pensión Hostal Mari-Luz

C/Palau 4 (93 317 34 63/www.pension mariluz.com). Metro Jaume I or Liceu. €.
The entrance and staircase of this 18th-century stone building are imposing, but you then have to climb several flights of stairs to reach the Mari-Luz. The effort is well worth it – stripped wood doors and old floor tiles add character to the otherwise plain but quiet rooms, some of which face a plant-filled inner courtyard. There are dorms as well as double and triple rooms.

Born & Sant Pere

Banys Orientals

C/Argenteria 37 (93 268 84 60/ www.hotelbanysorientals.com). Metro Jaume I. €€.
Banys Orientals is one of the best deals to be found in Barcelona. It exudes cool, from its location at the heart of the Born to the stylish shades-of-grey minimalism of its rooms, and nice touches such as complimentary mineral water on the landings. The main debit is the small size of some of the double rooms.

ESSENTIALS

Chic&basic

C/Princesa 50 (93 295 46 52/
www.chicandbasic.com). Metro Arc
de Triomf or Jaume I. €€.

This first floor *hostal* takes white-on-white to extremes, though not entirely unsuccessfully. Rooms come with white cotton linen, white floors, white walls, mirrored cornicing and glassed-in wet rooms in the centre. Elsewhere the playful vibe continues with a chill-out room furnished with fairytale sofas and pouffes; it also has tea- and coffee-making facilities and a fridge.

Ciutat Barcelona

C/Princesa 35 (93 269 74 75/
www.ciutatbarcelona.com). Metro
Jaume I. €€.

The Ciutat Barcelona is a jolly, primary-coloured affair, offering a refreshing contrast to the chocolate and charcoal shades of most of Barna's smart hotels. Retro shapes prevail in the furnishings and decoration, and rooms are very small but reasonably comfortable. The big draw, however, is a swanky wood-decked roof terrace complete with shaded tables and a decent-sized plunge pool.

Grand Hotel Central

Via Laietana 30 (93 295 79 00/
www.grandhotelcentral.com).
Metro Jaume I. €€€.

Another of the recent wave of Barcelona hotels to adhere to the unwritten design protocol that grey is the new black. The Central's shadowy, Hitchcockian corridors open up on to sleekly appointed rooms that come with flat-screen televisions, DVD players and Korres toiletries. But the real charm of the hotel lies on the roof, in the shape of a vertiginous infinity pool.

Pensió 2000

C/Sant Pere Més Alt 6, 1° (93 310
74 66/www.pensio2000.com). Metro
Urquinaona. €.

Pensió 2000 is a good-value *pensión* located opposite the Palau de la Música. Only two of the rooms are en suite, but the shared facilities are kept clean. The large rooms make it suitable for holidaying families.

Raval

Barceló Raval

NEW *Rambla del Raval 17-21 (93 320*
14 90/902 101 001/www.barcelo.com).
Metro Drassanes. €€.

This bleeding-edge, cylindrical building now dominates the Rambla del Raval and promises to become something of an icon of the *barrio*. The smart roof terrace offers 360° views (with key buildings labelled from a viewing platform) and a plunge pool. Bedrooms are starkly modern, with a technology port for all your multimedia needs and a Nespresso machine for those bleary mornings after.

Casa Camper

C/Elisabets 11 (93 342 62 80/
www.casacamper.com). Metro
Catalunya. €€€.

Devised by the Mallorcan footwear giant, this quirky concept-fest has as one of its USPs a bedroom-living room arrangement so that you get two spaces for the price of one. Less cleverly, the living rooms are situated across the corridor from the bedrooms, so to enjoy the cinema-sized TV and hammock, pack respectable pyjamas or risk the dash of shame. There are no minibars, but you can take free snacks from the café.

Hostal Gat Raval

C/Joaquin Costa 44, 2° (93 481 66 70/
www.gataccommodation.com). Metro
Universitat. €.

Smart, clean and funky with bright rooms, each boasting a work by a local artist. Some rooms have balconies while others have views of the MACBA. The only downsides are that nearly all the bathrooms are communal (though very clean) and there is no lift. Laptops can be hired. The same owners run the nearby Hostal Gat Xino (93 324 88 33), which has a similar cheap and chic vibe.

Hotel Ciutat Vella

Hotel Ciutat Vella

*C/Tallers 66 (93 481 37 99/www.hotel
ciutatvella.com). Metro Catalunya or
Universitat.* €€.

This is a fun and funky option when the budget's tight. Rooms and decor are done simply in white with splashes of pillarbox red. There's Wi-Fi and a hearty breakfast served in a lounge downstairs, and best of all a fabulously kitsch Astroturf rooftop terrace with hot tub.

Hotel Curious

NEW *C/Carme 25 (93 301 44 84/www.
hotelcurious.com). Metro Liceu.* €€.

Curious is an unusual new addition to the Raval with a more art-based approach to design. The rather funky mauve-hued lobby is in total contrast to more monotone bedrooms, which have giant black and white prints depicting Barcelona *barrios*.

Hotel Mesón Castilla

*C/Valldonzella 5 (93 318 21 82/
www.mesoncastilla.com). Metro
Universitat.* €€.

For a change from modern design, check into this chocolate-box hotel, which opened in 1952. Communal areas are full of antiques and artworks, while rooms have tiled floors and are decorated with hand-painted furniture from Olot in northern Catalonia. The best rooms have terraces, and there is a delightful plantfilled terrace off the breakfast room.

Hotel Sant Agustí

*Plaça Sant Agustí 3 (93 318 16 58/
www.hotelsa.com). Metro Liceu.* €€.

With its sandstone walls and huge, arched windows that look out on to the plaça, not to mention the pink-marble lobby filled with forest-green furniture, this imposing hotel is the oldest in town. Previously the Convent of St Augustine, the building was converted into a hotel in 1840. Rooms are spacious and comfortable, but there's no soundproofing. Good buffet breakfast.

Barceloneta & the Ports

Hotel AB Skipper

NEW *C/Litoral 10 (93 221 65 65/
www.hotelabskipper.com). Metro
Ciutadella.* €€€.

Situated near the Port Olímpic, the Skipper is a swish, American-style five-star reeling in long-weekenders with some good package deals. It's good on

Wanted.
Jumpers, coats and people with their knickers in a twist.

From the people who feel moved to bring us their old books and CDs, to the people fed up to the back teeth with our politicians' track record on climate change, Oxfam supporters have one thing in common. They're passionate. If you've got a little fire in your belly, we'd love to hear from you. Visit us at **oxfam.org.uk**

Be Humankind (✗) Oxfam

Registered charity No. 202918

outdoor space with a large heated pool, hammocks on the lawns, and a full-service spa. Additional treats include a lazy Sunday brunch, luxury rooftop pool and bar, and the AB Skipper yacht, which guests can charter for private use.

Hotel Arts

C/Marina 19-21 (93 221 10 00/ www.ritzcarlton.com). Metro Ciutadella-Vila Olímpica. €€€€.
The 44-storey, Ritz-Carlton-run Arts scores top marks for service. Bang & Olufsen CD players, interactive TV, sea and city views and a 'Club' floor for VIPs are just some of the perks. Avant-garde flower displays make the lobby a pleasant place to hang out. A beachfront pool overlooks Gehry's *Fish* sculpture, and a range of bars and restaurants cater to every taste. The Six Senses Spa has fabulous views and is open to non-guests.

Montjuïc & Poble Sec

Hostal BCN Port

Avda Paral·lel 15, entl (93 324 95 00/ www.hostalbcnport.com). Metro Drassanes or Paral·lel. €.
A smart *hostal* near the ferry port, the BCN Port has rooms that are furnished in a chic contemporary style with not a hint of the kitsch decor prevalent in more traditional budget places. All the rooms have en-suite bathrooms, as well as televisions and air-conditioning.

Eixample

Casanova BCN Hotel

NEW *Gran Via de les Corts Catalanes 559 (93 396 48 00/www.casanova bcnhotel.com). Metro Universitat or Urgell.* €€€.
A smart hotel where each room has its own Nespresso machine, suites have two bathrooms, giant candles are scattered through the lounge areas and there's a small spa. The rooftop pool should be in place for 2010. A cocktail and ceviche bar lends freshness to the usual tapas offerings.

Hostal d'Uxelles

Gran Via de les Corts Catalanes 688, pral (93 265 25 60/www.hotelduxelles. com). Metro Tetuán. €€.
A pretty, tastefully decorated *hostal*, with friendly staff, d'Uxelles is a delightful place to stay and a bargain to boot. The angels above reception are a hint of what's to come within: Modernista tiles, cream walls with gilt-framed mirrors, antique furnishings, canopies above the beds and bright, Andaluz-tiled bathrooms (all en suite). The best rooms have plant-filled balconies with tables and chairs, where you can have breakfast.

Hostal L'Antic Espai

Gran Via de les Corts Catalanes 660, pral (93 304 19 45/www.anticespai. com). Metro Passeig de Gràcia or Urquinaona. €.
A real find for lovers of character. Each room is rammed with antiques, be it an ornately carved wooden bedhead, a teardrop chandelier, a faux Louis XV dresser or a silken throw. All have ensuite bathrooms and 21st-century gadgetry such as flat-screen TVs and free Wi-Fi, some have balconies, and there's a patio with silk flowers.

Hostal Eden

C/Balmes 55, pral 1ª (93 452 66 20/ www.hostaleden.net). Metro Passeig de Gràcia. €.
Located on three floors of a Modernista building, this warm and relaxed *hostal* with friendly, helpful staff offers free internet access and has a sunny patio with a shower for you to cool off. The best rooms have marble bathrooms with corner baths, and Nos.114 and 115, at the rear, are quiet and have large windows overlooking the patio.

Hostal Girona

C/Girona 24, 1º 1ª (93 265 02 59/ www.hostalgirona.com). Metro Urquinaona. €.
A gem of a *hostal*, filled with antiques, chandeliers and oriental rugs. The rooms may be on the simple side, but all

A flat world

As the recession bites, self-catering becomes increasingly more attractive. The range of options is all-encompassing – splurge on aparthotels for extras like room service, cleaning and swimming pools. Save on flat rentals to spend it on food, wine and fun. So how do the two compare? What your money gets you:

Sky's the limit

Murmuri Apartments (aparthotel)
www.murmuri.com
- Elegant mews address
- Party planning
- Teak-decked terrace

'Sert II' (flat)
www.friendlyrentals.com
- Vast 2-bed loft space
- Exclusive gated sidestreet
- Suspended swing in sitting area

€300-€400

Suites Avenue (aparthotel)
www.derbyhotels.com/suitesavenue
- Building design by Toyo Ito
- Wine cabinet
- Personal shopper, chauffeur, PA
- Rooftop pool

'Principal' (flat)
www.destinationbcn.com
- Space (160sq m)
- Designer furniture
- Long egg-shaped bathtub
- Fridge-stocking service

€200-€300

Hispanos 7 Suiza (aparthotel)
www.hispanos7suiza.com
- Large terrace
- Hydro-massage shower
- Top-flight restaurant

'Sant Jaume' (flat)
www.destinationbcn.com
- Barri Gòtic penthouse
- Views of Plaça Sant Jaume
- Huge teak-decked terrace and BBQ

€100-€200

Boria BCN (aparthotel)
www.boriabcn.com
- Stylish suite in hip neighbourhood
- Tropical wood floors
- Library, DVD and stereo
- Rooftop terrace

'Summertime' (flat)
www.cocoonbarcelona.com
- Decorated in vibrant colours
- Sleeps eight
- Outdoor dining table
- Located in sleepy Gràcia

Less than €100

Barcelona Center Plaza (aparthotel)
www.barcelonacenterplaza.com
- No frills but comfortable studio
- Basic kitchen
- Balcony

'Rainbow' (flat)
www.gobcn.com
- Three bedrooms
- Jelly-bean colours
- Electric massage armchair

Hotel Murmuri p175

have charm, with tall windows and tiled floors. It's worth splashing out on rooms in the refurbished wing with ensuite bathrooms, although some in the old wing have ensuite showers. Brighter, outward-facing rooms have small balconies overlooking C/Girona or bigger balconies on to a huge and quiet patio.

Hostal Goya

C/Pau Claris 74, 1º (93 302 25 65/www. hostalgoya.com). Metro Urquinaona. **€€**.
Located in a typical Eixample building with fabulous tiled floors, the bedrooms are done out in chocolates and creams, with comfortable beds, chunky duvets and cushions; the bathrooms

are equally luxurious. The best rooms either give on to the street or the terrace at the back. Guests leaving the city in the evening can still use a bathroom to shower and change before they go.

Hostal San Remo

C/Ausiàs Marc 19, 1º-2ª (93 302 19 89/ www.hostalsanremo.com). Metro Urquinaona. **€**.
Staying in this bright, neat and peaceful apartment feels a bit like staying with an amenable relative. The friendly owner, Rosa, and her dog live on site and take good care of their guests. All seven rooms have air-conditioning and shiny bedspreads; five out of seven have

Villa Emilia p176

ensuite bathrooms, and most of them have a little balcony and double glazing.

Hotel Axel

C/Aribau 33 (93 323 93 93/www.axel hotels.com). Metro Universitat. €€€.
Housed in a Modernista building, with multi-coloured tiles in the lobby and bright rooms with bleached floors. The mostly gay, good-looking staff sport T-shirts with the logo 'heterofriendly', and everyone is made welcome. King-size beds come as standard, as does free mineral water and erotic artworks. The 'Superior' rooms have hydro-massage bathtubs and stained-glass gallery balconies. The Sky Bar on the rooftop is where it all happens, with a little pool, jacuzzi, sun deck, sauna and steam room.

Hotel Claris

C/Pau Claris 150 (93 487 62 62/ www.derbyhotels.com). Metro Passeig de Gràcia. €€€.
Antiques and contemporary design merge behind the neo-classical exterior of the Claris, which contains the largest private collection of Egyptian art in Spain. Some bedrooms are on the small side, while others are duplex, but all

have Chesterfield sofas and plenty of art. The rooftop pool is just about big enough to swim in, with plenty of loungers, and a cocktail bar and DJ.

Hotel Constanza

C/Bruc 33 (93 270 19 10/www.hotel constanza.com). Metro Urquinaona. €€.
This quiet and pleasant boutique has been around for a few years now and continues to please. The theme is oriental, with Japanese silk screens, orchid and pebble prints and sleek teak furniture creating an atmosphere of Zen-like calm. The best rooms are at the back, some with smart walled-in terraces, and it has comfortable single rooms. There's a good buffet breakfast.

Hotel Granados 83

C/Enric Granados 83 (93 492 96 70/ www.derbyhotels.com). Metro Diagonal. €€€.
The original ironwork structure of this former hospital lends an unexpectedly industrial feel to the Granados 83. The bare-bricked rooms include duplex and triplex versions, some with their own terraces and plunge pools. For mortals in the standard rooms, there is a rooftop pool and sun deck.

Hotel Majestic

Passeig de Gràcia 68 (93 488 17 17/ www.hotelmajestic.es). Metro Passeig de Gràcia. €€€€.

Behind a neo-classical façade lies a panoply of perks, such as a service that allows you to print a selection of international newspapers. Non-guests can enjoy the high life in the rooftop pool and gym, which offer wonderful views out over the city. Rooms are suitably opulent, decorated with classical flair. The Drolma restaurant is one of the finest, and priciest, in the city.

Hotel Murmuri

Rambla Catalunya 104 (93 550 06 00/ www.murmuri.com). Metro Diagonal. €€€€.

Murmuri has an effortless chic about it – creamy tones with gilt trim and sculpted flower arrangements give the interior a cool, calm atmosphere, attracting a well-heeled, grown-up crowd, and there's a lively lobby for drinks and a slick Thai restaurant. Bedrooms are spacious and airy, and generously stocked with Molton Brown toiletries. For a sophisticated shopping weekend at the heart of the designer quarter, few places beat it.

Hotel Omm

C/Rosselló 265 (93 445 40 00/www. hotelomm.es). Metro Diagonal. €€€.

Bedrooms are light and bright, as opposed to black on black corridors, and enjoy what may well be the city's comfiest beds and double bathrooms. The restaurant boasts a Michelin star, but there's also a healthy bistro alternative, as well as an extensive bar. A trendy club occupies the perfectly soundproofed basement, and a bar and pool area perches on the roof with views straight over Gaudí's La Pedrera next door.

Hotel Pulitzer

C/Bergara 8 (93 481 67 67/www. hotelpulitzer.es). Metro Catalunya. €€€.

A discreet façade reveals an impressive lobby that's stuffed with comfortable white leather sofas, a reading area and a swanky bar and restaurant. The rooftop terrace is a fabulous spot for a cocktail, with squishy loungers, scented candles and tropical plants, and views across the city. The rooms themselves are not big, but they are neatly decorated and come with cool grey marble, fluffy pillows and leather trim.

Hotel Soho

NEW *Gran Via de les Corts Catalanes 543-545 (93 552 96 10/www.nnhotels. com). Metro Urgell.* €€.

A duplex-height lobby filled with the light of numerous glass installations leads into a comfortable business space with library, desks, sofas, a small terrace and free internet. There's a cocktail bar and plunge pool on the roof. The large bedrooms have been done out in tasteful olive greens and wood, with gargantuan beds, LCD-screen TVs and glass bathrooms by Philippe Starck. The best have spacious terraces.

Market Hotel

Passatge Sant Antoni Abat 10 (93 325 12 05/www.markethotel.com.es). Metro Sant Antoni. €€.

The people who brought Barcelona the wildly successful Quinze Nits chain of restaurants have gone on to apply their low-budget, high-design approach to this hotel. The monochrome rooms, though not huge, are comfortable and stylish for the price and downstairs is a handsome and keenly priced restaurant, typical of the group.

Prestige Paseo de Gràcia

Passeig de Gràcia 62 (93 272 41 80/ www.prestigehotels.com). Metro Passeig de Gràcia. €€€€.

This sublime boutique hotel was created by architect Josep Juanpere, who took a 1930s building and revamped it with oriental-inspired minimalist design and Japanese gardens. The rooms are equipped with Bang & Olufsen TVs, intelligent lighting systems, free mini-bars and even umbrellas. Outside their rooms, the hotel's guests hang out in the cool Zeroom lounge-bar-library, where expert concierges are on hand.

the5rooms

C/Pau Claris 72 (93 342 78 80/www. thefiverooms.com). Metro Catalunya or Urquinaona. €€.

A chic and comfortable B&B in a handsome building, where the delightful Jessica Delgado makes every effort to encourage guests to feel at home. Books and magazines are dotted around the stylish sitting areas and bedrooms, and breakfast is served at any time of day. There are now two apartments in the neighbouring building and plans to add more rooms (and presumably, a new name) in late 2009.

Villa Emilia

NEW *C/Calàbria 115-117 (93 252 52 85/www.hotelvillaemilia.com). Metro Rocafort.* €€.

There's not much to discover in the immediate vicinity but Emilia compensates with the glam Zinc Bar in the lobby, complete with black chandeliers, red velvet sofas, and quality tapas. The pièce de résistance, however, is the open-air lounge on the rooftop, with sofas, candles, a well-stocked bar

and a buzzer for service. The rooms are decent with large comfortable beds, and aim for a good night's sleep rather than design awards.

Gràcia

Casa Fuster

Passeig de Gràcia 132 (93 255 30 00/ www.hotelcasafuster.com). Metro Diagonal. €€€€.

When the Fuster opened, many complained that this historic Modernista building should have been preserved as a public space. The famed on-site Café Viennese answers that demand somewhat, though when a cup of tea costs €15 you won't find many locals. Service is spot on; rooms, while rather small, feel regal in their muted tones, and there are fresh flowers daily. The rooftop pool has a jacuzzi and great views, while the gourmet restaurant has an insider feel.

Other districts

Barcelona Urbany

NEW *Avda Meridiana 90, Clot (93 245 84 14/www.barcelonaurbany. com). Metro Clot.* €

Forget the institutional youth hostels of old, with their mouldy showers and threadbare towels – the Urbany has brought about a paradigm shift in the market. For as little as €12 you can lie in a clean and comfortable dorm bed surfing the net, watch DVDs in a common room, swim in the pool or take a jacuzzi. Oh, and breakfast is included.

Hostal Poblenou

C/Taulat 30, Poblenou (93 221 26 01/ www.hostalpoblenou.com). Metro Poblenou. €.

Poblenou is a delightful *hostal* in an elegant restored building. The rooms are light and airy with their own bathrooms, and breakfast is served on a sunny terrace. Guests can help themselves to tea, coffee and mineral water at no extra cost. The owner, Mercedes, is on hand to provide any information you might need.

Getting Around

Arriving & leaving

By air

Aeroport de Barcelona

91 393 60 00/www.aena.es/
www.barcelona-airport.com
Barcelona's airport is at El Prat, just
south-west of the city. Each airline
works from one of the four main terminals. There are tourist information
desks and currency exchanges in terminals A and B.

Aerobús

The airport bus (information 93
415 60 20) runs from each terminal
to Plaça Catalunya, with stops at
Plaça Espanya, C/Urgell and Plaça
Universitat. Buses to the airport go
from Plaça Catalunya (in front of
El Corte Inglés), stopping at Sants
station and Plaça Espanya. Buses
run every 8-10mins, leaving the
airport from 6am-1am Mon-Fri
and 6.30am-1am at weekends,
returning from Plaça Catalunya
5.30am-12.15pm Mon-Fri and 6am-
12.15pm at weekends. The trip
takes 35-45mins; a single is €4.25,
a return €7.30. At night the N17
runs every hour, on the hour,
between the airport (from 10pm)
and Plaça Catalunya (from 11pm),
with several stops on the way,
including Plaça d'Espanya and
Plaça Universitat. Last departures
are at 5am. Journey time is 45 mins;
the cost is a single metro fare.

Airport trains

A long overhead walkway between
terminals A and B leads to the
airport train station. The Rodalies
line C10 leaves the airport at 29
and 59 mins past the hour, 6.29am-
10.59pm, with an extra train at
11.44pm daily, stopping at Sants

and Passeig de Gràcia. Trains to
the airport leave Sants at 25 and
55 past the hour, 5.25am-11.55pm
daily (five mins earlier from
Passeig de Gràcia). The journey
takes 20-30mins and costs €2.80
each way. Be aware that tickets are
valid only for 2hrs after purchase.
A little-publicised fact is that the
T-10 metro pass can also be used.

Taxis from the airport

The basic taxi fare from the airport
to central Barcelona should be
€18-€26, including a €3.10 airport
supplement. Fares are about 15
per cent higher after 9pm and at
weekends. There is a €1 supplement
for each large piece of luggage
placed in the car boot. All licensed
cab drivers use the ranks outside
the terminals.

By bus

Most long-distance coaches (both
national and international) stop or
terminate at **Estació d'Autobusos
Barcelona-Nord** (C/Alí Bei 80,
902 26 06 06, www.barcelona
nord.com). Some international
Eurolines services (information
93 490 40 00, www.eurolines.es)
begin and end journeys at Sants.

By train

Most long-distance services
operated by the Spanish state
railway company **RENFE** run
from Barcelona-Sants station,
easily reached by metro. A few
services from the French border
or south to Tarragona stop at the
Estació de França in the Born,
near the Barceloneta metro, but it's
otherwise sparsely served. Many
trains stop at **Passeig de Gràcia**

or Plaça Catalunya, which can be the handiest for the city centre.

RENFE

National 902 24 02 02/international 902 24 34 02/www.renfe.es. **Open** *National* 5am-10pm daily. *International* 7am-midnight daily.

RENFE tickets can be bought online, at train stations, travel agents or reserved over the phone and delivered to an address or hotel for a small extra fee. They have some English-speaking phone operators.

Public transport

Although it's run by different organisations, Barcelona public transport is highly integrated, with the same tickets valid for up to four changes of transport on bus, tram, local train and metro lines as long as you do it within 75 minutes. The **metro** is generally the quickest and easiest way of getting around the city. All metro lines operate from 5am to midnight Monday to Thursday, Sunday and public holidays; 5am to 2am Friday, and all through Saturday night. Buses run throughout the night and to areas not covered by the metro system. Local buses and the metro are run by the city transport authority (**TMB**). Two underground train lines connect with the metro but are run by Catalan government railways, the **FGC**. One runs north from Plaça Catalunya; the other runs west from Plaça Espanya to Cornellà. Two main tram routes are of limited use to visitors.

FGC information

Vestibule, Plaça Catalunya FGC station (93 205 15 15/www.fgc.net). **Open** 7am-9pm Mon-Fri. **Other locations**: FGC Provença (open 9am-7pm Mon-Fri, closed Aug); FGC Plaça d'Espanya (open 9am-2pm, 4-7pm Mon-Fri).

TMB information

Main vestibule, Metro Universitat, Eixample (93 318 70 74/www.tmb.net). **Open** 8am-8pm Mon-Fri. **Other locations**: vestibule, Metro Sants Estació & Sagrada Família (both 7am-9pm Mon-Fri; Sants also opens 9am-7pm Sat, 9am-2pm Sun); vestibule, Metro Diagonal (8am-8pm Mon-Fri).

Buses

Many city bus routes originate in or pass through the city centre, at Plaça Catalunya, Plaça Universitat and Plaça Urquinaona. However, they often run along different parallel streets, due to the city's one-way system. Not all stops are labelled and street signs are not always easy to locate. Most routes run 6am-10.30pm daily except Sundays. There's usually a bus every 10-15mins, but they're less frequent before 8am, after 9pm and on Saturdays. On Sundays, buses are less frequent still; a few do not run at all.

Board at the front and disembark through the middle or rear doors. Only single tickets can be bought from the driver; if you have a *targeta,* insert it into the machine behind the driver as you board.

Fares and tickets

Travel in the Barcelona urban area has a flat fare of €1.35 per journey, but multi-journey tickets or *targetes* are better value. The basic ten-trip *targeta* is the **T-10** (Catalan *Te-Deu*, Spanish *Te-Diez*) for €7.70, which can be shared by any number of people travelling simultaneously; the ticket is validated in the machines on the metro, train or bus once per person per journey. The T-10 offers access to all five of the city's main transport systems (local RENFE and FGC trains within the main metropolitan area, the metro, tram and buses). To transfer, insert your card into a machine a second time; unless 75 minutes have elapsed since your last journey, another unit will not be deducted. Single tickets don't allow free transfers.

You can buy T-10s at newsstands and Servi-Caixa cashpoints as well as metro and train stations, but not on buses.

Trams

Most tram lines only serve outlying neighbourhoods, but line **T5** can be useful – it runs from the far side of Ciutadella park to Glòries (where the Teatre Nacional and a large shopping mall are located, among other things) and on to Poblenou, Diagonal-Mar shopping centre and the Fòrum area.

All trams are fully accessible for wheelchair-users and are part of the integrated TMB *targeta* system: simply insert the ticket into the machine as you board. You can buy integrated tickets and single tickets from the machines at tram stops.

Tram information

Trambaix (902 19 32 75/www.tram bcn.com). **Open** 9am-2pm, 4-7pm Mon-Thur; 9am-2pm Fri.

Taxis

It's usually easy to find one of the 10,300 black and yellow taxis. There are ranks at railway and bus stations, in main squares and throughout the city, but taxis can also be hailed on the street when they show a green light on the roof and a sign saying '*lliure/libre*' (free) behind the windscreen. Information on taxi fares, ranks and regulations can be found at www.emt-amb.com.

Fares

Rates and supplements are shown inside cabs on a sticker in the rear side window (in English). The basic fare for a taxi hailed in the street to pick you up is €1.80 (or €1.90 at nights, weekends and holidays), which is what the meter should register when you set off. The basic rate, 82¢/km, applies 8am-8pm Mon-Fri; at other times, including public holidays, the rate is €1.04/km, plus a €4 supplement after midnight. There are supplements for luggage (€1), the airport (€3.10) and the port (€2.10), and for 'special nights' such as New Year's Eve (€3.10), as well as a waiting charge. Taxi drivers are not required to carry more than €20 in change; few accept credit cards.

Radio cabs

These companies take bookings 24 hours daily. Phone cabs start the meter when a call is answered but, by the time it picks you up, it should not display more than €3.22 during weekdays and €3.99 at night, at weekends or public holidays.

Barnataxi *93 357 77 55.*
Fono-Taxi *93 300 11 00.*
Ràdio Taxi '033' *93 303 30 33.*
Servi-Taxi *93 330 03 00.*
Taxi Groc *93 322 22 22.*
Taxi Miramar *93 433 10 20.*

Driving

Car & motorbike hire

Car hire is relatively pricey, but it's a competitive market so shop around. Check carefully what's included: ideally, you want unlimited mileage, 16% VAT (IVA) included and full insurance cover (*seguro todo riesgo*) rather than the third-party minimum (*seguro obligatorio*). You'll need a credit card as a guarantee. Most companies require you to have had a licence for at least a year; many also enforce a minimum age limit.

ESSENTIALS

Europcar *93 491 48 22, reservations 902 10 50 30, www.europcar.com.*
Motissimo *93 490 84 01, www.motissimo.es.*
Pepecar *807 41 42 43, www.pepecar.com.*
Vanguard *93 439 38 80, www.vanguardrent.com.*

Parking

Parking is fiendishly complicated, and municipal police are quick to hand out tickets or tow away cars. In some parts of the old city, access is limited to residents for much of the day. In some Old City streets, time-controlled bollards pop up, meaning your car may get stuck. Wherever you are, don't park in front of doors signed '*Gual Permanent*', indicating an entry with 24-hour right of access.

Pay and display areas
The Area Verda contains zones exclusively for residents' use (most of the old city), and 'partial zones' (found in Gràcia, Barceloneta and the Eixample) where non-residents pay €2.80 an hour with a one- or two-hour maximum stay, as indicated on the meter.

If you overstay by no more than an hour, you can cancel the fine by paying an extra €6; to do so, press *Anul·lar denúncia* on the machine, insert €6, then press Ticket. Some machines accept credit cards (MC, V); none accepts notes or gives change. For information, call 010 or see www.bcn.cat/areaverda.

Car parks
Car parks ('*parkings*') are signalled by a white 'P' on a blue sign. SABA (Plaça Catalunya, Plaça Urquinaona, Rambla Catalunya, Avda Catedral, airport and elsewhere; 93 230 56 00, 902 28 30 80, www.saba.es) costs around €2.60/hr, while SMASSA car parks (Plaça Catalunya 23, C/Hospital 25-29, Avda Francesc Cambó 10, Passeig de Gràcia 60, and elsewhere; 93 409 20 21, www.bsmsa.es/mobilitat) cost €2.30-€2.70/hr.

Towed vehicles
If the police have towed your car, they should leave a triangular sticker on the pavement where it stood. The sticker should let you know to which pound it's been taken. If not, call 901 513 151; staff generally don't speak English. Recovering your vehicle within 4hrs costs €146.30, with each extra hour costing €1.60, or €19 per day. You'll also have to pay a fine to the police, which varies. You'll need your passport and documentation, or the rental contract, to prove ownership.

Petrol

Most gasolineres (petrol stations) have unleaded (*sense plom/sin plomo*), regular (super) and diesel (gas-oil). Petrol is cheaper in Spain than it is in most northern European countries.

Cycling

There's a network of bike lanes (*carrils bici*) along major avenues and by the seafront; local authorities are keen to promote cycling. However, weekday traffic can be risky, despite legislation that states that drivers must slow down near cyclists. No more than two bikes may ride side by side. Cycling information can be found at www.bcn.cat/bicicleta.

Bicicleta Barcelona (bicycle hire)
C/Esparteria 3, Born (93 268 21 05/ www.bicicletabarcelona.com). Metro Barceloneta or Jaume I. **Open** 10am-7pm Mon-Sat; 10am-2pm Sun.

Resources A-Z

Accident & emergency

The following lines are available 24 hours a day.

Emergency services 112. Police, fire or ambulance.

Ambulance/Ambulància 061. In a medical emergency, go to the casualty department (*Urgències*) of any of the main public hospitals. All are open 24 hours daily.

Centre d'Urgències Perecamps Avda Drassanes 13-15, Raval (93 441 06 00). Metro Drassanes or Paral·lel.

Hospital Clínic C/Villarroel 170, Eixample (93 227 54 00). Metro Hospital Clínic.

Hospital del Mar Passeig Marítim 25-29, Barceloneta (93 248 30 00). Metro Ciutadella-Vila Olímpica.

Hospital Dos de Maig C/Dos de Maig 301, Eixample (93 507 27 00). Metro Hospital de Sant Pau.

Hospital de Sant Pau C/Sant Antoni Maria Claret 167, Eixample (93 291 90 00). Metro Hospital de Sant Pau.

Pharmacies

Pharmacies (*farmàcies/farmacias*) are signalled by large green and red neon crosses. Most are open 9am-1.30pm and 4.30-8pm weekdays, and 9am-1.30pm on Saturdays. About a dozen operate around the clock, while more have late opening hours; some of the most central are listed below. The full list of chemists that stay open late (usually till 10pm) and overnight on any given night is posted daily outside every pharmacy door and given in the day's papers. You can also call the 010 and 098 info lines. At night, duty pharmacies often appear closed, but knock on the shutters and you'll be attended to.

Farmàcia Alvarez Passeig de Gràcia 26, Eixample (93 302 11 24). Metro Passeig de Gràcia. **Open** 8am-10.30pm Mon-Thur; 8am-midnight Fri; 9am-midnight Sat.

Farmàcia Cervera C/Muntaner 254, Eixample (93 200 09 96). Metro Diagonal/FGC Gràcia. **Open** 24hrs daily.

Farmàcia Clapés La Rambla 98, Barri Gòtic (93 301 28 43). Metro Liceu. **Open** 24hrs daily.

Farmàcia Vilar Vestíbule, Estació de Sants, Sants (93 490 92 07). Metro Sants Estació. **Open** 7am-10.30pm Mon-Fri; 8am-10.30pm Sat, Sun.

Consulates

Australian Consulate Plaça Gal·la Placidia 1, Gràcia (93 490 90 13/www.spain.embassy.gov.au). FGC Gràcia. **Open** 10am-noon Mon-Fri. Closed Aug.

British Consulate Avda Diagonal 477 13°, Eixample (93 366 62 00/ www.ukinspain.com). Metro Hospital Clínic. **Open** Mid Sept-mid June 9.30am-2pm Mon-Fri. Mid June-mid Sept 8.30am-1.30pm Mon-Fri.

Canadian Consulate C/Elisenda de Pinós 10, Sarrià (93 204 27 00/ www.canada-es.org). FGC Reina Elisenda. **Open** 10am-1pm Mon-Fri.

Irish Consulate Gran Via Carles III 94, Les Corts (93 491 50 21). Metro Maria Cristina. **Open** 10am-1pm Mon-Fri.

New Zealand Consulate Travessera de Gràcia 64, 2°, Gràcia (93 209 03 99). Metro Diagonal. **Open** 9am-2pm, 4-7pm Mon-Fri.

South African Consulate Parque Empresarial Mas Blau II, Alta Ribagorza 6-8, El Prat de Llobregat (93 506 91 00/laffont@indukern.es). **Open** 9.30am-noon Mon-Fri.

US Consulate Passeig Reina Elisenda 23, Sarrià (93 280 22 27/www.embusa .es). FGC Reina Elisenda. **Open** 9am-1pm Mon-Fri.

ESSENTIALS

Credit card loss

Each of these lines has English-speaking staff and is open 24 hours a day.

American Express *902 11 11 35.*
Diners Club *901 10 10 11.*
MasterCard *900 97 12 31.*
Visa *900 99 11 24.*

Customs

Customs declarations are not usually necessary if you arrive in Spain from another EU country and are carrying only legal goods for personal use. The amounts given below are guidelines only:

- 800 cigarettes, 400 small cigars, 200 cigars or 1kg loose tobacco
- 10 litres of spirits (over 22% alcohol), 90 litres of wine (under 22% alcohol) or 110 litres of beer

From a non-EU country or the Canary Islands, you can bring:

- 200 cigarettes, 100 small cigars, 50 regular cigars or 250g (8.82oz) of tobacco
- 1 litre of spirits (over 22% alcohol) or 2 litres of wine or beer (under 22%)
- 50g (1.76oz) of perfume
- 500g coffee; 100g tea

Visitors can also carry up to €6,000 in cash without having to declare it. Non-EU residents are able to reclaim VAT (IVA) on some purchases when they leave.

Disabled travellers

The website www.accessible barcelona.com is a useful resource for disabled travellers.

Institut Municipal de Persones amb Disminució

Avda Diagonal 233, Eixample (93 413 27 75/www.bcn.cat/accessible). Metro Glòries or Monumental/56, 62 bus. **Open** 9am-2pm Mon-Fri.

The city's organisation for the disabled has information on access to venues and can provide a map with wheelchair-friendly itineraries.

Transport

Access for disabled people to local transport still leaves quite a lot to be desired. For wheelchair-users, buses and taxis are usually the best bets. For transport information, call TMB (93 318 70 74) or 010. Transport maps, which can be picked up from transport information offices and metro stations, indicate wheelchair access points and adapted bus routes. For a list of accessible metro stations and bus lines, check www.tmb.net and click on 'Transport for everyone'.

Electricity

The standard current in Spain is 220V. Plugs are of the type that has two round pins. You'll need a plug adaptor to use British-bought electrical devices. If you have US (110V) equipment, you will need a transformer as well as an adaptor.

Estancs/estancos

Government-run tobacco shops, known as an *estanc/estanco* (at times, just *'tabac'*) and identified by a brown and yellow sign, are important institutions. Along with tobacco, they also supply postage stamps and envelopes, public transport *targetes* and phonecards.

Internet

There are internet centres all over Barcelona, and the city council has undertaken to bring free Wi-Fi access to 500 public spaces by 2010.

Bornet Internet Café

C/Barra de Ferro 3, Born (93 268 15 07/www.bornet-bcn.com). Metro Jaume I.

Open 10am-11pm Mon-Fri; noon-11pm Sat, Sun. No credit cards.
There are ten terminals in this small café and six more for laptops. One hour is €2.80.

easyEverything

La Rambla 31 (93 301 75 07/ www.easyeverything.com). Metro Drassanes or Liceu. **Open** 8am-2am daily. No credit cards.
There are 330 terminals here and 240 at Ronda Universitat 35 (8am-2am daily). Buy credit from the machines; price then increases with demand.

Opening times

Most shops open from 9/10am to 1/2pm, and then 4/5pm to 8/9pm, Monday to Saturday. Many smaller businesses don't reopen on Saturday afternoons. All-day opening is becoming more common, especially for larger establishments.

Markets open at 7/8am; most stalls shut by 2pm, but many open on Fridays and Saturdays until 8pm.

Note that in summer, many of Barcelona's shops and restaurants shut for all or part of August. Many museums close one day each week, usually Mondays.

Police

If you're robbed or attacked, report the incident as soon as possible at the nearest police station (*comisaría*), or dial 112. The most convenient is the 24hr Guàrdia Urbana station (La Rambla 43, 092 or 93 256 24 30), which often has English-speaking officers on duty; they may eventually transfer you to the Mossos d'Esquadra (C/Nou de la Rambla 76, 088 or 93 306 23 00) to formally report the crime.

To do this, you'll need to make an official statement (*denuncia*). It's highly improbable that you will recover your property, but you need the *denuncia* to make an insurance claim. You can also make this statement over the phone or online (902 10 21 12, www.policia.es; except for crimes involving physical violence, or if the perpetrator has been identified). You'll still have to go to the *comisaría* within 72 hours to sign the *denuncia*, but you'll skip some queues.

Post

Letters and postcards weighing up to 20g cost 32¢ within Spain; 62¢ to the rest of Europe; 78¢ to the rest of the world – though anything in a large or non-rectangular envelope costs more. Prices normally rise on 1 Jan. It's usually easiest to buy stamps at *estancs* (p182). Mail sent abroad is slow: 5-6 working days in Europe, 8-10 to the USA. Postboxes in the street are yellow, sometimes with a white or blue horn insignia. Postal information is available at www.correos.es or on 902 197 197.

Correu Central

Plaça Antonio López, Barri Gòtic (93 486 80 50). Metro Barceloneta or Jaume I. **Open** 8.30am-9.30pm Mon-Fri; 8.30am-2pm Sat.
Other locations Ronda Universitat 23, Eixample; C/Aragó 282, Eixample (both 8.30am-8.30pm Mon-Fri, 9.30am-1pm Sat).

Smoking

Laws were passed in 2006 that required all bars and restaurants over 100sq m (1,080sq ft) to have a non-smoking area; smaller establishments can elect to be non-smoking or not, but those that do not can no longer admit under-18s. The enforcement of this law is rather hit-and-miss. Most hotels have non-smoking rooms or floors, although if you ask for a non-smoking room, some hotels may

ESSENTIALS

just give you a room that has had the ashtrays removed. Smoking bans in cinemas, theatres and on trains are generally respected, though smoking in banks, offices and on station platforms is still quite common.

Telephones

Normal Spanish phone numbers have nine digits; the area code (93 in the province of Barcelona) must be dialled with all calls, both local and long-distance. Spanish mobile numbers always begin with 6. Numbers starting 900 are freephone lines, while other 90 numbers are special-rate services.

International & long-distance calls

To make an international call, dial 00 and then the country code, followed by the area code (omitting the first zero in UK numbers), and then the number you wish to call. Country codes are as follows: Australia 61; Canada 1; Irish Republic 353; New Zealand 64; South Africa 27; United Kingdom 44; USA 1. To phone Spain from abroad, you should dial the international access code, followed by 34, followed by the required number.

Public phones

The most common type of payphone accepts coins (5¢ up), phonecards and credit cards. There is a multilingual digital display (press 'L' to change language) and written instructions in English and other languages. Calls to directory enquiries on 11818 are free from payphones, but you'll usually have to insert a coin to make the call (it will be returned when you hang up).

Telefónica phonecards (*targetes telefònica/tarjetas telefónica*) are sold at newsstands and *estancs* (p182).

Other cards sold at phone centres, shops and newsstands give cheaper rates on all but local calls. This latter type of card contains a toll-free number to call from any phone.

Tickets

FNAC (p135) has an efficient ticket desk on its ground floor: it sells tickets to theme parks and sights, but it's especially good for contemporary music concerts and events (it's also one of the main outlets for tickets to Sónar, p40). Concert tickets for smaller venues are often sold in record shops and at the venues themselves; check posters for further details. If you want to get tickets to the football, see the listings on p151.

Servi-Caixa – La Caixa

902 33 22 11/www.servicaixa.com.
Use the special Servi-Caixa ATMs (most larger branches of La Caixa have them), dial 902 33 22 11 or check the website to purchase tickets for cinemas, concerts, plays, museums, amusement parks and Barça games. You'll need the card with which you made the payment when you collect the tickets.

Tel-entrada – Caixa Catalunya

902 10 12 12/www.telentrada.com.
Through Tel-entrada you can purchase tickets for theatre performances, cinemas (including the IMAX), concerts, museums and sights over the phone, online or over the counter at any branch of the Caixa Catalunya savings bank. Tickets can be collected from Caixa Catalunya ATMs or the tourist office at Plaça Catalunya (below).

Time

Spain is one hour ahead of London, six hours ahead of New York, eight hours behind Sydney and ten hours behind Wellington. In all EU countries clocks are moved forward one hour on the last weekend of March and back on the last weekend of October.

Tipping

There are no fixed rules for tipping in Barcelona, but locals generally don't tip much. It's fair to leave 5-10 per cent in restaurants, but don't feel you have to if the service has been bad. People sometimes leave a little change in bars: not expected, but appreciated. In taxis, tipping is not standard, but many people will round up to the nearest euro. It's usual to tip hotel porters.

Tourist information

Centre d'Informació de la Virreina

Palau de la Virreina, La Rambla 99 (93 316 10 00/www.bcn.cat/cultura). Metro Liceu. **Open** 10am-8pm Mon-Sat; 11am-3pm Sun. *Ticket sales* 11am-8pm Tue-Sat; 11am-3pm Sun.
The information office of the city's culture department, with details of shows, exhibitions and special events.

Oficines d'Informació Turística

Plaça Catalunya, Eixample (information 807 11 72 22/from outside Spain +34 93 285 38 34/www.bcn.cat/ www.barcelonaturisme.com). Metro Catalunya. **Open** *Office* 9am-9pm daily. *Call centre* 9am-8pm Mon-Fri.
The main office of the city tourist board is underground on the Corte Inglés side of the square: look for big red signs with 'i' in white. It has information, money exchange, a shop and a hotel booking service, and sells phonecards, tickets for shows, sights and public transport.
Other locations C/Ciutat 2, Barri Gòtic; C/Sardenya (located opposite the Sagrada Familia), Eixample; Plaça Portal Pau (located opposite Monument a Colom), Port Vell; Sants station; La Rambla 115; corner of Plaça d'Espanya and Avda Maria Cristina; airport.

Palau Robert

Passeig de Gràcia 107, Eixample (93 238 80 91/www.gencat.net/probert). Metro Diagonal. **Open** 10am-7pm Mon-Sat; 10am-2.30pm Sun.
The Generalitat's lavishly equipped centre has maps and other essentials for the whole of Catalonia.

010 phoneline

Open 8am-10pm Mon-Sat.
This city-run information line is aimed mainly at locals, but it manages to do an impeccable job of answering all kinds of queries. There are sometimes English-speaking operators.

Visas

EU nationals and citizens of the US, Canada, Australia and New Zealand do not need visas for stays of up to three months. For EU citizens a passport or national ID card valid for travel abroad is sufficient; non-EU citizens must have full passports.

What's on

The main papers all have daily 'what's on' events listings, with entertainment supplements on Fridays (most run TV schedules on Saturdays). For monthly listings, see *Metropolitan* and the freesheets such as *Mondo Sonoro* and *AB* (these can be found in bars and music shops).

Guía del Ocio

A weekly listings magazine available at any kiosk. Its listings aren't always 100% up to date or accurate but it is a useful starting point. It's also online at www.guiadelociobcn.es.

Time Out Barcelona

A comprehensive weekly listings magazine, in Catalan (www.timeout.cat).

Catalan Vocabulary

Catalan phonetics are significantly different from those of Spanish, with a wider range of vowel sounds and soft consonants. Catalans use the familiar (*tu*) rather than the polite (*vosté*) second-person forms very freely, but for convenience verbs are given here in the polite form.

Useful expressions

hello *hola*; good morning *bon dia*; good afternoon *bona tarda*; good evening/night *bona nit*; goodbye *adéu* please *si us plau*; very good/OK *molt bé*; thank you (very much) *(moltes) gràcies*; you're welcome *de res* do you speak English? *parla anglés?* I'm sorry, I don't speak Catalan *ho sento, no parlo català;* I don't understand *no ho entenc* what's your name? *com es diu?* Sir/Mr *senyor (sr);* Madam/Mrs *senyora (sra);* Miss *senyoreta (srta)* excuse me/ sorry *perdoni/disculpi;* excuse me, please *escolti* (literally, 'listen to me'); OK/fine *val/d'acord* how much is it? *quant val?* why? *perqué?* when? *quan?* who? *qui?* what? *qué?* where? *on?* how? *com?* where is…? *on és…?* who is it? *qui és?* is/are there any…? *hi ha…?/n'hi ha de…?* very *molt;* and *i* or *o;* with *amb;* without sense; enough *prou* open *obert;* closed *tancat* entrance *entrada;* exit *sortida* I would like *vull;* how many would you like? *quants en vol?* I like *m'agrada;* I don't like *no m'agrada* good *bo/bona;* bad *dolent/a;* well/badly *bé/malament;* small *petit/a;* big *gran;* expensive *car/a;* cheap *barat/a;* hot (food, drink) *calent/a;* cold *fred/a* something *alguna cosa;* nothing *res;* more *més;* less *menys;* more or less *més o menys* toilets *els banys/els serveis/ els lavabos*

Getting around

a ticket *un bitllet;* return *de anada i tornada;* left *esquerra;* right *dreta;* here *aquí;* there *allí;* straight on *tot recte;* at the corner *a la cantonada;* as far as *fins a;* towards *cap a;* near *a prop;* far *lluny;* is it far? *és lluny?*

Time

now *ara;* later *més tard;* yesterday *ahir;* today *avui;* tomorrow *demà;* morning *el matí;* midday *migdia;* afternoon *la tarda;* evening *el vespre;* night *la nit;* late night (roughly, 1-6am) *la matinada;* at what time…? *a quina hora…?* in an hour *en una hora;* at 2 *a les dues;* at 8pm *a les vuit del vespre;* at 1.30 *a dos quarts de dues/ a la una i mitja;* at 5.15 *a un quart de sis/a las cinc i quart;* at 22.30 *a vint-i-dos-trenta*

Numbers

0 *zero;* 1 *u, un, una;* 2 *dos, dues;* 3 *tres;* 4 *quatre;* 5 *cinc;* 6 *sis;* 7 *set;* 8 *vuit;* 9 *nou;* 10 *deu;* 11 *onze;* 12 *dotze;* 13 *tretze;* 14 *catorze;* 15 *quinze;* 16 *setze;* 17 *disset;* 18 *divuit;* 19 *dinou;* 20 *vint;* 21 *vint-i-u;* 22 *vint-i-dos, vin t-i-dues;* 30 *trenta;* 40 *quaranta;* 50 *cinquanta;* 60 *seixanta;* 70 *setanta;* 80 *vuitanta;* 90 *noranta;* 100 *cent;* 200 *dos-cents, dues-centes;* 1,000 *mil*

Days & months

Monday *dilluns;* Tuesday *dimarts;* Wednesday *dimecres;* Thursday *dijous;* Friday *divendres;* Saturday *dissabte;* Sunday *diumenge* January *gener;* February *febrer;* March *març;* April *abril;* May *maig;* June *juny;* July *juliol;* August *agost;* September *setembre;* October *octubre;* November *novembre;* December *desembre*

Spanish Vocabulary

Although many locals prefer to speak Catalan, everyone in the city can speak Spanish. The Spanish familiar form for 'you' (*tú*) is used very freely, but it's safer to use the more formal *usted* with older people and strangers (verbs below are given in the *usted* form).

Useful expressions

hello *hola*; **good morning** *buenos días*; **good afternoon, good evening** *buenas tardes*; **good evening** (after dark); **good night** *buenas noches*; **goodbye** *adiós* **please** *por favor*; **very good/OK** *muy bien;* **thank you (very much)** *(muchas) gracias*; **you're welcome** *de nada*; **do you speak English?** *¿habla inglés?* **I don't speak Spanish** *no hablo castellano*; **I don't understand** *no lo entiendo* **OK/fine** *vale* **what's your name?** *¿cómo se llama?* **Sir/Mr** *señor (sr)*; **Madam/Mrs** *señora (sra)*; **Miss** *señorita (srta)* **excuse me/sorry** *perdón*; **excuse me, please** *oiga* (to attract someone's attention, politely; literally, 'hear me') **where is…?** *¿dónde está…?* **why?** *¿por qué?* **when?** *¿cuándo?* **who?** *¿quién?* **what?** *¿qué?* **where?** *¿dónde?* **how?** *¿cómo?* **who is it?** *¿quién es?* **is/are there any…?** *¿hay…?* **very** *muy*; **and** *y*; **or** *o*; **with** *con*; **without** *sin;* **enough** *bastante* **open** *abierto*; **closed** *cerrado*; **entrance** *entrada*; **exit** *salida* **I would like** *quiero*; **how many would you like?** *¿cuántos quiere?* **how much is it** *¿cuánto es?* **I like** *me gusta*; **I don't like** *no me gusta* **good** *bueno/a*; **bad** *malo/a*; **well/badly** *bien/mal*; **small** *pequeño/a*; **big** *gran, grande*; **expensive** *caro/a*; **cheap** *barato/a*; **hot** (food, drink) *caliente*; **cold** *frío/a*; **something** *algo*; **nothing** *nada;* **more/less** *más/menos*; **more or less** *más o menos* **toilets** *los baños/los servicios/los lavabos*

Getting around

a ticket *un billete*; **return** *de ida y vuelta*; **the next stop** *la próxima parada*; **left** *izquierda*; **right** *derecha* **here** *aquí*; **there** *allí*; **straight on** *todo recto*; **to the end of the street** *al final de la calle*; **as far as** *hasta*; **towards** *hacia*; **near** *cerca*; **far** *lejos*

Time

now *ahora*; **later** *más tarde;* **yesterday** *ayer*; **today** *hoy*; **tomorrow** *mañana*; **morning** *la mañana*; **midday** *mediodía*; **afternoon/evening** *la tarde*; **night** *la noche*; **late night** (roughly 1-6am) *la madrugada* **at what time…?** *¿a qué hora…?* **at 2** *a las dos*; **at 8pm** *a las ocho de la tarde*; **at 1.30** *a la una y media*; **at 5.15** *a las cinco y cuarto*; **in an hour** *en una hora*

Numbers

0 *cero*; 1 *un, uno, una*; 2 *dos*; 3 *tres*; 4 *cuatro*; 5 *cinco*; 6 *seis*; 7 *siete*; 8 *ocho*; 9 *nueve*; 10 *diez*; 11 *once*; 12 *doce*; 13 *trece*; 14 *catorce*; 15 *quince*; 16 *dieciséis*; 17 *diecisiete*; 18 *dieciocho*; 19 *diecinueve*; 20 *veinte*; 21 *veintiuno*; 22 *veintidós*; 30 *treinta*; 40 *cuarenta*; 50 *cincuenta*; 60 *sesenta*; 70 *setenta*; 80 *ochenta*; 90 *noventa*; 100 *cien*; 200 *doscientos*; 1,000 *mil*

Days & months

Monday *lunes*; **Tuesday** *martes*; **Wednesday** *miércoles*; **Thursday** *jueves*; **Friday** *viernes*; **Saturday** *sábado*; **Sunday** *domingo* **January** *enero*; **February** *febrero*; **March** *marzo*; **April** *abril*; **May** *mayo*; **June** *junio*; **July** *julio*; **August** *agosto*; **September** *septiembre*; **October** *octubre*; **November** *noviembre*; **December** *diciembre*

Menu Glossary

Basics

Catalan	Spanish	English
una cullera	una cuchara	a spoon
una forquilla	un tenedor	a fork
un ganivet	un cuchillo	a knife
una ampolla de	una botella de	a bottle of
vi negre	vino tinto	red wine
vi rosat	vino rosado	rosé
vi blanc	vino blanco	white wine
una altra	otra	another (one)
més	más	more
pa	pan	bread
oli d'oliva	aceite de oliva	olive oil
sal i pebre	sal y pimienta	salt and pepper
amanida	ensalada	salad
truita	tortilla	omelette

(note: **truita** refers to either an omelette or a trout.)

Catalan	Spanish	English
la nota	la cuenta	the bill
un cendrer	un cenicero	ashtray
bon profit	aproveche	enjoy your meal
sóc…	soy…	I'm a…
vegetarià/ana	vegetariano/a	vegetarian
diabètic/a	diabético/a	diabetic

Cooking terms

Catalan	Spanish	English
a la brasa	a la brasa	chargrilled
a la graella/planxa	a la plancha	grilled on a hot metal plate
a la romana	a la romana	fried in batter
al forn	al horno	baked
al vapor	al vapor	steamed
fregit	frito	fried
rostit	asado	roast
ben fet	bien hecho	well done
a punt	medio hecho	medium
poc fet	poco hecho	rare

Carn/Carne/Meat

Catalan	Spanish	English
bou	buey	beef
cabrit	cabrito	kid
conill	conejo	rabbit
embotits	embotidos	cold cuts
fetge	higado	liver
garrí	cochinillo	suckling pig
llebre	liebre	hare
llengua	lengua	tongue
llom	lomo	loin (usually pork)
pernil (serrà)	jamón serrano	dry-cured ham
pernil dolç	jamón york	cooked ham
peus de porc	manos de cerdo	pigs' trotters
porc	cerdo	pork
porc senglar	jabalí	wild boar
vedella	ternera	veal
xai/be	cordero	lamb

Aviram/Aves/Poultry

Catalan	Spanish	English
ànec	pato	duck
gall dindi	pavo	turkey
guatlla	codorniz	quail
oca	oca	goose
ous	huevos	eggs
perdiu	perdiz	partridge
colomí	pichón	pigeon
pintada	gallina de Guinea	guinea fowl
pollastre	pollo	chicken

Peix/Pescado/Fish

Catalan	Spanish	English
anxoves	anchoas	anchovies
bacallà	bacalao	salt cod

besuc	besugo	sea bream
caballa	verat	mackerel
calamarsos	calamares	squid
llenguado	lenguado	sole
llobarro	lubina	sea bass
lluç	merluza	hake
moll	salmonete	red mullet
musclos	mejillones	mussels
pop	pulpo	octopus
rap	rape	monkfish
rèmol	rodaballo	turbot
salmó	salmón	salmon
sardines	sardinas	sardines
sípia	sepia	squid
tonyina	atún	tuna
truita	trucha	trout

(note: *truita* can also mean omelette.)

Marisc/Mariscos/Shellfish

Catalan	Spanish	English
calamarsos	calamares	squid
cloïsses	almejas	clams
cranc	cangrejo	crab
escamarlans	cigalas	crayfish
escopinyes	berberechos	cockles
espardenyes	espardeñas	sea cucumbers
gambes	gambas	prawns
llagosta	langosta	spiny lobster
llagostins	langostinos	langoustines
llamàntol	bogavante	lobster
musclos	mejillones	mussels
navalles	navajas	razor clams
percebes	percebes	barnacles
pop	pulpo	octopus
sípia	sepia	squid
tallarines	tallarinas	wedge clams

Verdures/Legumbre/Vegetables

Catalan	Spanish	English
albergínia	berenjena	aubergine
all	ajo	garlic
alvocat	aguacate	avocado
bolets	setas	wild mushrooms
carbassós	calabacines	courgette
carxofes	alcachofas	artichokes
ceba	cebolla	onion
cigrons	garbanzos	chickpeas
col	col	cabbage
enciam	lechuga	lettuce
endivies	endivias	chicory
espinacs	espinacas	spinach
mongetes blanques	judías blancas	haricot beans
mongetes verdes	judías verdes	French beans
pastanagues	zanahorias	carrot
patates	patatas	potatoes
pebrots	pimientos	peppers
pèsols	guisantes	peas
porros	puerros	leek
tomàquets	tomates	tomatoes
xampinyons	champiñones	mushrooms

Postres/Postres/Desserts

Catalan	Spanish	English
flam	flan	crème caramel
formatge	queso	cheese
gelat	helado	ice-cream
música	música	dried fruit and nuts with muscatel
pastís	pastel	cake
tarta	tarta	tart

Fruïta/Fruta/Fruit

Catalan	Spanish	English
figues	higos	figs
gerds	frambuesas	raspberries
maduixes	fresas	strawberries
pera	pera	pear
pinya	piña	pineapple
plàtan	plátano	banana
poma	manzana	apple
préssec	melocotón	peach
prunes	ciruelas	plums
raïm	uvas	grapes
taronja	naranja	orange

ESSENTIALS

Index

Sights & Areas

a
Ajuntament (City Hall) p56
Antic Hospital de la Santa
    Creu & La Capella p88

b
Barceloneta p98
Barri Gòtic p54
Born p73
Bus Montjuïc Turístic
    p111

c
CaixaForum p111
Casa Amatller p121
Casa Àsia p121
Casa Batlló p121
Catedral p56
CCCB (Centre de Cultura
    Contemporània de
    Barcelona) p88
Cementiri Sud-Oest p111
Centre d'Art Santa Mònica
    p57
Collserola p152
Corts, Les p150
CosmoCaixa p154

d
Dalí Barcelona Real
    Cercle Artístic p57
Disseny Hub Barcelona/
    Museu de Ceràmica
    p154

e
Eixample p120

f
Font Màgica de Montjuïc
    p111
Fundació Antoni Tàpies
    p121
Fundació Foto Colectània
    p140
Fundació Joan Brossa p125
Fundació Joan Miró p111
Fundació Suñol p125
Fundación Alorda Derksen
    p125
Fundación Francisco Godia
    p126

g
Gràcia p140

h
Horta p160
Hospital de la Santa Creu
    i Sant Pau p126

j
Jardí Botànic p112
Jardins de Joan Brossa p113
Jardins Mossèn Costa i
    Llobera p113

m
MACBA (Museu d'Art
    Contemporani de
    Barcelona) p88
MNAC (Museu Nacional
    d'Art de Catalunya) p113
Monestir de Pedralbes p155
Montjuïc p108
Monument a Colom p99
Museu Barbier-Mueller
    d'Art Precolombí p73
Museu d'Arqueologia
    de Catalunya p114
Museu d'Història de
    Catalunya p99
Museu d'Història de la
    Ciutat p58
Museu de Carrosses
    Fúnebres p127
Museu de Cera p57
Museu de Ceràmica p154
Museu de Ciències Naturals
    p74
Museu de l'Eròtica p57
Museu de la Música p127
Museu de la Xocolata p74
Museu del Calçat (Shoe
    Museum) p57
Museu del Perfum p127
Museu Diocesà p58
Museu Egipci de Barcelona
    p127
Museu Etnològic p114
Museu Frederic Marès p58
Museu Marítim p99
Museu Olímpic i de l'Esport
    p115
Museu Picasso p76

p
Palau de la Generalitat p58
Palau de la Música Catalana
    p76
Palau Güell p90
Parc de l'Espanya Industrial
    p150

Parc de l'Estació del Nord
    p127
Parc de la Ciutadella p77
Parc de la Creueta del Coll
    p155
Parc del Laberint p160
Parc Joan Miró (Parc de
    l'Escorxador) p128
Park Güell p141
Pavelló Mies van der Rohe
    p115
Pavellons de la Finca Güell
    p155
Pedrera, La (Casa Milà)
    p128
Poble Espanyol p115
Poble Sec p108
Poblenou p157
Ports, The p98

r
Rambla, La p54
Raval p86
Refugi 307 p116

s
Sagrada Família p129
Sant Pau del Camp p90
Sant Pere p73
Santa Maria del Mar p77
Sants p150
Sinagoga Shlomo Ben
    Adret p59

t
Telefèric de Montjuïc
    (cable car) p116
Temple Romà d'Augusti p59
Tibidabo p152
Tibidabo Funfair p152
Torre de Collserola p152
Tramvia Blau p156

z
Zona Alta p153
Zoo p78

Eating & Drinking

a
Ácoma p59
Agua p102
Alkimia p129
Artkuisine p156
Atril, El p78
Au Port de la Lune
    p90

ESSENTIALS

ESSENTIALS

Get the local experience

Over 50 of the world's top destinations available.